THE SCOTT AND LAURIE OKI SERIES
IN ASIAN AMERICAN STUDIES

To Rev. Dr. Willie,

Thanks for the psychological
and spiritual insights,

Steve

THE SCOTT AND LAURIE OKI SERIES
IN ASIAN AMERICAN STUDIES

Altered Lives, Enduring Community

JAPANESE AMERICANS REMEMBER THEIR
WORLD WAR II INCARCERATION

Stephen S. Fugita
Marilyn Fernandez

University of Washington Press
Seattle and London

This book is published with the assistance of a grant from the Scott and Laurie Oki Endowed Fund for the publication of Asian American Studies.

University of Washington Press
PO Box 50096, Seattle, WA 98145
www.washington.edu/uwpress

LIBRARY OF CONGRESS CATALOGING-IN-PUBLICATION DATA

Fugita, Stephen.
    Altered lives, enduring community : Japanese Americans remember their World War II incarceration / Stephen S. Fugita, Marilyn Fernandez.
        p. cm.—(The Scott and Laurie Oki series in Asian American studies)
    Includes bibliographical references and index.
    ISBN 0-295-98380-9 (alk. paper)—ISBN 0-295-98381-7 (pbk. : alk. paper)
    1. Japanese Americans—Evacuation and relocation, 1942–1945.
    2. Japanese Americans—Cultural assimilation.   3. Japanese Americans—Ethnic identity.   4. Japanese Americans—Social conditions—20th century.
    5. Japanese Americans—Economic conditions—20th century.   I. Fernandez, Marilyn.   II. Title.   III. Series.
    D769.8.A6F78   2003
    940.53'17'089956073—dc22   2003065757

The paper used in this publication is acid-free and recycled from 10 percent post-consumer and at least 50 percent pre-consumer waste. It meets the minimum requirements of American National Standard for Information Sciences—Permanence of Paper for Printed Library Materials, ANSI z39.48–1984.

This book is dedicated to
S. Frank Miyamoto,
pioneer, *sensei,* and friend

Contents

Acknowledgments

This book is the culmination of the efforts of a team of individuals. Tom Ikeda, the director of Denshō: The Japanese American Legacy Project, has supported the data collection from the Project's inception. He provided leadership and committed resources at numerous critical junctures. Becky Fukuda identified and selected the pool of quotes from Denshō visual history narrators and critiqued portions of the manuscript. Erin Kimura and Larry Hashima contacted, coordinated, and conducted survey interviews. Erin also entered the data into the statistical analysis program. Dana Hoshide made available the photographs. The following individuals served as survey interviewers: Ivy Arai, Dee Goto, Alyssa Grossman, Sheri Nakashima, and Tomoyo Yamada. Others who provided valuable comments on portions of the manuscript were Art Hansen, Lance Laird, Tim Lukes, Setsuko Matsunaga Nishi, Stephen Warner, Joe Yasutake, and especially Frank Miyamoto. Frank spent countless hours drawing upon his unique knowledge to strengthen the manuscript. This manuscript was smoothly shepherded through the University of Washington Press by Naomi Pascal and Marilyn Trueblood. Mary Ribesky skillfully copyedited the text. Santa Clara University provided both the computing facilities for data analysis and a supportive environment in which to write. The survey respondents and visual history narrators who generously shared their rich experiences and perspectives, of course, made this effort possible. Finally, on a personal note, we would like to express our appreciation to our spouses, Karen Fugita and Peter D'Souza, for their continuous support. Any errors or faulty interpretations, of course, remain ours.

Altered Lives,
Enduring Community

ONE

Introduction

The more I think of it—as I get a little older—I think the damage
done by the internment and the destroying of self-esteem, directly
or indirectly, has really taken its toll, and it will take its toll for the
next couple of generations. (Tomio Moriguchi, denshovh-motomio-
02-0017[1])

Soon after Japanese fighter-bombers shocked the nation with their crippling attack on U.S. naval ships in Pearl Harbor, some 110,000 persons
of Japanese ancestry, the majority of whom were American citizens, were
forcibly removed from their Pacific Coast homes and incarcerated in desolate camps in the interior of the country. Here they were held, on average,
for two to three years before they were allowed to rejoin the society from
which they had been abruptly and harshly removed. They suffered perni-
cious and disorienting attacks on their self-concept and identity, jarring
upheavals to their family and community life, and, frequently, crippling economic losses. The fundamental causes of this monumental breach of constitutional rights, according to a congressional commission, were "Racism,
wartime hysteria, and the failure of political leadership" (Commission on
Wartime Relocation and Internment of Civilians, 1997).

More than sixty years have passed since that unprecedented suspension
of civil rights took place. At the time of the uprooting and incarceration,
about one-third of those detained were Issei or immigrant generation, and
about two-thirds were Nisei, or American-born. Almost all of the older first
or Issei generation have now passed on. The majority of their children, the

3

American-born, second-generation Nisei, however, are still living. When they were excluded from the Pacific Coast, the average Nisei was about seventeen years of age; most were children or young adults. Now, they are generally in their seventies and eighties, and some are even in their nineties.

The aging of the Nisei is a serious concern for social scientists and historians, as this population constitutes the last remaining group who directly experienced the wartime exclusion and incarceration. Given the unprecedented nature of the forceful uprooting of this population during World War II, it seems imperative to preserve the experiences of those who were subjected to the event. Moreover, not only are their wartime experiences of great interest, but so are their accounts of how they reentered American society and reestablished themselves following their wartime trauma. Surprisingly, there have been few social scientific attempts to collect detailed information from a representative group of former incarcerees, a lacuna, no doubt, caused by the difficulties inherent in securing such information.

Voluminous literature describes the expulsion of Japanese Americans from the West Coast and their daily lives in the "internment"[2] camps. During the war, the federal government collected extensive records about the incarcerees, and university-based researchers mounted numerous social scientific efforts to study the camps and their residents. Many researchers viewed the camps as massive "social laboratories" (e.g., Leighton 1945; Thomas 1952; Thomas and Nishimoto 1946; War Relocation Authority 1946b, 1946c). After the war, many scholars extensively examined these and other records to document more clearly why the incarceration took place and evolved in the way that it did (e.g., Bosworth 1967; Broom and Kitsuse 1956; Commission on Wartime Relocation and Internment of Civilians 1997; Daniels 1993; Daniels, Taylor, and Kitano 1991; Girdner and Loftis 1969; Weglyn 1976). A large-scale effort administered from UCLA, the Japanese American Research Project (JARP), collected historical, interview, and survey data during the 1960's on Japanese Americans, many of whom had been incarcerated (e.g., Bonacich and Modell 1980; Levine and Rhodes 1981; Montero 1980). Nagata (1993) has examined communication about the incarceration between Nisei parents and their Sansei (third-generation) children. Further, a substantial number of narrative and autobiographical accounts that give personal views of the human impact of the incarceration have become available (e.g., Gorfinkel 1995; Hansen 1991; Harris 1999; Tateishi 1984; Uchida 1982).

The majority of the foregoing studies, however, are either archival historical analyses or reports in which the authors extract and interpret accounts provided by those who were in the wartime camps. The historically oriented works are invaluable as they chronicle the political, economic, legal, and administrative aspects of the incarceration. For their part, the personal narratives make available the human drama of some of those who were directly impacted. However, with the latter, one is uncertain of the extent to which these individual perspectives are representative of the larger group of incarcerees. Even those studies which employed a large number of respondents (for example, the JARP project, which was a major three-generation effort examining the broader nature of the Japanese American community rather than the incarceration per se, and Nagata's [1993] mail survey) drew their samples from community organization lists. We are thus uncertain of the extent to which the results are truly generalizable to all incarcerees. Therefore, the difficult problem of representativeness remains.

OUR MAIN SOURCE OF DATA: THE DENSHŌ SURVEY

Concern over losing firsthand accounts of the wartime incarceration and postwar adaptation prompted a group of concerned individuals in Seattle to establish in 1996 Denshō: The Japanese American Legacy Project. As several of the founders of this group had strong backgrounds in the computer industry, the Project started with a multi-media, visual history orientation. The basic idea was to videotape and digitize a large representative group of former incarcerees who lived in the greater Seattle area. The Project continues to shoot and digitally process additional visual histories, but its current focus is now on producing educational materials about the World War II incarceration. Much of this material is available on Denshō's Web site (www.densho.org). The majority of the quoted material in this book is drawn from the visual histories collected by the Project.[3]

Despite their vividness, visual histories also give rise to certain inherent limitations. Because many individuals are uncomfortable being videotaped, particularly among this population, the question of representativeness is again raised. Moreover, since the objective is generally to allow the respondents to present their own perspectives, the questioning is oftentimes minimally guided, and thus there is no assurance that particular critical topics will be covered.

Thus, soon after the Project was initiated, a second approach, a representative sample survey that would complement the visual histories, was launched. This survey was based upon a random sample of virtually all Japanese

American registered voters living in King County (in which Seattle is located) in 1997. One of the authors of this monograph (Fugita) was involved, along with several members of the Denshō staff and an advisory group of social scientists, in designing and directing the survey. The survey instrument was written to contain many items that would permit the statistical analysis of responses. Having a survey done under the auspices of Denshō not only made available the financial resources needed to mount such an effort, but it also provided to the community the legitimacy necessary to obtain widespread cooperation and willingness to discuss the still sensitive topic of the incarceration.

The final survey sample of 183 former incarcerees consisted of individuals who were at least five years of age at the time of their imprisonment. Because of the geogenerational age distribution found among Japanese Americans, the vast majority of these individuals were Nisei. Trained interviewers administered all of the surveys, usually in the homes of the respondents. See appendix A and chapter 2 for additional details about sampling, survey items, and other methodological issues.

MAJOR OBJECTIVES OF THIS STUDY

The main purpose of this study is to examine the impact of the World War II experiences of exclusion and incarceration of Japanese Americans on their postwar efforts to reestablish themselves in American society. Given the haste with which they were forced from their homes and communities, the living conditions into which they were placed, the disruptions to their education or careers, and the humiliation to which they were exposed, one might expect to observe both long-term socioeconomic consequences as well as persistent, if subtle, psychological effects. Our principal focus, using the Denshō survey, will be on the socioeconomic consequences, which are more readily measurable with traditional survey and historical methodologies. Secondarily, we explore the psychological effects, which are considerably more difficult to document and may have a course of development quite distinct from the socioeconomic ones. The Denshō survey responses provide some information about psychological effects, but for a better understanding of this area, we draw upon the Denshō oral and visual histories as well as other historical documentation.

A cursory examination of Japanese Americans today does not immediately suggest that their lives were seriously disrupted by their World War II experience. Even if we focus on only the Nisei, who directly experienced the incarceration, census figures document that they are better educated and have higher incomes than the white majority (e.g., Fong 1998, 57–65). This was already evident in 1970, only twenty-five years after their wartime incarceration (U.S. Bureau of the Census 1973). In the social arena, they continue to have extensive ethnic friendship networks as well as numerous and active organizations, particularly on the Pacific Coast (e.g., Fugita and O'Brien 1991; Kitano 1993, 107–9). Observations such as these have caused some social scientists to go so far as to dub them "the model minority" because of their apparent economic and social achievements in the face of persistent adversity (e.g., Peterson 1966). However, if we explore below these aggregate surface indicators, does this apparently sanguine picture still hold up? Surely, one would expect that, given the degree of disruption of individuals' lives and the assaults on their identities and self-concepts, there would be significant long-term negative effects.

These questions are extremely difficult to answer with any degree of certainty. No single social scientific or historical approach, such as the use of surveys, archival data, oral histories, or participant observation, can hope to provide definitive answers to many of these intriguing questions. If we consider our preferred methodological tool of surveys, several problematic issues immediately become apparent, such as the accuracy of retrospective reconstruction, the plethora of events that have intervened since World War II, and other methodological conundrums. However, by utilizing a combination of distinct disciplinary and methodological approaches, a rich and compelling understanding can be crafted. Therefore, even though the foundation of our work is an extensive contemporary survey, our study draws liberally from several disciplinary approaches and literatures. In particular, we emphasize the historical literature and oral histories to better understand the prewar and wartime periods. These help "set the stage" for interpreting our Denshō survey results, which are most relevant to postwar and contemporary issues.

NEED FOR HISTORICAL CONTEXT

To understand the influence of the incarceration on individual Seattle Nisei respondents as well as on their community, we need to comprehend what their lives were like before the war. Although the Denshō survey does provide some information about the prewar period, a much more detailed and nuanced understanding is necessary. In order to facilitate this, we develop a historical and sociological framework in this chapter and then devote the entire next chapter to presenting the historical documentation needed to capture the major features of this period in the lives of Seattle Nisei.

Our review of the literature suggests that examining three macro-level topics can help us better understand the consequences of the incarceration of the Nisei: the U.S.– Japan relationship, the U.S. societal context, and the character of the ethnic or Japanese American community.

U.S.– Japan relationship. Relations between the United States and Japan have evolved from that of being reviled enemies prior to World War II to that of highly interdependent allies in the geopolitics of the volatile Pacific Rim region. Escalating tensions between the two countries in the 1930's strongly influenced Americans' view of the Issei and their young Nisei progeny. Moreover, differences between Issei born and raised in Japan and their American-born Nisei children in how they viewed Japan's political and military actions during this era and throughout World War II frequently produced tensions within families as well as in the larger ethnic community. After the war, this externally imposed international pressure on the community and individuals became, for the most part, nonexistent. This is not to imply that there have not been periods of tension between the two countries after the war, most notably skirmishes in trade and, more broadly, economic competition. In fact, these periods have occasionally produced negative fallout for not only Japanese Americans but other Asian Americans as well (e.g., Fong 1998, 152–54).

U.S. societal context. American society has itself changed dramatically in a multitude of ways since the beginning of the twentieth century, when the Issei began to arrive in significant numbers. The aspect of change that is probably most germane to our study is that of race relations. In the prewar era, not only was de facto discrimination against racial minorities the norm, but de jure discrimination was also a daily reality for many groups. For Japanese Americans, the larger society was "semi-permeable" or "castelike" during this period (Miyamoto 1984, ix–xi). The Issei could not become naturalized citizens or buy land during most of this period and, in 1924, their immigration to the United States was completely halted. This discrimination constrained their economic development in agriculture and small business as well as their integration into the larger society. Social intermingling across ethnic and racial boundaries was limited. These boundaries were also the product of language difficulties among the immigrant Issei and the natural proclivity of recently arrived groups to seek refuge among their own people. Most of the Nisei attended integrated public schools, where they became highly acculturated. However, when they came of age, many were blocked from entering desirable occupations, such as the unionized trades and the professions (e.g., Modell 1977, 127–153).

After the tumult of World War II, the country became engaged in an uneven and wrenching movement towards greater equality for all of its citizens. For Japanese Americans, discriminatory laws directed towards them were removed fairly rapidly from the books during this period. Economic, political, and social opportunities became much more widespread. Still, various forms of informal discrimination persisted. Starting in the 1960s, racial and ethnic minorities experienced dramatic changes in how they came to view themselves, their communities, and their cultures. This process was confounded with, and probably as significant as, the breaking down of discriminatory barriers.

Japanese American community. Due to certain cultural predispositions and social and educational resources, many Issei were able before the war to move up from wage-labor positions in industries such as agriculture to become sharecroppers, then leasers, and finally independent farmers. They also started a multitude of urban small businesses, most notably hotels, stores, and restaurants. To a degree, they were forced into these small business niches because of the discrimination they faced in other occupational areas. Social and cultural resources such as communal solidarity were critical to the formation and maintenance of this economic form (e.g., Bonacich and Modell 1980, 34–63). Once established, this ethnic economy both supported, and was supported by, a wide variety of highly organized, interlinked institutions.

Part of this propensity to build extensive formal and informal ethnic ties was a function of cultural templates brought over by the Issei from Japan (e.g., Miyamoto, Fugita, and Kashima 2002). The Meiji-era Japanese society in which the Issei were socialized emphasized group or organizational responses to handling everyday exigencies. This cultural orientation, in combination with difficulties in securing occupational and social opportunities in the larger American society, made the Issei turn their energies inward to develop wide-ranging economic and social networks in their own community. So, in many ways, for Japanese Americans before World War II, parallel communities existed; one was ethnic and dominated by Issei organizations and leaders, and the other was a frequently impenetrable yet, in many ways, beckoning larger white world.

The wartime exclusion from their Pacific Coast homes and confinement in isolated War Relocation Authority (WRA) and Department of Justice (DOJ) camps severely damaged both the economic and social networks that the Issei and older Nisei had developed. Fortunately, as a consequence of the government process of "evacuating" families together in a given locale, a substantial number of ties between individuals and families were preserved during this period. Generally, families from the same area were sent to the same camp. The government's policy, from the outset of the removal program, was not to split families or communities (Broom and Kitsuse 1956, 37).

When the Nisei, and later the Issei, were released from the camps, many did not return immediately to their former West Coast homes but detoured, sometimes permanently, to new, unfamiliar places, principally in the Midwest and East. The incarcerees were not permitted to return to their former Pacific Coast homes until January 2, 1945. The resultant diaspora was consistent with the WRA's assimilationist orientation to dealing with "the Japanese problem." The government actively encouraged the former incarcerees to disperse and not reestablish the tight ethnic communities they lived in before the war. Moreover, many incarcerees felt that they would face less hostility in these new areas than back on the Pacific Coast. The Issei, who were now in their fifties and sixties, were, in the main, unable to start over again and never reestablished their dominant position in the community. Their prewar organizations, for example, the ubiquitous Japanese Associations, except in rare instances such as in New York City, were never re-formed.

The postwar generational transfer of community leadership initially made the Nisei the community's interface with the larger society, while the Issei were the active organizers and fund raisers within the community. Soon, however, the Nisei's strong need for contact with one another drove them to be an energetic force for the building or rebuilding of ethnic churches, athletic leagues, Japanese American Citizens League chapters, and service organizations wherever they resettled (e.g., Nishi 1998–99). As a result, and because of the displacement of the Issei during the war, the Nisei became the main ethnic community players after the war. Nonetheless, these new and rebuilt ethnic communities never regained the size or importance they had before the war because the highly acculturated Nisei could now more easily navigate the increasingly open U.S. society. One consequence of the Issei losing their farms and small businesses, as they generally did not have the capital to reestablish them, and of the more open postwar opportunity structure was a shift from the prewar small capitalist occupations to an occupational pattern after the war that was distinctly more Nisei driven and oriented toward mainstream society and wage and salary earners. In short, the postwar ethnic community exhibited both continuities and discontinuities with its prewar form.

SOME SENSITIZING CONCEPTS

The three macro, overarching themes just discussed (U.S.–Japan relationship, U.S. societal context, and Japanese American community) help us to contextualize the lives of our Nisei respondents historically and socially. In addition, several other more micro sociological concepts, which are listed below, are utilized throughout the book to sensitize us to certain outcomes.

Life course. This perspective focuses our attention on survey participants' responses to new challenges over their entire lives (e.g., Elder 1986; Elder and Liker 1982; Elder, Liker, and Cross 1984; Mayer 1988; Pavalko and Elder 1990). The approach assumes that, throughout life, individuals assess and react to situations in light of their personal biographies (e.g., Elder and Liker 1982). Thus, more temporally distal as well as more proximal consequences of major life experiences and individuals' responses can receive analytic attention. In fact, this approach has produced significant insights about the differential impact of major life events such as economic depression and military service (so-called "turning points") on individuals who varied in their access to different types of resources (e.g., Elder 1974, 1986; Pavalko and Elder, 1990). With respect to our particular problem, an examination of how individuals with differing characteristics and resources responded to and reconstructed their incarceration experience, World War II produced a similar "turning point" in the lives of the Denshō Nisei respondents.

Age and gender. A major analytic distinction within the life-course framework that we foreground is "age" or "life-stage." Following Elder's "life-stage principle" (Elder 1986, 1987), we pay careful attention to the points in the former incarcerees' life courses where survey respondents experienced events surrounding World War II. Incarcerees' age (or more appropriately the underlying processes associated with this marker variable) at the time of their incarceration is complexly related to differences in both the nature of an individual's experiences as well as their current meaning. A fundamental expectation is that individuals of various ages came to the World War II period with diverse biographies, social roles, and resources and consequently were impacted by and remember their imprisonment quite differently.

To put it another way, the incarceration was a major disruption to the age-graded developmental tasks facing various cohorts of incarcerees, and thus it is expected to have differential effects as a function of the respondents' life-stage. For example, older Nisei were more likely to have experienced a major disruption in their career trajectory as a by-product of the incarceration. Many of these individuals also had pressing family responsibilities that had to be managed as best as possible under the circumstances. Others who were somewhat younger had their opportunities to obtain higher education taken away or, in rarer cases, enhanced by the student relocation efforts of outside groups.

Also, given the highly gendered nature of Japanese American, and indeed, mainstream American society during the World War II period, we explore a wide range of potential gender-related effects. For instance, one might speculate that college-aged Nisei women were more negatively impacted by the incarceration because the scarce financial resources that were available to families might be more likely invested in a son's education than in a daughter's. Acting in concert with this, older daughters may have felt greater role responsibility to care for their aging Issei parents and younger siblings than older sons.

Financial, human, social, and cultural capital. The incarceration itself was a very leveling experience for the Japanese Americans who experienced it. Regardless of what individuals' stations in life were before the war, their treatment within the barbed-wire confines of their camp was usually quite similar. Nonetheless, as would be expected in any large human group, individuals faced their imprisonment with diverse amounts of material, psychic, social, and cultural resources. How incarcerees dealt with and felt about their expulsion, incarceration, and resettlement was and still is strongly influenced by their access to and ability to mobilize these types of resources. Thus, another major analytic concern of our study in the way Nisei incarcerees coped is to better understand the consequences of having differential access to financial, human, social, and cultural capital.

Brief descriptions of these different types of resources are useful here. Financial capital is typically defined as wealth or income. Human capital refers to the resources that an individual-qua-individual brings to situations and is usually indexed by a proxy variable, such as the level of formal education a person has attained. Social capital is the quantity and quality of resources the individual is able to secure through various social institutions and networks such as family and friends (e.g., Putnam 1995, 2000). Cultural capital is the ability to understand and utilize normatively preferred cultural forms, such as middle-class interpersonal style and artistic expression (e.g., Coleman 1988). Classifying our respondents along these dimensions guides us to a more systematic and nuanced picture of how the incarceration impacted individuals over their life courses.

ORGANIZATION OF THE BOOK

The presentation of our findings is basically temporal. We have begun in this chapter by introducing the topic and briefly discussing a number of the most significant historical factors and analytic concepts. Chapter 2 describes prewar Japanese America, focusing especially on the Seattle community and the larger American context in which it was then embedded. Chapter 3 focuses on the incarceration itself. Chapter 4 examines the postwar experiences of those incarcerees who either entered the military or resisted the draft during wartime. These topics are followed by discussions of the postwar resettlement (chapter 5) and marriage and the family (chapter 6). Next, occupational achievement patterns (chapter 7) and religion and its role in shaping memories of the incarceration (chapter 8) are described. Chapter 9 is a summary and discussion of the implications of our findings.

TWO

The Pre–World War II Community

I remember always having older women, *obachan,* not *obaachan* but *obaasan,* just older women that could tell us what to do and we would snap to it because you just did it [laughs]. I found that it's funny because even when I was adult and married and had my own kids, when I ran into them I felt like a little kid again because they reminded me of the times . . . if my mother wasn't there, they could tell me what to do and I would have to do it, which was fine. (May K. Sasaki, denshovh-smay-01-0005)

In this second chapter, we give the reader a sense of the world of our Nisei respondents prior to the turmoil of World War II. Along with a description of the Denshō survey respondents and information about their prewar lives, this sets the stage for our main focus, the reactions of former incarcerees to their exclusion and detention. Since the community in which our Nisei respondents grew up was dominated by their Issei parents, we start by examining the worldviews, values, and social templates which this immigrant generation brought with them from turn-of-the-century Meiji Japan. This leads into the more germane question about how the Issei's aspirations and resources meshed with the conditions they found on the Pacific Coast in the early twentieth century. What kind of "beachhead" were they able to establish for themselves and their children in the three or four decades they were in the country before the incarceration? What were the contours of their relationship with the larger American society?

As we outline the answers to these questions, we focus on the Seattle area, as it is the region where the majority of our survey respondents were raised. Nonetheless, the social ecology of this area was quite similar to other major West Coast cities where significant numbers of Issei settled. In those instances where the Pacific Northwest was unique, we will attempt to draw attention to these differences.

THE ISSEI

What the Issei Brought to the United States

The Issei were born and socialized in Japan during the Meiji Restoration period, which began in 1868. This era was characterized by rapid industrialization, modernization, and an attempt to quickly shift Japan's social structure from feudalism to one that was more supportive of imperialism. After the humiliating, forcible opening of their country by Admiral Perry's gunboats in 1853, Japan's leaders feared that their country would be colonized or, in other ways, become a victim of Western imperialism. They were all too aware of the dismal fate of their weak neighbors such as China (e.g., Duus 1976, 60–64).

As part of the effort to build a powerful nation, the leaders promulgated the concept of a familistic state with the Imperial Family as the original stem. In the Japanese social system, the family (ie) was the key unit. Moreover, the Japanese concept of family went beyond being simply a group of individuals; it also involved the family's ancestral line, house, and property. In both the Civil and Criminal Code of Japan at the time, the family, not the individual, was the principal unit of society (Miyamoto 1984, 28). Thus, in the Japanese system, it was very important to preserve the status or "name" of the family, much more so than that of the individual. Loyalty and filial piety were emphasized to counter "self-conscious individualism" which was incompatible with the kind of "divine country" the leaders desired (Fukutake 1989, 11–16).

At the time of the Meiji restoration, 90 percent of the Japanese lived in villages (muras). These were characterized by dense, multiplex relationships among families; even in the cities, neighborhood ties were strong. These relationships made possible a great deal of mutual assistance in instrumental activities such as rice production and home building as well as on important social occasions, such as weddings and funerals. In addition, new organizations such as cooperatives, women's institutes, and youth groups were encouraged (e.g.,

Norbeck 1972). Even these secondary, functional groups took on a familistic structure and atmosphere.

As a way to support these groups, much stronger emphasis was placed on interpersonal harmony as contrasted with individual autonomy. One manifestation of this was the encouragement of unanimous decision-making in groups. Also, custom and authority were preferred over conscience and judgment, as they were more likely to lead to interpersonal harmony. In short, a type of "familistic communitarianism" was strongly emphasized in the name of country and emperor (Fukutake 1989,18–43, 70).

Given the intense and rising nationalism of the period, one might ask why a significant number of the Issei chose to leave their homeland. One "push" factor was the Meiji government's imposition of a series of land tax reforms to finance the drive for modernization. These fell most heavily on the farming class (Moriyama 1985, 2–5). This sector of society ultimately provided the majority of immigrants who came first to Hawaii and subsequently to the U.S. mainland (Ichioka 1988, 42–48).

Another factor that encouraged emigration was the *dekasegi* tradition of mostly young, rural workers supplementing their meager incomes by traveling to urban areas to temporarily work. This internal migration helped to legitimize the idea of temporarily traveling abroad to better one's economic status (Moriyama 1985, 6; Wilson and Hosokawa 1980, 28).

These factors, combined with Japan's rigid social structure, caused many ambitious young men to begin to dream of the exciting new possibilities they heard about in America. Guides to America, contacts with returnees, and letters from earlier migrants frequently painted an idealized picture of the economic opportunities in the United States (Ichioka 1988, 11–13; Ito 1973, 5–6). Significantly, the Issei's initial motivation to immigrate was based upon the perceived opportunity to raise their status in Japan, the so-called sojourner orientation. For many, this orientation changed over the years, although a substantial number who had the weakest identification with America returned to Japan when they were forced to deal with increasing discrimination and the Depression. In addition, although the precise numbers cannot be known, many young men were also motivated to avoid conscription (Ichihashi 1932, 87–88; Ichioka 1988, 13–14).

Not surprisingly, those who did immigrate to the United States brought with them Meiji-era characteristics, values, and worldviews: a high level of educational motivation and attainment (for the period) due to Japan's requirement for universal education, status drive for upward mobility, and perhaps most importantly, a capacity for group cooperation and action (e.g., Miyamoto 1984, 6–7; Thomas 1952, 47–53).

The latter group orientation was based upon fundamental social relational norms such as *wa* (meaning "peace" or "harmony"). The *wa* concept, difficult to define in English, refers less to "peace-loving" in an ideological sense and more to "conflict-avoidance" (Miyamoto, Fugita, and Kashima 2002). This value often makes it possible for the Japanese to work in groups without more individualistic orientations disrupting shared goals. So important was this concept to Japanese society that it was written into the first article of Prince Shōtoku's seventh-century constitution (Nakamura 1968, 633).

Another pervasive and long-standing Japanese social orientation that the Issei strongly held was *giri-ninjô* (e.g., Hayashi and Kuroda 1997, 26–30). This complex set of social attitudes roughly refers to "obligation and duty" *(giri)* and "responsiveness to the deeper feelings of others" *(ninjô)* (Miyamoto, Fugita, and Kashima 2002). These values were reinforced by the religious institutions of Buddhism and Shintoism (Wierzbica 1991). Social orientations such as these predisposed the Issei to make group-oriented responses to the exigencies they found in early twentieth-century America.

The Community that the Issei Built

As previously mentioned, our discussion of the prewar Japanese American community emphasizes Seattle and King County, since this is the area where the majority of Denshō survey respondents spent their youth. Their immigrant parents not only built their own ethnic community in what was, at the time, a raw frontier, but they also ultimately made very substantial contributions to the larger agricultural and small business sectors of the region's economy.

Frontier period. During the 1880s and 1890s, some 250 Japanese settled in Seattle. Subsequently, around the turn of the century, the rate of immigration to the area sharply increased, as did the class of immigrant individuals. While most were laborers, there were also a small number of college-educated Issei. As previously noted, the majority of these Issei were single men who were economically motivated sojourners or "birds of passage." Most initially hoped to stay in the United States some three to five years before returning to Japan as wealthy individuals (e.g., Ito 1973, 16–17, 30, 33).

During the period that the Issei arrived in Seattle, the area was experiencing booming growth. From 1890 to 1900 the population of the city almost doubled from 42,837 to 80,671, and then it virtually tripled to 237,174 from 1900 to 1910 (Sale 1976, 51). Many of the young Issei men took jobs in the surrounding rough-hewn logging camps, sawmills, canneries, and railroads and visited the city for supplies and recreation. As most of these arduous laboring jobs did not provide the rapid economic advancement to which the sojourners aspired, it was not long before many began to move into entrepreneurship.

Farming. As elsewhere on the Pacific Coast, one of the main entrepreneurial endeavors the Japanese took up was small-scale, intensive farming. In the Seattle area, the Issei did much of the grueling work necessary to clear the forests and drain the marshes in exchange for their initial use. Ultimately, they grew a variety of vegetables and berries and sold much of it through ethnically linked produce houses and marketing cooperatives as well as at the Pike Place Market. By the beginning of World War I, Japanese occupied some 70 percent of the stalls in the bustling waterfront market. Further, by one estimate, in the 1920s they grew 75 percent of the region's vegetables and produced half its milk (Takami 1998, 20). This economic success in agriculture, again similar to other areas of the West Coast, particularly California, drew the ire of competing groups. Thus, in 1921, the Washington State Legislature passed an alien land law that was designed to restrict Japanese farming by preventing them from not only owning land but leasing it as well. This legislation was modeled after a similar California law that was originally passed in 1913 and strengthened in 1920. As "aliens ineligible for citizenship," the Issei lacked the right to vote and thus were easy targets for politicians.

The legal impediments posed by the Alien Land Law created a great deal of uncertainty. Ultimately, the Issei growers developed a variety of techniques that helped them skirt the law; they became "managers" for whites who technically owned the land, entered into verbal agreements, or bought the land in the name of Nisei who had reached their majority. Even though they were often able to evade the land law, it was frightening to the Issei because it threatened their very livelihood (Ichioka 1988, 226–43). The Seattle Japanese newspaper *Taihoku Nippō* editorialized that it created "a great panic" and equated the situation of the Issei to that of the *eta,* or pariah caste in Japan (cited in Ichioka 1988, 234). The loophole of making citizen

Nisei the "owners" was closed by an amendment to the Alien Land Law in 1923. As a result, the number of acres cultivated by the Issei was significantly reduced. Still, by the outbreak of World War II, the Japanese farmed approximately 56 percent of all agricultural land in King County (Takami, 1998, 24–25).

Nihonmachi. After Jackson Street was regraded in 1908 to reduce its steep elevation, many Japanese moved from Pioneer Square to the Jackson and Yesler Street or "skid road" neighborhood that is now part of the International District (e.g., Chin 2001, 10, 40–41). This section of the city, which was immediately south of downtown, was a high-crime, polyethnic, working-class area. As significant numbers of Issei moved into the locale, it became known as Japantown, or Nihonmachi. It reached its economic and social peak in the 1920s. The passage of the 1924 Immigration Act, which cut off the stream of newcomers who needed the area's supplies and services, and increasing residential dispersion subsequently reduced its vitality. Nonetheless, Nihonmachi was the heart of Japanese American life in the Pacific Northwest until the uprooting of the community soon after Pearl Harbor.

Shifting Immigration and Labor Patterns

As previously noted, the initial frontier-stage of the Issei community had a disproportionate number of male laborers. This changed dramatically after the passage of the so-called "gentlemen's agreement" of 1907–8, which was put in place to stop the immigration of male laborers. However, much to the chagrin of the exclusionists, it stimulated the picture bride mechanism, which allowed women technically married to Japanese businessmen and farmers already in the United States to enter the country (Daniels 1993, 17–19; Ichioka 1988, 71–72). This influx of women, which had already started on a smaller scale, made possible the next phase in the development of the Japanese community, the so-called "settling period" (Miyamoto 1984, 11). Not only was the male-dominated, frontier society transformed into a family-oriented one, there was also a large-scale movement into entrepreneurial as contrasted with wage-earner occupations. The extra hands of a wife (and later children) made viable many marginal, labor-intensive small businesses. But the lives of those in these small businesses were far from easy. The following two quotes from Denshō visual history narrators provide a glimpse into the rigorous lifestyle associated with these businesses. The first recalls the arduous routine of an Issei mother and her children; the second of a young teenage Nisei:

> She gets up at four-thirty in the morning and makes breakfast for the workers. And, not make lunch but make the makings for lunch so that they can pack their own lunch before they go to work. Then have dinner ready when they come back from work. So our job as kids were to come back from school and get the *furo,* the bathtub ready. Clean it, fill it up with water and build a fire up under it, so it'll be good and hot by the time they finish their dinner, so they can, so everybody can take baths, you know, among other things. And then the kitchen help, so forth, you know. Of course, no washing machines. (Harvey Watanabe, denshovh-wharvey-01-0007)

> We had to start working at a very young age. Nowadays, I wouldn't think of telling my son, go take a truckload of produce to Seattle when he was thirteen years old. But I used to do that from thirteen, no driver's license. And I drove every, six days a week to take a load of produce into Seattle wholesale market, and made it home before, in time to make the next day's load and load it up and work until nine, ten o'clock at night I remember some nights. And first thing in the morning, I used to get up at four o'clock in the morning to go and get it all done before school. (Seichi Hayashida, denshovh-hseichi-01-0005)

The outbreak of World War I brought many white workers to Seattle's shipbuilding industry. These laborers needed the services, such as working-class hotels and restaurants, that the Japanese small businesses provided. By the 1930s, 46 percent of the Japanese in Seattle were entrepreneurs in the trades or services, and another 25 percent were directly dependent upon them. See table 2.1 for a listing of the large number and variety of Japanese businesses in the city in 1935. The size of Seattle's Japanese laboring class was thus quite small. An important consequence of this relatively homogeneous, small capitalist occupational pattern was the relative lack of class-consciousness within the community. This was an important feature of the community, as it minimized class-based cleavages from developing, which would have reduced the cohesiveness of the ethnic group (Miyamoto 1984, 16–17).

The large number and variety of retail shops and services that were found

Table 2.1. Ten Most Important Trades Among the Japanese in Seattle

Trades	No. of Establishments
Hotels	183
Groceries	148
Dye works	94
Public-market stands	64
Produce houses	57
Gardeners	42
Restaurants	36
Barber shops	36
Laundries	31
Peddlers (fruit and vegetables)	24

Source: Seattle Japanese Occupational Census of 1935, published by the Seattle Japanese
Chamber of Commerce. (Miyamoto 1984).

in Nihonmachi provided for virtually all the needs and wants of the Issei. Especially on weekends, farmers and laborers flooded into the area for supplies and recreation. At its peak in the 1920s, Nihonmachi contained a large number of bustling barbershops, bathhouses, groceries, dry goods stores, laundries, bakeries, fish and meat markets, confectionary and cigar stores, bookstores, restaurants, and gambling houses. One example of the latter was the Toyo Club, which was the second largest gambling house on the West Coast. Also, the services of tailors, physicians, dentists, and lawyers were available. There were two Japanese-language newspapers that provided news about Japan and the local community, the *Hokubei Jiji* (North American Times) and *Taihoku Nippō* (Great Northern Daily News). In addition, from 1928 up until World War II, an English-language paper, the *Japanese American Courier*, served the rapidly increasing Nisei segment of the community (Ito 1973, 140; Takami 1998, 36).

A Rich Web of Institutions

One of the key characteristics of the Seattle Japanese community (and most other pre—World War II Japanese enclaves) was its plethora of institutions. Whatever the need or interest, if there were over a handful of likeminded individuals, an organization seemed to emerge. This quality of the Japanese was apparent even to outsiders. The Carnegie-sponsored "Studies of Americanization" described them as "the most efficiently and completely organized among the immigrant groups" (Thomas 1952, 50).

Churches. Given the strong predominance of Buddhism and Shintoism compared with Christianity in Japan, one wonders why, in Seattle, there came to be more Japanese who were members of Christian churches than Buddhist and Shinto temples. One likely reason was that the Christian churches made available important services to newcomers that were previously provided to the Issei by their family and village. For instance, Christian churches served as employment agencies and taught the Issei English and American customs. Buddhism had no tradition of social welfare since, in Japan, kin and fellow villagers provided most of the necessary services.

The Baptists were the first to establish a church in 1899 that had a mission for Japanese women. The Methodist Episcopal Church followed soon after. Nisei Spady Koyama describes how this process worked in Spokane's Japanese Methodist Church.

> After we finished our regular schooling, we would all go to what we call a Japanese mission, located right next door to the Central Methodist Church, which had a very active and energetic women's society of the Central Methodist Ladies. They, in turn, took upon themselves the fact that they noticed all these coming, incoming women from Japan, don't know the language, nor do they know how to use knives, forks and spoons, nor know when and how to gets shots for their school kids. So they took upon themselves to create a Japanese mission right next door and they would come over and [it was] run by the ladies of the Central Methodist Church and that explains why today most of Spokane young people, second as well as third generation, are members of the Highland Park Methodist Church. (Spady Koyama, denshovh-kspady-01-0006)

The Issei who converted to Protestantism, even though they usually attended segregated churches, were likely to become somewhat more assimilated than Buddhists. This was due to the greater emphasis on mainstream cultural elements such as the celebration of Christmas and Easter as well as to greater contact with non-Japanese within the larger church organization.

Despite the strong Christian connection, Buddhism also flourished. The Seattle Buddhist Temple was started in 1901 and moved several times to larger quarters as it grew. It was a critical institution in promoting a Japanese language school for the Nisei (e.g., Chin 2001, 28; Miyamoto 1984, 45—50).

Nippon Kan. The community "gathering place" was the Nippon Kan The-
ater. Built with community funds in 1909, it was in constant use, hosting a
variety of political debates, plays, Japanese movies, operas, symphonies,
kabuki, puppet shows, martial arts competitions, church fund raisers, sports
team banquets, and Japanese-language school events such as the celebration
of *Tenchosetsu* (Emperor's Birthday). Educational, business, sports, church,
and cultural groups as well as university students used the hall (Chin 2001,
26; Dubrow 2002, 62–79). David Takami (1998, 29) relates, "Most of the
entertainers were delightfully unprofessional, sometimes forgetting their lines
and struggling to improvise. Between performances, children ran up and
down the balcony staircases and their parents caught up with the latest community gossip."

Learning the ropes: Ken connections. One wonders how the Issei who came
from mostly farming families were able to learn the necessary skills to run
the many new small businesses that they started. Moreover, how did they
procure the necessary capital? Generally, "pioneers" learned the basics of
the trade and then would subsequently hire others whom they would train
and later help get started in their own businesses. In particular, if a fellow
Issei was from the same prefecture or ken in Japan, established individuals
felt an obligation to extend a hand. For the employer, this pro-social perspective and subsequent relationship had the advantage of ensuring greater
loyalty and effort from the employee. This process thus produced a tendency
for people from the same ken to be in the same line of work (Miyamoto
1984, 20).

Tanomoshi. Although much of the capital to start small businesses came from
"sweat equity," the Issei in Seattle (as in other Japanese communities) frequently used the *tanomoshi,* or rotating credit mechanism (e.g., Light 1972,
27–30; Miyamoto 1984, 21–22). There were a number of variations on how
this financial arrangement was practiced, but its key feature was that a group
of trusted individuals made systematic contributions to a common "pot"
that became available for one person to use, for example, as a down pay-
ment on a piece of property. The social aspects of this arrangement were
critical. Typically, a small group of friends brought together some fifteen to
twenty friends or vouched-for individuals for a dinner meeting. The individual who got access to the "pot" frequently showed his appreciation by
paying for the dinner or providing small gifts. At subsequent gatherings, indi-

viduals bid for the "pot" until everyone had obtained the pooled sum. Clearly, the crucial element that made the rotating credit mechanism possible was trust among the individuals. The fact that *tanomoshi* were common during this period among unrelated community members involved in commercial transactions attests to the primary group nature of relationships among many in the community (Miyamoto 1984, 21–22).

Sociopolitical organizations. The most influential and widespread Issei organizations were the Japanese Associations. These organizations dealt with a wide range of issues, including assisting new arrivals, fighting anti-Japanese legislation, supporting social and educational programs, acting as quasi-Japanese government offices, and promoting the immigrant community's economic interests (e.g., Ichioka 1977). They were found in virtually all Japanese communities of any size. In Seattle, the Japanese Association of Washington State was founded in 1900. That year, the first problem it dealt with was a boycott against Western-style Japanese restaurants, one that it successfully mediated. Not surprisingly, internal economic and other rivalries often surfaced and, in 1910, a faction split off and formed the Seattle Japanese Association. The two associations reunited in 1912. In 1913, ten Japanese Associations in the Pacific Northwest joined the Seattle organization, and in 1915, the group grew to encompass fifteen regional associations. One of the ways the Japanese Association in Seattle supported itself was by issuing "Consular Certificates" to visit Japan. In so doing, it acted as a semi-official arm of the Japanese government (Ichioka 1977; Ito 1973, 143).

The Japanese Association of Washington State became the umbrella organization for an amazing number of groups. By the late 1920s, the following organizations sent representatives to the Association: thirty-three prefectural associations, U.C. Club, Asia Club, Seattle Japanese Youth Club, Nitto Club, Japanese Chef's Friendship Association, Barber's Association, Washington State Farmers' Association, Washington State Shoemakers' League, Launderers' Association, Japanese Businessmen's Club, Pike Place Market Association, Dye Works Association, (Western) Restaurant Association, and Hotel Operators' Association (Ito 1973, 144–46).

As sociological principles of ingroup/outgroup dynamics would predict, when identifiable anti-Japanese pressures arose, the constantly bickering factions tended to put aside their differences. For example, in the drive to obtain naturalization rights, not only did the local groups unite, but the Japanese Associations in Washington, Oregon, California, and even British Columbia came together (Ito 1973, 147). This highly developed network of social and economic ties allowed the Issei to successfully fight attempts to drive them out of specific businesses. They could threaten boycotts of particular firms, or they could promise to channel all Japanese businesses to a single cooperative firm (Miyamoto 1984, 22). It should also be noted that it was felt to be a great honor to be a representative to the Japanese Association, warranting a telegram to one's home in Japan (Ito 1973, 163). They were the community "big shots."

The Seattle Japanese Chamber of Commerce was, in effect, the commercial branch of the Japanese Association. It represented some twenty-two business associations, such as the Hotel Operator's Association, Dye Works Association, and Restaurant Association. These associations attempted to regulate competition within the trade by, for example, mandating the distance between shops, length of workday, and prices. In addition, it represented the businesses to the larger white world. Another major function was social: to promote good will among the owners (e.g., Ito 1973, 132; Miyamoto 1984, 23).

The extensive interconnectedness among the Japanese associations also made it possible for them to exercise a high degree of social control over community members in different geographic areas. A good example of this relates to the inherent difficulties that were a part of the so-called picture bride mechanism. This process, which was a natural extension of the practice of arranged marriages in Japan, became common after the "gentlemen's agreement" of 1907–8 blocked male laborers from immigrating. On occasion, this mechanism of procuring young women from Japan as wives for single immigrant men in America produced, from the woman's perspective, less than hoped-for results. Men sometimes enhanced their physical attractiveness by touching up or sending an outdated photograph or by claiming, for example, to be a successful hotel operator when they actually ran a small boardinghouse. Every now and then an intolerable situation caused the woman to desert her husband, creating the scandal known as *kakeochi*. The Japanese Association often published a photograph and extensive identifying information about the "errant" wife in the immigrant press. In effect, the associations acted as moral "watchdogs" by treating the missing wife as an outcast to be located. The associations communicated with each other to such an extent that the wife could not hide wherever there were any other Japanese living (Ichioka 1980).

There were occasions when the Japanese sense of social responsibility proved to be a hindrance to the group's vitality. For instance, there was a widely felt obligation to patronize fellow Japanese, particularly friends and fellow ken members. The net result was feelings of reciprocal obligation such that the Issei expected special consideration from their fellow countrymen. This caused resentment on the part of the vendor or shop owner because it entailed primary group norms and social sensibilities in what would otherwise be a market-oriented, secondary relationship. This confounding of primary and secondary group norms also showed up in requests for credit or loans, which were not treated as arms-length commercial transactions. Thus, many noneconomic transactions were made which impeded the growth of Issei enterprises. In fact, because of these within-group, quasi-kin attitudes, the Japanese frequently repaid their debts to outsiders before they did so to their fellow countrymen. This created a positive image of Japanese creditworthiness to outsiders but produced economic strains within the community (cf. Miyamoto 1984, 23–27).

THE NISEI

The Nisei Come of Age

The passage of the Immigration Act of 1924 marked the end of a period of new and severe legal disadvantages wrought upon the Issei. The first of these, the Washington Alien Land Law of 1921, attempted to drive them out of agriculture. Then came the 1922 Ozawa naturalization test case in which the U.S. Supreme Court made it impossible for the Issei to become American citizens. Finally, the Immigration Act of 1924 virtually slammed the door shut on new immigration from Japan. In response to these serious impediments, and seeing no future in the country, many disillusioned Issei returned to Japan. But the majority reluctantly concluded that even though they would never be able to become first-class citizens, at least their maturing, Nisei children would be able to do so. In 1920, Nisei were about one-quarter of Seattle's 7,874 Japanese population. By 1930, nearly half of the Japanese population of 8,448 was American born (Takami 1998, 32).

Kibei. A sometimes overlooked but unique group of Nisei were the Kibei. They were Nisei who were sent to Japan for a significant proportion of their education but ultimately returned to the United States. By one estimate, they formed 9 percent of this geogeneration. When in Japan, they often lived with grandparents while their parents concentrated on working in America, struggling to realize the dream of returning to Japan wealthy. When the Kibei returned to the United States, they sometimes had difficulty establishing affectionate bonds with their parents and siblings. This was due to their residual feelings of having been rejected and their divergent cultural and political perspectives (e.g., Takahashi 1997, 78). Being "too Japanesy," they frequently had trouble fitting into the Nisei subculture. At the time, many teenage Nisei were self-consciously trying to disassociate themselves from things Japanese, particularly during the 1930s, when tensions between the United States and Japan were mounting (e.g., Kitano 1976, 159–60; Sone 1979, 126–30).

Family and social life: A (sometimes conflicting) mix of Japanese and American. There was usually a large "generation gap" between Issei parents and their Nisei children. For one, communication was difficult given the poor English of most Issei and the weak Japanese of most Nisei. Moreover, the direct expression of emotion favored by American culture, and to a lesser degree by the Nisei, was frequently at odds with the more indirect emotional style of the Issei. In addition, the formal, hierarchical Japanese cultural schemata of the Issei were frequently off-putting to their more Americanized Nisei children. As the Nisei entered their teenage years, their decidedly American interests and perspectives were a source of tension, and sometimes open conflict, with their parents. Common problem areas were personal appearance and social activities such as hairstyles, clothing, dancing, and dating (Takahashi 1997, 44–46). Girls, especially, were highly restricted when viewed through an American "lens."

The homes of most Nisei children were usually a "low or middlebrow" mixture of Japanese and mainstream culture. Meals, as well as home furnishings, were typically a combination of American and Japanese fare. Chizuko Norton describes her mother's culinary patterns:

I grew up eating not just Japanese food, but other food as well. . . . [My mother] said that when she came, she was just eighteen, and didn't know how to cook, didn't even know how to cook rice. And what she would do, since she lived in Seattle in that Yesler area that she would go to the neighbors and watched the lady of the house cooking dinner, and then, she would go and purchase these items and then go home and try it. Whether they were Jewish people or Russian. (Chizuko Norton, denshovh-nchizuko-01-0006)

As illustrated in the opening quote to this chapter by Nisei May Sasaki, not only did Issei parents have tight control over their children, but the family also generally worked synchronously with the community. Family control was thus not simply parental control but community control. Gossip traveled rapidly, and parents were quick to rein in their errant children lest the family name be besmirched. In many ways, for the Issei, their primary group ways of relating extended to secondary groups. For example, if a girl at the Bon Odori festival multi-generation dance had her obi misaligned on her kimono, most adults, regardless of relationship, would feel compelled to fix it, and comfortable doing so (e.g., Miyamoto 1984, 40–42).

Education of the Seattle Nisei

Mainstream education. Most Nisei children attended public schools in the neighborhood. Many vividly remember the strict tutelage of a particular principal, beloved Ada Mahon, first at Main Street School at Sixth and Main and later at nearby Bailey Gatzert School. One Seattle Nisei recalls:

> The principal there was Ada J. Mahon, and she was a staunch American in the true sense. Singing "Star Spangled Banner" and "God Bless America" and we marched to the "Stars and Stripes Forever" and all the John Phillip Sousa marches. And you march out of the school everyday, hearing this "Stars and Stripes Forever" and this kind of marching music. Kind of indoctrinating us on how to become good Americans, I guess. And she did a helluva good job. In fact, she did such a good job that we weren't able to see the perspective of being Japanese American. We were trying to be so totally American that it prevented us from looking at our parents' culture and truly reflecting on what we could gain by being both Japanese and American. (Henry Miyatake, denshovh-mhenry-01-0006)

The Nisei went on to area high schools, where many achieved outstanding academic records. Their parents subtly pushed them, as this Denshō narrator recalls:

> Well, they said that because we're different, and we're gonna be, have a lot of prejudice, says "Study harder, and do the best you can, and then compete and then get honors." And so most of the Oriental people got the honor,

like honor society, or scholarship, because of the fact they studied harder.
(Kay Matsuoka, denshovh-mkay-01-0005)

Miyamoto (1984, 54) has shown that Nisei were overrepresented in their
class salutatorian and valedictorian categories.

Japanese Language School. Another very significant part of the Nisei's education was Japanese Language School, or *Nihon gakkō*. Originally started in
1902 in a commercial building, it first moved to the Buddhist Temple and
finally, in 1913, to its current location on the periphery of Nihonmachi. At
its peak in the 1930s it was housed in two large wooden buildings and served
almost two thousand students. The majority of Nisei spent almost eight years
in Japanese Language School. Classes were usually an hour and a half every
weekday after a full day of public school classes.

Rather than spend the additional time in yet another classroom, most
of the Nisei, especially the boys, would have strongly preferred to have spent
the time playing sports or participating in other "American" after-school
activities. However, their Issei parents felt that they should not only learn
the Issei's native tongue but also Japanese etiquette and moral values. Nonetheless, the actual outcome was that the majority of Nisei ended up with a
rather rudimentary grasp of the intricacies of the Japanese language even
after eight years of instruction. One Nisei recalls his years in the school.

> I used to go to *Nihon gakkō*. I used to be there from about four o'clock to
> maybe five thirty or so. And so I was a student of Japanese language for quite
> a few years, from when I was six 'til I was twelve, so about six years. So I
> should have been pretty good in Japanese, but we were more interested in
> goofing around than studying. And I had a very good teacher; Mrs. Hashi-
> guchi was my teacher. And she tried her best to try to get us to learn Japa-
> nese because she knew we weren't dumb, but we acted like we were dumb.
> And we wouldn't do the things she told us to do. My mother would say, after
> I got a term paper or exam, I would bring it to her and she would shake her
> head and say, oh, just mutter to herself. (Henry Miyatake, denshovh-mhenry-
> 01-0011)

Eagerly anticipated was the annual language school picnic in Jefferson Park.
Hundreds of Japanese turned out for a full day of games with prizes for all

of the children, folk songs and dances, marching drills, baseball, and a veritable mountain of home-cooked Japanese food that the mothers toiled long hours to prepare (Sone 1979, 71–80).

The time spent in this almost universally attended community institution very likely affected the young Nisei more than they or their parents realized at the time. Not only were they exposed to Japanese social ethics and courtesies, but they formed an extensive network of friendships that frequently lasted a lifetime (e.g., Miyamoto 1984, xvi). This cultural and social capital was to serve the Nisei well in the years following the incarceration, when it was crucial to forming and accessing needed material, social, and psychic resources.

Social, Political, and Occupational Life of the Nisei

Sports. Another very important aspect of Nisei life, particularly for males, was sports. From a very young age, boys started to play baseball in the streets and in the open areas between buildings. As early as 1906, some Issei formed the Nippon Club. The first Nisei team, the Cherries, was started in 1911. The following year, some Mikado players joined the Cherries to form the Asahi Club. Initially, these teams played in the City League, but as the Nisei increased in number, they formed their own leagues, stratified by age and ability levels. Significantly, these leagues were organized long before Little Leagues and Babe Ruth Leagues were established in the larger white community (Chin 2001, 54; Miyamoto 1984, xviii).

As in virtually all Japanese communities, the Seattle Issei were supportive of the Nisei playing baseball because they felt it would keep them out of trouble. Some drove the teams to other towns to play other Nisei teams, contributed money for uniforms, and took the team out for *Chinameshi* (Chinese food) to celebrate after big games. Parents and siblings turned out to cheer on their sons and brothers.

The English-language, four-page Nisei newspaper the *Japanese American Courier* organized and promoted the extensive Courier Leagues, which included baseball, basketball, and football. It even sponsored a girls' basketball league. In the late 1930s, an annual Fourth of July Japanese state baseball tournament was started. This all-weekend event drew hundreds to enjoy the food and game booths as well as the baseball competition (Chin 2001, 54–55). Other sports groups that had followings in the community were a golfers' association, a tennis club, a fishermen's club (at one time,

there were eight Japanese tackle shops), a judo club, a *kendo* club and a bowling league.

Japanese American Courier. As noted above, a key factor in organizing and
publicizing sports in the Seattle area was James Sakamoto's *Japanese American Courier.* Sakamoto was a gifted athlete from Seattle who moved to New
York City and became the English editor of the immigrant newspaper the
Japanese American News. While pursuing journalism, he started boxing pro-
fessionally, eventually working his way up to a few matches in Madison Square
Garden. In 1926, his athletic career ended when he was almost blinded in
the ring. This injury caused him to return to Seattle in 1927. He and his
wife, Misao, started the *Courier* in 1928, the first English-language newspaper for the Japanese in the country (Chin 2001, 56; Ichioka 1986–87).

Besides sports, the *Courier* covered a wide range of other Nisei activities.
It reported on church activities, the two student clubs at the University of
Washington, the Girls' Club, and the Business Girls' Club, which sponsored
socials and dances, oratorical contests, and flower arranging exhibits. The
paper also reported on many music and dance groups, a ham radio club, and
a camera club, and covered the activities of organizations in the then outlying farming areas, such as Bellevue and Green Lake. These groups often
had functions that were coordinated with those in Nihonmachi. The *Courier*
supported this plethora of organizations and activities by keeping Nihonmachi's residents and those who lived outside its boundaries informed of
the wide range of activities (Miyamoto 1984, xviii–xix).

Nisei interpersonal style. Miyamoto (1984, xix) argues that during the 1930s,
even though the Nisei were mostly monolingual English speakers with
interests similar to mainstream Americans, they exhibited the same broad
social orientation as their Issei parents. This included a unique interpersonal
style, which although Japanese in its emphasis on being highly responsive
to the feelings of the other, was adjusted to fit better within the American
context. One example of the outcome was lowered spontaneity. Monica
Sone (1979, 131) describes how Nisei high school students felt about speaking out.

> Almost all the students of Japanese blood sat like rocks during discussion
> period. Something compellingly Japanese made us feel it was better to seem
> stupid in a quiet way rather than to make boners out loud. I began to think

of the Japanese as the Silent People, and I envied my fellow students who clamored to be heard.

Joking was also characteristic of the Nisei, as it protected interpersonal sensitivities by sending the meta message that what was being said was not to be taken seriously (Miyamoto 1986–87). One persistent consequence of the creation of this unique interpersonal style is that Nisei are most comfortable interacting with their own, thus further reinforcing group solidarity (Fugita, Miyamoto, and Kashima 2002).

The Japanese American Citizens League (JACL). James Sakamoto also played a critical role in the formation of the Japanese American Citizens League, the largest and most influential Nisei organization before and after World War II. In 1921, when the Washington Alien Land Law and other anti-Japanese legislation were being drafted, a small group of older Nisei, with the encouragement of the Issei, formed the Seattle Progressive Citizens League. This fledgling organization hoped to combat discrimination against the Japanese. It floundered until Sakamoto returned to Seattle in 1927. At that time, there was a serious conflict within the Seattle community between the two major athletic groups, the Nippon A.C. and Taiyo A.C. He saw the Citizens League as a mechanism to potentially bring together the warring factions. Subsequently, he used the *Courier* to promote the Citizens League and its ideology.

As similar Nisei anti-discrimination groups, such as chapters of the American Loyalty League, were emerging in California, a decision was made to form a national organization, the National Council of the Japanese American Citizens League, at a meeting in San Francisco in 1929. Because of Sakamoto's and his friends' leadership, the first national convention of the JACL was held in Seattle in 1930. One of Sakamoto's boyhood friends, Clarence Arai, became the first national JACL president. Sakamoto himself was elected president of the Seattle chapter in 1931 and went on to become the national president from 1936 to 1938. Like Sakamoto and Arai, those active in the JACL were generally older Nisei who were college-educated businessmen or professionals. They were "prominent" in the community and generally were affiliated with the Republican Party (Takahashi 1997, 54–58). Yet, during the 1930s, the JACL struggled to maintain itself. Its main activities involved sponsoring various social functions, such as an annual banquet, dances, and "Japan Day" (Chin 2001, 56; Miyamoto 1984, xix).

The JACL's political positions were quite similar to those of the Japanese Association and, in fact, it received financial support from the Association. It defended Japan's involvement in Manchuria and Japan's role in the Far East generally. For example, after the Marco Polo Bridge Incident in 1937, Sakamoto claimed that Japan had preserved law and order against Chinese warlordism and communist insurgency and had protected Japanese nationals and their investments (Takahashi 1997, 59; Thomas 1952, 53).

The Nisei as a bridge of understanding. After the passage of the Immigration Act of 1924 and its negative implications for Issei, some leaders began to suggest that the Nisei could play a pivotal role in Japan-U.S. relationships by being a "bridge of understanding." One of the key voices pushing this perspective was Kyūtarō Abiko, the publisher of the most influential Japanese immigrant daily, the *Nichibei Shimbun*. Supporting the bridge concept was the idea of the Pacific era. Advocates of this latter notion saw Japan and the United States as the dominant powers of what was going to become a new Pacific culture combining the best of the two increasingly dominant regions of the world. In this new culture, Nisei were portrayed as major interpreters and transmitters, helping to create necessary stability and understanding (Ichioka 1986–87; Takahashi 1997, 49–53).

With the so-called "Manchurian Incident," when some Japanese junior officers created the pretext for Japan to militarily occupy Manchuria and create the puppet state of Manchukuo, tensions between the United States and Japan sharply increased. This caused the bridge-of-understanding concept to shift its focus somewhat from the Nisei teaching Americans about the Japanese to include a more international element, that of explaining events in the Far East to Americans from Japan's perspective. James Sakamoto was a strong supporter of the bridge-of-understanding concept and used the *Courier* to advocate this point of view. To be better able to act in this role, he called for the Nisei to master the Japanese language and visit Japan by going on *kengakudan* (study tours). However, to most ordinary Issei and Nisei, the bridge-of-understanding ideology was too abstract and removed from their daily concerns. Nonetheless, it does reveal some of the cross-pressures to which the Nisei were exposed.

Ultimately, international events made the bridge concept totally untenable, even to its most ardent supporters. As the Issei got their news of world events from Japanese language newspapers, which in turn obtained their information from Japanese wire services, the Japanese line influenced them. Not surprisingly, when the Sino-Japanese War began in 1937, for the most part they rallied behind Japan. Emergency committees distributed propaganda favorable to Japan, money was collected for national defense and war relief, gift packets called *imonbukuro* filled with nonperishable toiletries, tobacco, and food were sent to soldiers on the China front, and celebrations of Japanese military victories were held (Ichioka 1986–87). For most Nisei at the time, these activities had more of a humanitarian thrust than a "pro-Japan" one.

Issei-Nisei tensions escalate. As Japan-U.S. relations continued to deteriorate, some Nisei actively worked against the position advocated by most Issei. For example, some visibly supported the boycott against sending scrap iron to Japan (e.g., Wada 1986–87). In many families with older Nisei, "bottled-up" tension between the two generations occasionally threatened to burst out. The following recollection by Sone (1979, 148) may have been typical.

> Discussion of politics, especially Japan versus America, had become taboo in our family for it sent tempers skyrocketing. Henry and I used to criticize Japan's aggressions in China and Manchuria while Father and Mother condemned Great Britain and America's superior attitude toward Asiatics and their interference with Japan's economic growth. During these arguments, we had eyed each other like strangers, parents against children.

Perhaps fortunately, most Nisei were too young to be actively involved in these and similar debates.

Amidst the intergenerational tensions, to counteract the American public's inability to differentiate between the Issei and even the Nisei and the Japanese military, the JACL and the *Courier* began to advocate a form of hyper patriotism. In Southern California, some JACL leaders provided information to naval intelligence, the FBI, and other agencies about Issei, Kibei, and Nisei who were suspected of being disloyal. As quoted in Ichioka (1986–87, 72), Togo Tanaka, a journalist and the unofficial historian of the JACL at the time, reported that "a segment of J.A.C.L. leadership in 1939 and 1940 began to arrogate to itself the authority to judge and evaluate the loyalty of members of the Japanese community."

Employment prospects. As the Nisei came of age, most hoped for less ardu-ous, more prestigious "clean jobs" beyond the family farms and small shops of the ethnic community. However, those who made forays into the wider job market often were humiliated when they were forced to return to Nihon-machi and work for the Issei. In 1940, only two out of every ten Nisei in Seattle worked for a white firm. Even this was higher than in San Francisco and Los Angeles, where the figure was less than one out every ten Nisei (Thomas 1952, 41). One narrator recalled:

> Well, as a young man I knew that I could never get a job in the airplane industry. Those were off limits, you know. And you couldn't get a job in teamster work because you join the Teamster Union. So, there were the areas that you worked around. (Harvey Watanabe, denshovh-wharvey-01-0006)

Thus, employment was another facet of life where the Nisei faced a great deal of uncertainty.

THE DENSHŌ SURVEY

Now that we have presented an outline of the prewar world of the Nisei, we would like to introduce the reader to the respondents whose lives we examine for the remainder of this book. They are mostly Nisei who were children, teenagers or, less frequently, young adults during the years imme-diately preceding Pearl Harbor. They form a representative sample of those who were incarcerated and are currently living in King County, Washing-ton (the greater Seattle area). Since the sampling and interviewing proce-dures are described in detail in appendix A, only their most important features will be mentioned here. The respondents were randomly selected from a sampling frame of Japanese American registered voters who were living in King County during 1997. They were screened to ensure that they were at least five years of age in 1942. This was done to increase the likelihood that only those who had at least some memories of their camp experience would be surveyed. The sample size was 183 persons with a refusal rate of 28%. Respondents were either interviewed in their homes or at the Denshō office (then in the old Japanese Language School building), which is located on the periphery of what used to be Nihonmachi.

Demographic Characteristics
of the Denshō Survey Respondents

Geogeneration. The bulk of our survey sample of former incarcerees were born and raised in the United States, having little experience with life in Japan. As shown in table 2.2, 84.2% were "straight" Nisei. A small subset of Nisei was Kibei (5.5%). The remainder of the sample was Sansei (third generation, 2.7%), Issei (1.6%), and those of mixed geogenerational status (5.5%). The numbers of Sansei, Issei, and mixed generation individuals were too small to be separately analyzed.[1]

Gender, age, and religion. There were equivalent numbers of males (50.8%) and females (49.2%) among our respondents even though we did not stratify our sample selection by gender. This serendipitous outcome allowed more precise cross-gender comparisons. The mean age of the respondents at the time they were surveyed (1997) was 72.8 years. They ranged in age from 57 to 90. With respect to religion, the largest number were Protestant (36.1%) at the time they were surveyed. A slightly smaller percentage indicated that they were Buddhist (29.5%). Those reporting that they were Catholic were 4.4%, and 18.6% were placed in the residual category of "other." Finally, 11.5% said that they had no religious faith.

Time in Japan. In order to better gauge how much experience survey respondents had had living in Japan before World War II, we asked whether they had lived there before World War II and how old they were when they left Japan and came back to the United States. Two-thirds (67.8%) indicated that they had spent no time in Japan. Of those who had been to Japan, the vast majority (84.5%) were sent when they were children under 11 years of age. Most respondents also returned to the United States as children under 11 years of age (70.5%). Six and four-tenths percent came back between the ages of 12 and 17. A substantially larger number returned in the college-age bracket of 18 to 22 years (21.3%). Only 1.6% indicated that they came back to the United States during their early adulthood, that is, when they were 23 years or older.

Prewar Family Economic Characteristics

Occupations of families. The vast majority of our Nisei respondents grew up in households where their Issei fathers were small businessmen of some type

Table 2.2. Demographic Characteristics: Geogeneration, Gender, Religion, and Prewar Ties to Japan

Variable		Value
Generation (%)	Issei	1.6
	Kibei	5.5
	Nisei	84.2
	Sansei	2.7
	Mixed	5.5
	Other	0.5
	Number of cases	183
Gender (%)	Males	50.8
	Females	49.2
	Number of cases	183
Age at time of survey: Mean (*SD*)		72.8 (6.7)
Religion (%)	Buddhist	29.5
	Protestants	36.1
	Catholics	4.4
	Other	18.6
	None	11.5
	Number of cases	183
Been to Japan before?	Yes	32.2
	No	67.8
	Number of cases	183
How old when went to Japan?	Under 11 years old	84.5
	12–17	6.8
	18–22	6.8
	23+	1.7
	Number of cases	58
Age when returned from Japan	Under 11 years old	70.5
	12–17	6.4
	18–22	21.3
	23+	1.6
	Number of cases	61

Table 2.3. Family's Prewar Financial Resources

Variable		Value
Father self-employed? (%)	Yes	86.3
	No	13.7
	Number of cases	175
Job sector in which father worked (%)	Executive, administrative, & managerial occup.	15.7
	Engineers and other	0.6
	Health professionals	1.2
	Writers, artists, entertainers	1.2
	Sales occupations	20.9
	Private household service	1.2
	Protective and other	11.0
	Farming related	39.5
	Forestry and logging	0.6
	Fishers, hunters, trappers	0.6
	Manual laborers	7.6
	Number of cases	172
Mean TSEI[1] score for father's job	Mean	31.36
	SD	8.49
	Number of cases	172
Did respondent or parents own a farm? (%)	Own farm—self	6.7
	Own farm—parents	30.0
	Lease/sharecrop—self	5.0
	Lease/sharecrop—parents	48.3
	Farm worker—parents	1.7
	Other	8.3
	Number of cases	60
Did family own house, farm, store, or other property before the war? (%)	Yes	37.2
	No	61.2
	Don't know	1.6
	Number of cases	183

[1] TSEI score = socioeconomic index for occupations developed by Hauser and Warren (1997).

(86.3%). Further, as shown in table 2.3, the majority of these Issei were involved in some aspect of agriculture (39.5%). Sales, at 20.9%, was a distant second with respect to the occupation of the fathers of the Nisei respondents. The third most common Issei occupational category, at 15.7%, combined executive, administrative, and managerial jobs such as hotel managers and railroad and cannery foremen.

Owned vs. leased/sharecropped farm operations. Of those families working in farming, most of the Issei parents of our respondents leased or sharecropped (48.3%) rather than owned their land (30.0%). One and seven-tenths percent of those in agriculture had Issei parents who were farm laborers. Another 8.3% of the immigrant generation were in some other aspect of agriculture, such as packing shed or shipping operations. A small number of Nisei respondents were old enough to be running farming operations themselves at the outbreak of the war; 5.0% leased or sharecropped while 6.7% owned a farm. The impact of the Alien Land Law can be seen in the greater proportion of Nisei who owned as opposed to leased/sharecropped land compared with the Issei, who were much more senior.

Ownership of property. A more general question about prewar property ownership involved whether the respondent's family owned their own house, farm, or other property. Those who answered affirmatively were 37.2%, and 61.2% answered negatively. Again, the Alien Land Law, no doubt, suppressed ownership.

Denshō Respondents at the Time of Their Incarceration

Several of our survey items assessed the human, social, and financial capital of our respondents at the time they were incarcerated. These data are helpful in that they not only describe the general characteristics of our Nisei sample, but also illustrate the diversity within the group. This helps us understand not only how the events surrounding World War II impacted the Nisei as a group, but also how these same events interacted with the personal and social resources of individuals, sometimes producing markedly different outcomes.

Age at incarceration. We used the age at which a respondent was incarcerated as a primary marker. Drawing on Elder's (1986, 1987) life-stage principle, the assumption was made that the age at which respondents were incarcerated would strongly influence both the nature of their World War II experiences as well as their recollection of the events surrounding these experiences.

As shown in table 2.4, the mean age of our respondents at the time of their mass removal from the West Coast or so-called "evacuation" (1942) was 17.4 years. Their ages ranged from 5 to 35. Twenty-one percent were children between the ages of 5 and 11 years at the time of their exclusion. The largest percentage of respondents, 29.3%, fell into the adolescent age

Table 2.4. Age and Marital Status at Evacuation

Variable		Value
Age at exclusion (%)	5–11	21.0
	12–17	29.3
	18–22	28.7
	23+	21.0
	Mean (*SD*)	17.4 (6.6)
	Number of cases	181
When married? (%)		
	Before or during camp	21.2
	After leaving camp	78.8
	Number of cases	184

bracket of 12 to 17 years, although only by a small margin. An almost equal percentage (28.7%) was in the college-age group, ranging from 18 to 22 years of age. Those in their early adult years of 23 and older comprised 21.0% of the sample. Thus, the survey respondents were fairly evenly spread across these four designated life-stage brackets. Our sample's mean age is similar to the median age of 17 years that Thomas (1952, 19) reported for Nisei in all ten of the War Relocation Authority (WRA) camps in 1942.

Marital status at incarceration. Since marital status is such a central determinant of social roles and responsibilities, we asked our respondents if they were married, and if so, the date of the event. Among those who were married, we determined if they were married before or during their incarceration or after leaving the WRA camps. About a fifth of the sample (21.2%) were married either before or during camp, while 78.8% were married after leaving the compounds (table 2.4). This pattern is in keeping with the young mean age of our respondents at the time of their incarceration.

Ethnicity of friends. As previously illustrated, the interpersonal networks of the Nisei were principally located within the ethnic community. To empirically examine this, we asked the Denshō respondents how many of their three best friends in 1941 were Japanese. As shown in table 2.5, the mean number of such best friends was 2.5. This figure was similar for both

Table 2.5. Prewar Friendships

Variable	All Respondents	Gender	
		Male	*Female*
Of three best friends in 1941, how many Japanese? (%)			
None	7.1	7.5	6.7
One	6.0	5.4	6.7
Two	13.2	16.1	10.1
Three	73.6	71.0	76.4
Number of cases	182	93	89
Mean (*SD*)	2.5 (0.9)	2.5 (0.9)	2.6 (0.9)

men and women (2.5 for males and 2.6 for females). There were also no significant age differences among the respondents with regard to prewar friendships.

Schooling at the time of incarceration. At the time of their exclusion, most of the respondents were attending school (60.7%; see table 2.6). Significantly more males (65.6%) were in school than were females (55.6%). One-half (50.8%) were in their primary school years, kindergarten through the eighth grade. Approximately one-third (34.1%) were in high school (ninth through twelfth grade). A relatively small percentage of older Nisei were attending college as undergraduates (14.1%). Almost twice as many males (17.5%) as females (9.8%) were students in colleges or universities at the time. No one in the sample was attending graduate school when they were excluded from the Pacific Coast.

Educational aspirations. As we have noted before, the Japanese-oriented culture to which our Nisei were exposed placed a high value upon educational attainment. A college education was seen as a measure of family status and prestige as well as instrumental for economic mobility (Broom and Kitsuse 1956, 7). Thus, even though the ultimate utility of higher education was often not clear to the Nisei before World War II, many individuals hoped to earn a college degree. In order to have an indication of respondents' prewar aspirations, we asked them whether they were planning to attend col-

Table 2.6. Education: Status and Aspirations at Exclusion

Variable	All Respondents	Gender	
		Male	*Female*
Was respondent in school in 1942? (%)			
Yes	60.7	65.6	55.6
No	39.3	34.4	44.4
Number of cases	183	93	90
Grade at exclusion (%)			
No formal schooling	0.9	0.0	2.0
Kindergarten–8th grade	50.8	55.6	45.1
9th grade–12th grade	34.1	27.0	43.1
1st–4th year of college	14.1	17.5	9.8
5th year of college and higher	0.0	0.0	0.0
Number of cases	114	63	51
College plans at time of exclusion of those aged 14–18 (%)			
Was planning to attend	34.8	45.5	25.0
Was planning not to attend	10.9	9.1	12.5
Decided on working	8.7	4.5	12.5
Too young	32.6	22.7	41.7
Other	13.0	18.2	8.3
Number of cases	46	22	24

lege (table 2.6). Since educational aspirations usually become highly salient for most individuals when they are attending high school, we focused on those who were 14 to 18 years of age at the time of the incarceration ($n =$ 46). Over one-third (34.8%) of this group said they planned to attend college. Males, not surprisingly, had higher aspirations than females. Among the males, a strikingly high 45.5% said they planned to attend college. The figure for females was 25.0%. Taking both genders together, only 19.6% either were planning not to attend or had decided to work. A total of 45.6% said they were either too young to have made a decision or had otherwise not been able to decide whether to attend.

It is quite significant that among prewar high-school-aged Nisei, substantially more planned to attend college (35%) than did not (20%). Part of this high ambition may be due to the confident, unrealistic ambitions exhibited by adolescents in general (Cross and Markus 1991; Weinstein 1980). Yet, given the very real and widespread job discrimination that the Nisei faced during this period and ultimately the exceptionally low likelihood that they would be able to "directly use" a degree in the society at large, these figures are remarkable. Apparently, their socialization produced not only a powerful kind of determination and optimism but also something perhaps more akin to self-delusion (Modell 1977, 128). Monica Sone's (1979, 229) prewar recollection provides an illustration of this complex feeling.

> I had been intimidated by the racial barriers in the business and professional world and I wasn't brave enough to explore or develop my other interests. It seemed useless to do so in the face of closed doors. So when I entered the University of Washington, I clung to literature, my first love, saying to my friends that I wanted to teach. We all knew this was a fancy too, destined to wither.

Employment at exclusion. Among those who were working at the time of their mass removal ($n = 57$), one third were employed in some aspect of agriculture (33.3%; see table 2.7). Almost twice as many men (44.4%) were working in this economic sector as were women (23.3%). The second most common occupation was sales (19.3%), with more women (23.3%) than men (14.8%) employed in this occupational category. These data are entirely consistent with the historical narrative we discussed earlier in the chapter.

Occupational aspirations. If we examine the type of occupations that respondents were planning to enter at the time of the incarceration, the same pattern of high aspirations as was evident in the educational arena emerges. Specifically, the relevant survey item asked, "In 1941, what occupation were you planning on making your life's work?" The most common responses were administrative support and clerical (16.3%) and farming related (15.0%; see table 2.7). These two occupations were very gendered in that 29.7% of the women planned on an administrative support career, while only 4.7% of the men did so. Conversely, 23.3% of the men and only 5.4% of the women planned on entering farming.

Consistent with the surprisingly high educational aspirations of our Nisei respondents, 35.1% of the sample indicated that they planned to enter one of the professions. With respect to the type of professional occupation they planned on entering, 12.5% hoped for careers in the health professions. Many more women (21.6%) wanted to work in this sector of the economy than men (4.7%), most likely as nurses. The second most popular planned pro-

Table 2.7. Employment: Experience and Aspirations at Exclusion

Variable	All Respondents	Gender	
		Male	*Female*
Job sector in which respondent worked at exclusion (%)			
Executive, administrative, managerial	3.5	0.0	6.7
Health professionals	1.8	0.0	3.3
Teachers, post–secondary	1.8	3.7	0.0
Sales occupations	19.3	14.8	23.3
Admin. support occupations, clerical	14.0	7.4	20.0
Protective and other	14.0	7.4	20.0
Farming related	33.3	44.4	23.3
Manual laborers	12.3	22.2	3.3
Number of cases	57	27	30
TSEI score of respondent's occupation at exclusion			
Mean	28.0	27.2	28.7
SD	10.4	10.5	10.4
Number of cases	57	27	30
Job sector: Respondent's planned occupation (%)			
Executive, admin., managerial	3.8	7.0	0.0***
Engineers and other	11.3	20.9	0.0
Health professionals	12.5	4.7	21.6
Teachers, post–secondary	5.0	4.7	5.4
Social scientists, lawyers	2.5	2.3	2.7
Writers, artists, entertainers	5.0	7.0	2.7
Health technicians	2.5	2.3	2.7
Sales occupations	12.5	11.6	13.5
Admin. support occup., clerical	16.3	4.7	29.7
Protective and other	6.3	0.0	13.5
Farming related	15.0	23.3	5.4
Manual laborers	7.5	11.6	2.7
Number of cases	80	43	37
Mean TSEI score of respondent's planned occupation:			
Mean	42.3	44.9	39.3
SD	21.9	17.5	15.0
Number of cases	80	43	37

***Gender differences are significant at $p < .001$ level (two-tailed).

fessional career was engineering. Overall, 11.3% expected to enter this field (20.9% men, 0.0% women). Five percent planned to become teachers. The remaining professional job categories that our respondents indicated that they planned on entering before the war were social science and law (2.5%) and executive or managerial (3.8%). Of the latter category, 7.0% of respondents were male, and zero respondents were female. Overall, what continues to be striking is the high percentages who were aiming for occupations that had few openings for Nisei at the time. Perhaps those who were planning on health, law, and managerial careers thought that they could use the ethnic economy as a "fall back position." However, those who planned on engineering or teaching careers, which were virtually all in the general economy, had very significant, perhaps not fully recognized, hurdles to surmount. Some of these respondents may have entertained the possibility of going to Japan to work.

> I used to see the older Nisei that had even graduated college with degrees in aeronautical engineering and can't—no job here. So they'd go to Japan. Or they'd have a degree in accounting, or this and that, and you see 'em working in Public Market or in the grocery store. (Tad Sato, denshovh-stad-01-0010)

THE NISEI AND THE PREWAR JAPANESE COMMUNITY

During many of the years that the Nisei were growing up, tensions between the Japanese and the U.S. governments were increasing as the Japanese expanded their sphere of influence in the Far East. This combined with general attitudes toward racial minorities then extant in the country and, in the case of Japanese Americans, economic competition, prevented them from participating in many aspects of the larger society. Nonetheless, even in the face of much de jure and de facto discrimination, and partly because of it, the Issei built an economically viable ethnic economy whose foundation was built upon family-run small businesses, particularly in agriculture.

As noted earlier, as a consequence of these impediments placed in their path, the Issei shifted many of their aspirations to their citizen children who, they hoped, would become first-class citizens. As the Issei continued to build both their businesses and their community, the Nisei were the natural benefactors. They could become involved in a plethora of church activities, sports leagues, cultural productions, social clubs, and community festivals in the ethnic community.

This is not to say that all was well. Pressures were building in the family and in the community. The Nisei were becoming, in many ways, highly acculturated because of their experiences in the public schools and the "Anglo conformity" ideology that was dominant in the larger society at the time. Few Nisei had spent time in Japan before World War II and among those that did, most did so in response to their parents' desires. Due to the very large cultural and linguistic gap between Issei parents and their Nisei children, meaningful communication was difficult, although there was little outright rebellion, given most families' embeddedness in the primary group–oriented ethnic community.

Importantly, because of support from their parents and community for the pursuit of education, the Nisei had educational and occupational aspirations that appeared to be headed for a serious collision with reality. This was already apparent among the leading edge of Nisei who were well educated and sought employment in the larger society. They were, in the main, blocked from utilizing their education except by going to Japan or returning to the difficult situation of working for the Issei in lower-prestige, ethnic economy jobs. In some occupations, it was possible to become an independent professional serving the Japanese community.

Our survey data clearly document these high educational and occupational aspirations among the Nisei before 1941. Almost half of high-school-aged males and a quarter of the females said that they planned to attend college before the war. Further, 40 percent intended to enter the professions. Although it must have been very unclear to them what the future might hold, the Nisei were hopeful. Of course, not all were able to achieve their dreams. What resources and situations helped those who eventually achieved or exceeded their dreams, and what factors were responsible for frustrating others in their attempts to do so? In the following chapters, we will follow these Nisei through the traumatic disruptions and anguish of the World War II period and into their subsequent postwar lives.

THREE

The Incarceration

Yeah, if you're a prisoner in a concentration camp at seven years old,
you think everybody is. I mean, you don't know your circumstances
are so unusual. You have no idea to compare with anyone else's life
so you just assume that this is life. No one tells you any different. You
get an undertone of something is wrong. I know right out of camp,
a librarian asked me how was it to be in camp, and I know that my
answer I thought was a correct answer. "It was fine, ma'am." That was
what I was supposed to say when an adult asks me. I was supposed
to put the best foot forward. And then she turned around and told
her assistant, "You see, some people in camp enjoyed it," and I felt
betrayed. That was not the response that she was supposed to give her
assistant. She was supposed to compliment me . . . 'cause I knew that
camp was not a place where all of us were happy, where it was pleas-
ant to be. It was confusing to me. Why? I don't think my mom or
dad ever explained to me why I was in camp. I don't think anybody
ever did. I think it came kind of slowly, I started to talk to people and
to wonder at what point, like a victim of rape, is it okay to talk about?
Do you bring more harm? Do you bring more denigration to yourself
by admitting that something bad happened to you? You really don't
know so you kind of let it go. (Mako Nakagawa, denshovh-nmako-
01-0014)

The complex political forces and historical particulars that led to the
exclusion and incarceration of Japanese Americans have been the sub-

47

ject of a great deal of scholarly attention (e.g., Bosworth 1967; Daniels 1986, 1993; Girdner and Loftis 1969; Grodzins 1949; Commission on Wartime Relocation and Internment of Civilians 1997; Robinson 2001; Weglyn 1976). Further, a substantial amount of anecdotal material and several oral-history projects have addressed the more personal perspectives and consequences of the upheaval (e.g., Denshō 1997; Hansen 1991; Tateishi 1984). In this chapter, we draw upon these rich and very significant materials to put our survey data into historical perspective and set the social context. The specific and unique contribution that we hope to make is to illuminate how former incarcerees with differing amounts of capital, particularly financial, human, and social, reacted to and, most importantly, now remember their traumatic exclusion and incarceration some sixty years later.

Some questions immediately come to mind. Among former incarcerees, is there still a great deal of suppressed anguish and anger, as was evident among those who testified during the redress hearings held in the early 1980s? As the individuals who came forward were a small minority of all incarcerees, to what extent were their feelings representative of the entire group? Perhaps the process involved in winning redress provided a kind of "relief valve" or catharsis for the community, and therefore many former incarcerees now have a very different perspective. What are the outlines of the undoubtedly complex relationships of access to material, human, and social resources to memories and feelings about this tumultuous period? Did, for example, having more human capital help one cope with the uprooting and confinement, or did it make more salient the indignities and oppression and therefore increase the pain of the experience?

The life-course approach that we have adopted also suggests additional questions. How did the individual's life-stage at the time influence how events are recalled? Surely the interpretive lens through which an elementary schoolchild viewed the incarceration was dramatically different from that of a young adult. The former had to cope with upheavals in his or her family support system at, perhaps, a "sensitive period" in their lives. The latter, on the other hand, had to confront not only the reality of his or her family's financial and occupational losses but also a very uncertain future in their own country. What of gender-related effects? Were women's or men's plans for pursuing higher education or specific occupations differentially impacted? More generally, how do individual's prewar biographies, especially with respect to socioeconomic resources, influence the assessment of their camp experiences? Further, we explore whether our respondents' present-day socioeconomic characteristics and ethnic community ties appear to color the reconstruction of their incarceration period.

UPROOTING AND INCARCERATION

Rapidly Escalating Tensions

On Sunday December 7, 1941, the FBI started picking up Issei community leaders: Japanese Association officials, Japanese language schoolteachers, Buddhists priests, and other prominent community people. Frank Fujii, then a child, still remembers the day vividly.

> Well, one hour after Pearl Harbor, I was very, you know, this innocent kid that opens the door. And this is one hour after Pearl Harbor now and here two big white gentlemen would say, "We're the FBI, where is Mr. Jimmie Raisaku Fujii?" And I say, "Oh Dad's here somewhere." And I get him and they took him. I didn't see him after that for three-and-a-half years. (Frank Fujii, denshovh-ffrank-01-0008)

People frantically called close friends until late into the evening to try to decipher what lay ahead. Initially, most Nisei felt that even though their "enemy alien" parents might be detained, since they were American citizens, they were "safe." Soon, though, confidence in even this basic assumption began to erode. Akiko Kurose relates:

> When I went back to school that following morning, you know, December 8th, one of the teachers said, "You people bombed Pearl Harbor." And I'm going, "My people?" All of a sudden my Japaneseness became very aware to me. (Akiko Kurose, denshovh-kakiko-01-0013)

At first, politicians and newspapers in the Seattle area urged restraint in the treatment of the local Japanese. But soon, as U.S. military losses in the Pacific began to mount, shrill calls for excluding them from the entire Pacific Coast began to increase. Several nationally prominent journalists, for example, Walter Lippman, Edward R. Murrow, and Henry McLemore, as well as economic interest groups such as growers associations, increased the pressure on the federal government to act (e.g., Daniels 1993, 32–34; Takami 1998, 43). McLemore wrote the following:

I am for the immediate removal of every Japanese on the West Coast to a point deep in the interior. I don't mean a nice part of the interior either. Herd 'em up, pack 'em off and give 'em the inside room in the badlands. Let 'em be pinched, hurt, hungry and dead up against it. . . . (tenBroek, Barnhart, and Matson 1954, 75)

The young Nisei Japanese American Citizens League (JACL) officers who were thrust into leadership roles due to the FBI pickup of the Issei leaders took an accommodationist line. They hoped that cooperation would lead to greater ultimate consideration (Daniels 1993, 79–80). Given the rising paranoia about their loyalty, community members tried to distance themselves from anything Japanese. They destroyed or hid items that might be seen as indicating ties to Japan, such as kendo swords, Japanese books, Japanese flags, Japanese records, and pictures of trips to Japan (e.g., Broom and Kitsuse 1956, 12–13).

On March 2, the U.S. Army encouraged the Japanese to voluntarily move out of the Pacific coastal zone. After hastily selling their businesses, homes, and possessions, some who attempted to act on this were met by hostile local citizens in the receiving interior states. Thus, on March 27, the Japanese were forbidden to migrate. Now frozen in place and subject to a travel curfew, a widespread sense of self-consciousness, vulnerability, and insecurity gripped the community (Broom and Kitsuse 1956, 15).

Three months after Pearl Harbor, Attorney General Francis Biddle and his Department of Justice, which opposed mass exclusion from the Pacific Coast based upon constitutional principles, lost the "Japanese question" to a jittery War Department. A largely indifferent, distracted, and short-term-oriented President Roosevelt signed Executive Order 9066 on February 19, and thus made it possible for the Army to uproot virtually an entire minority group, some 110,000 individuals, from their communities (Robinson 2001, 240–58).

Lieutenant General John L. DeWitt, head of Western Defense Command, and Captain Karl R. Bendetsen, who was soon to be promoted to colonel, became the chief architects of the exclusion and subsequent incarceration. DeWitt appointed Bendetsen head of the Wartime Civil Control Administration (WCCA), the Army agency tasked with moving the Japanese off of the Pacific Coast and housing them in temporary "assembly centers."[1] A civilian agency, the War Relocation Authority (WRA) was created to oversee ten "permanent" camps to be built in the interior of the country. On March 30, Japanese Americans from Bainbridge Island in the Puget Sound area became the first group to be forcibly removed and incarcerated in what was initially an "assembly center" and which subsequently became a WRA camp at Manzanar, California. In Seattle, "evacuation" announcements were posted on April 21 on telephone poles and bulletin boards, and community members were ordered to leave in three separate groups (Takami 1998, 48).

Exclusion and Incarceration: The King County Sample

Army "assembly centers." Since our sample was drawn from King County, it is not surprising that nearly three-fourths of survey respondents lived in this county prior to World War II (73.6 %). Those who were living in the City of Seattle at the time of the expulsion were initially sent to Puyallup Assembly Center. This county fairground is located approximately thirty-five miles south of Seattle. The detainees were moved there in buses, vans, and private autos. Two-thirds (66.7%) of our sample were temporarily housed there when they were first evicted from their homes (see table 3.1). Another 20% of the respondents were sent to the newly constructed Pinedale Assembly Center, which was located just north of Fresno, California. Those who were living in the then rural areas surrounding Seattle, such as Bellevue and the White River Valley, were sent to hot and arid Pinedale. Overall, some 93% of our respondents report having been initially detained in a temporary "assembly center." Most said they entered one of the two temporary camps in either April or May 1942. The majority left for a "permanent" WRA "relocation center" in either August (42.5%) or September (31.5%) 1942. Therefore, on average, the Denshō respondents were held in temporary detention sites for four to five months.

As the "assembly centers" had to be pressed into service quickly, they were characterized by makeshift and generally very poorly conceived arrangements. They were administered by an Army agency and thus, in some aspects, resembled the military. Most of the living quarters were very primitive, although there was some variation. For example, at Puyallup, some of the "apartments" were in what had been animal exhibition areas just a few weeks before the incarcerees moved in. The more fortunate were assigned to new barracks-type living quarters in the former fairground parking lot. As one visual history narrator recalls,

Table 3.1. Descriptive Statistics on Incarceration Experience

Variable		%
Were you sent to an "assembly center"?		
	Yes	93.4
	No	6.6
	Number of cases	183
Which "assembly center"?		
	Fresno	2.3
	Marysville	0.6
	Pinedale	20.5
	Portland	6.4
	Puyallup	66.7
	Santa Anita	1.8
	Stockton	0.6
	Tanforan	0.6
	Tulare	0.6
	Number of cases	171
Date entered "assembly center"	Before April 1942	4.1
	April 1942	35.5
	May 1942	54.7
	June 1942–Nov. 1942	5.9
	Number of cases	172
Date left "assembly center"	Before July 1942	5.8
	July 1942	11.0
	August 1942	47.7
	Sept. 1942	30.2
	Oct. 1942– Dec. 1942	5.3
	Number of cases	172
Number of months in "assembly center"	1 month	2.9
	2 months	14.5
	3 months	33.7
	4 months	29.0
	5 months	15.1
	6–7 months	4.7
	Number of cases	172
Were you sent to a War Relocation Authority (WRA)"relocation center" or internment camp?	Yes	97.3
	No	2.7
	Number of cases	183
Asked only of Issei: Were you placed into a Justice Department camp (INS) or Army camp (e.g., Lordsburg, NM)?	Yes	0.0
	No	100.0
	Number of cases	3

Table 3.1. continued

Variable		%
Which WRA camp were you in?	Amache, CO	0.5
	Gila River, AZ	1.1
	Heart Mountain, WY	1.1
	Jerome, AR	0.5
	Manzanar, CA	2.2
	Minidoka, ID	65.0
	Poston, AZ	1.6
	Rohwer, AR	0.5
	Topaz, UT	1.1
	Tule Lake, CA	25.1
	Number of cases	183
When did you enter the WRA camp?	Before July 1942	10.5
	July 1942	9.9
	August 1942	42.5
	September 1942	31.5
	Oct. 1942–July 31, 1943	5.7
	Number of cases	181
When did you leave the WRA camp?	Before October 1943	33.0
	Oct. 1943–Dec. 1944	18.7
	After Dec. 1944	48.4
	Number of cases	182
Were you sent to two camps?	Yes	20.2
	No	79.8
	Number of cases	183
Which was the first of two camps you were sent to?	Gila River, AZ	2.6
	Jerome, AR	5.3
	Manzanar, CA	7.9
	Minidoka, ID	15.8
	Rohwer, AR	2.6
	Topaz, UT	2.6
	Tule Lake, CA	63.2
	Number of cases	38
When did you arrive at the first camp?	1942	94.6
	1943	5.4
	Number of cases	38
Year when you left first camp:	1942	7.9
	1943	73.7
	1944	15.8
	1945	2.6
	Number of cases	38

continued

Table 3.1. Continued.

Variable		%
Length of stay in first camp:	Less than 1 year	7.9
	1 year	76.3
	2 years	13.2
	3 years	2.6
	Number of cases	38
Which was the second of two camps you were sent to?	Amache, CO	2.6
	Heart Mountain, WY	23.1
	Minidoka, ID	46.2
	Rohwer, AR	5.1
	Topaz, UT	2.6
	Tule Lake, CA	15.4
	Crystal City, TX	5.1
	Number of cases	39
When did you leave the second camp?	1943	10.5
	1944	18.4
	1945	63.2
	1946	7.9
	Number of cases	38

They were sheds. The partitions between the sections only went up to as high as 7 feet and above that was the ceiling. And so if any child was not feeling well and would awaken during the night and start crying for water or whatever, it kept everybody else in that shed from sleeping. I remember there was one child who had a peculiar cry I remember. It sounded, that sound reminded me of some unhappy woman who was sobbing. . . . They didn't have proper toilet facilities, all they had was a pit dug. And the toilet seat was just a board with holes in there. And so the place, the stench was overwhelming. No real preparations had been made. (Shosuke Sasaki, denshovh-sshosuke-01-0014)

When needed services were not forthcoming in the austere temporary incarceration camps, the "evacuees" quickly developed them themselves. For example, there were no provisions for formal schooling for the approximately one-quarter of the residents who had been attending educational institutions. In order to keep the desire to learn alive in the students in addition to simply keeping them occupied, the incarcerees themselves organized and

1. Japanese Fishing Tackle Dealers Association float, Seattle, 1930s.
Denshopd-p13-00003, Mamiya Family Collection, Denshō.

2. Community picnic foot race, Seattle, c. 1918. *Denshopd-p13-00006, Mamiya Family Collection, Denshō.*

3. Grand opening of the Jackson Café, Seattle, 1930s. The café was located on Jackson Street in Nihonmachi and served Western food, such as stew, steak, sandwiches, and pastries. The café closed in the early 1970s. *Denshopd-p53-00009, Denshō.*

The Japanese American Courier

TRUTH ☆☆☆ JUSTICE ☆☆☆ TOLERANCE

| Volume XV, No. 741 | Seattle, Wash., Friday, March 27, 1942 | Five Cents A Copy |

JAPANESE WARNED CAN'T LEAVE AREA STARTING MONDAY

Orderly Evacuation Slated Object; Protection Also Would Be Afforded

FARM TRANSFER VIEWED

A warning that no Japanese or Americans of Japanese ancestry will be allowed to leave Military Area No. 1, voluntarily after Sunday, March 29, was issued Wednesday by Gen. John L. DeWitt at San Francisco. Previously these people had been urged to evacuate voluntarily.

The statement said this was for the purpose of orderly evacuation, and for the protection of the Japanese. It was reported.

In California several fairgrounds and other public sites have been taken over for concentration of the Japanese, it was reported.

Other Regulations Remain

As the statement was reported to declare that all existing regulations will remain in effect, it was considered that the Japanese will be restricted in five-mile areas under the curfew at present.

At the same time, State Selective Service headquarters at Camp Murray that farmers who might replace Japanese on Bainbridge Island would be deferred from military service if they could prove they were experienced and key men on farms. It was said all key features in the state may be deferred.

Japanese on Bainbridge were registered Wednesday in preparation for their evacuation by noon next Monday.

Valuable Crop Area Left

The Kitsap County agent said the Bainbridge Japanese farmers will leave an estimated 633 acres in crops, most of which had been contracted for by canneries and produce companies. This includes 400 acres strawberries, 156 acres in peas and about 40 acres in other berries.

In Seattle the curfew order was to go into effect Friday morning at 5 o'clock. It was pointed out that in addition to other downtown...

[remainder illegible]

VANCOUVER, B. C.—Two citizens of asserted violations of regulations by Japanese were reported here this week.

Saburo Tazabushi, 22, of [illegible]...

All Should Report Residence Changes

Although it had been understood that any German, Japanese or Italian alien in Military Area No. 1 must notify federal officials of change in residence, it is stated in an order from General DeWitt that this also applies to any person of Japanese ancestry.

The Emergency Defense Council of the JACL stresses this requirement as important, and asks full co-operation. It is further emphasized that all requirements such as travel permits and curfew should be fully met, to avoid any misunderstanding.

UTAH FOLKS GIVE FIVE-POINT PLAN

Agricultural Groups Ready To Receive Japanese On Certain Conditions

SALT LAKE CITY.—In a conference here between Gov. Herbert B. Maw, Tom Clark, alien co-ordinator, the Utah Farm Bureau Federation and other agricultural groups, a program was mapped out with regard to alien control and immigration in this state.

As Utah is considered a potential area for evacuees, the program was of importance. The combined farm groups adopted the following five-point statement clarifying their attitude.

First, the statement said, agriculture is entirely opposed to sale of Utah land to Japanese or to leases which extend beyond duration of war.

Second, agriculture approves employment of Japanese immigrants in harvest and other farm work, provided they do not displace local labor and are kept out of strategic areas.

Third, agriculture favors a system under which all immigrant Japanese will report to the U. S. Employment service on their arrival in the state.

Fourth, the proper state agencies should make surveys of possible work projects which might be inaugurated to provide employment for Japanese.

And fifth the State Bureau [illegible] and other groups recommended a program of care [illegible] supervision of immigrants and approved Gov. Maw's action in loaning all instruction available to federal authorities and to be [illegible].

HUGE LAND TRACT TO GET EVACUEES

Ninety Thousand Acres In Arizona Taken Over For 20,000 Japanese

WASHINGTON. — Plans for evacuating Japanese from the West Coast and war production, connected with labor unions, were the outstanding features of government activity this week.

Most of the important and developing evacuation project was revealed in the announcement by the War Relocation Authority that 90,000 acres of land in the Colorado Ind in Reservation at Parker, Ariz., had been taken over, and would ultimately provide homes for 20,000 Japanese.

The battle over production raged this week, with Donald M. Nelson, production chief, warning both labor and management that production must proceed without interruption. Legislation before the Congress to ban the 40-hour week caused the discussion. The President is against the legislation.

But Speaker Rayburn came out with a statement saying that time and a half pay should begin only after 48 hours.

The government this week put a price ceiling on eight articles—refrigerators, typewriters, vacuum cleaners, washing machines, irons, radios, phonographs, and cooking and heating stoves.

Thurman Arnold, assistant attorney general, at a hearing said of men and machines. He charged organized labor with injuring defense, holding farmers and consumers at its mercy. He said no other group could "get away" with what labor has...

[remainder illegible]

Care Provided For Pets For Evacuees

LOS ANGELES—One humane interest phase of the evacuation of the Japanese people from this area that developed this week is the necessity of caring for household pets. It came about that a large number of evacuees had pets, such as dogs, cats and birds that they feared they would have to abandon.

To remedy this situation and provide for humane care of the pets. It was announced that the City Animal Shelter would look after this need. Shelter agents will call for pets, or they may be taken there.

SERVICE CENTERS TO AID FARMERS

Agencies Combine For Help To Evacuees; Offices In Many Coast Cities

Although the status of Japanese farmers remained somewhat indefinite this week as plans for evacuation went forward, the federal agencies concerned again urged that the work still this week continued to prepare for disposing of their property for operation.

The Wartime Civilian Control Administration has taken over with the opening of offices in more than 60 West Coast cities. In Seattle the office is functioning at 808 Second Ave. The plan is to assist Japanese to dispose of property, or to give assistance in operating.

In San Francisco the Agricultural Coordinator of the JACL for Northern California is asking the Leagues along the Coast to help distribute a leaflet issued by the Farm Security Administration of the Department of Agriculture.

The FSA leaflet explains the purpose of the agency, and also submits a list of questions and answers. This list, however is... [illegible]

Disposal of Property Will Be Given Attention; Also To Provide Storage

CLERICAL HELP ASKED

SAN FRANCISCO.—The local JACL chapter has appointed committees to gather information on the evacuation. One committee will look into property disposal and protection. This is headed by Koji Murata and Tamotsu Sakai.

Another committee directed by Motoki Kudo and Dr. Kazuo Togasaki will look after plans for disposal of storage of personal property, such as furniture. The JACL has called for volunteer clerical workers.

SALT LAKE CITY.—George A. Fisher, former executive secretary of the State Land Board is said to have offered his 4,000-acre ranch near this place to Japanese evacuees. About 40 families could be accommodated. However, the county commissioners of Utah at a meeting here recently went on record as opposing receiving any Japanese in their districts. They met with Gov. Herbert B. Maw.

SAN FRANCISCO.—Dr. Monroe E. Deutsch, vice president and provost of the University of California, expressed the opinion here recently that Axis alien students would be allowed to complete their college courses this semester. Federal officials refused to comment.

SACRAMENTO, Calif.—The State Personnel Board has received copies of charges filed against 13 suspected Japanese employes of the State Board of Equalization. The employes are charged with "acts incompatible" with or inimical to continued employment in public service." Heads of several other state agencies said they would not dismiss employes unless requested by military authorities.

FRESNO, Calif.—The local chapter of the JACL is conducting an emergency fund drive to plan funds to carry on needed work here. This money would be distributed... [illegible]

---

4. The front page of the *Japanese American Courier*, Seattle, March 27, 1942. The *Courier* was the first all-English newspaper for Nisei in the United States; this edition was released shortly before their forced removal. *Denshopd-p21-00001, Denshō.*

Form NJACL-OA-1

JAPANESE AMERICAN CITIZENS LEAGUE

OATH OF ALLEGIANCE

(N. B. Taken by the undersigned individual as a prerequisite to membership in the Japanese American Citizen League for the year 1942. This organization is composed entirely of American citizens, is national in scope, and is pledged "For Better Americans In A Greater America." It has over sixty chapters and a membership of some 20,000 in over 300 communities in the United States.)

I, the undersigned, do solemnly swear (or affirm) that I will support and defend the Constitution of the United States of America against all enemies, foreign and domestic; that I will bear true faith and allegiance to the same; that I do hereby forswear and repudiate any other allegiance which I knowingly or unknowingly may have held heretofore; and that I take these obligations freely, without any mental reservation whatsoever or purpose of evasion. So help me God.

Subscribed and sworn to before me this ..6..
day of ......Apr....., 1942.

Notary Public in and for the County
of **Notary Public in and for the State of** ......, State
of **Washington residing at Kent.**

My commission expires..**OCT 10 1942**..

Mae Sadako Iseri
(Signature)

Route 2   Box 126
(Street Address)

Kent,   Washington
(City)   (State)

Valley Civic League
(Chapter Name)

Right Index Finger	Photograph	Certificate of Identification

JACL Valley Civic League Chapter

Name ..Iseri, Sadako Mae..

Address ..Route 2   Box 126..
    ..Kent, Washington..

Height..5..feet....1..inches. Weight..115..

Distinctive marks ....

Birthplace ....
        Street or R. F. D.

    Kent,   Washington
    City   State

Birthdate Aug.   22   1916
        Month   Day   Year

5. After Pearl Harbor but before the forced removal and incarceration, the Japanese American Citizens League encouraged Nisei to carry identification papers voluntarily. Thomas, Washington, 1942. *Denshopd-p25-00015, Iseri Family Collection, Denshō.*

6. Original *Seattle Post-Intelligencer* caption: "Novel audience—Scene in the old the-
ater at 1319 Ranier Ave., which has been converted into a civil control station for
evacuation of Japanese from Seattle this week." The Japanese passed from table to
table, and when the "show" was over, they were ready for their trip to the assembly
center in Puyallup, Washington, 1942. *Courtesy Museum of History and Industry; photo
Seattle Post-Intelligencer, PI-28063.*

7. Issei couple being removed from their home, Bainbridge Island, Washington, 1942.
Denshopd-i34-00066, Bainbridge Island Japanese American Community, Denshō.

8. The Puyallup Assembly Center, also known as "Camp Harmony," was located on the Puyallup Fairgrounds in Washington State. It was open from April 28 through September 23, 1942. Barracks housed the incarcerees, who were mostly from Seattle. *Courtesy Museum of History and Industry; photo* Seattle Post-Intelligencer, *86.5, Puyallup-Japanese Colony.*

9. Tule Lake War Relocation Authority camp with Castle Rock in the background. Tule Lake, California, 1940s. *Denshopd-p2-00033, Bain Family Collection, Denshō.*

10. The Higo Ten-Cent Store in Nihonmachi after exclusion. The owners were able to reopen the store after the war as they were able to pay property taxes while incarcerated. Seattle, 1942. *Courtesy Museum of History and Industry; photo* Seattle Post-Intelligencer, *PI-28868.*

11. A New Year's dance held in the Tule Lake camp hospital. Tule Lake, California, January 5, 1945. *Denshopd-i37-00128, National Archives and Records Administration, Denshō.*

12. Original War Relocation Authority caption: "The 1944 league baseball season got under way at the Tule Lake center on April 19. Project Director Ray R. Best tossed out the first ball. Nearly half of the 17,000 residents of the center were present for the opening game." Tule Lake, California, April 14, 1944. *Denshopd-i37-00381, National Archives and Records Administration, Denshō.*

13. An embroidery class at Mindoka camp. Minidoka, Idaho, ca. 1943. *Denshopd-i39-00013, Wing Luke Asian Museum, Hatate Collection, 1992-41-4 CD, Denshō.*

14. Christmas decorations in Block 1 dining hall of the Minidoka camp. Minidoka, Idaho, December 1943. *Denshopd-i37-00012, National Archives and Records Administration, Denshō.*

15. Original War Relocation Authority caption: "Segregee is fingerprinted." Tule Lake, California, September 1943. *Denshopd-i37-00275, National Archives and Records Administration, Denshō.*

16. Original War Relocation Authority caption: "Bugle Corps Hokoku Seinen Dan gather at Gate 1 to give proper send off to 125 of their number being sent to Santa Fe Internment Camp March 4, 1945." Tule Lake, California. *Denshopd-i37-00183, National Archives and Records Administration, Denshō.*

17. Nisei of 552nd Field Artillery, 442nd Regimental Combat Team fire 105-mm howitzer in battle for Leghorn (Livorno), Italy, July 12, 1944. *Denshopd-i37-00343, National Archives and Records Administration, Denshō.*

18. Books about possible resettlement areas displayed in the Minidoka community library. Minidoka, Idaho, January 1944. *Denshopd-i37-00044, National Archives and Records Administration, Denshō.*

19. Original War Relocation Authority caption: "Scene showing the results of vandalism at the Nichiren Buddhist Temple, 2800 East 3rd Street, Los Angeles, CA – 1944." *Denshopd-i37-00283, National Archives and Records Administration, Denshō.*

20. Photo from War Relocation Authority campaign to encourage incarcerees to relocate outside of the exclusion zone. Part of the original WRA caption reads: "Every man likes to put on his slippers, light up his favorite pipe, and read the evening paper before the fireplace." Milwaukee, 1944. *Denshopd-p7-00008, Kaneko Family Collection, Denshō.*

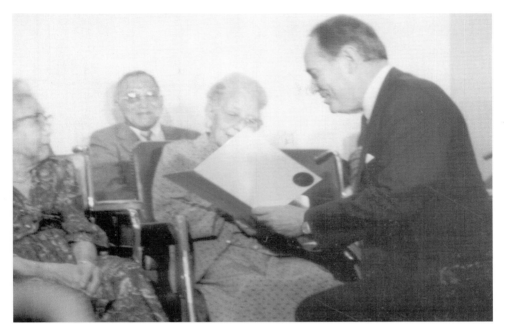

21. Assistant Attorney General John Dunne presenting one of the first redress checks to an Issei woman. Washington, D.C., October 9, 1990. *Denshopd-p25-00131, Yamada Family Collection, Denshō.*

22. Tule Lake incarcerees erected this cross on top of a formation called Castle Rock. The area below is the former site of the camp. Tule Lake, California, July 1998. *Denshopd-p11-00006, Klimek Family Collection, Denshō.*

23. The Bon Odori is an annual community event held in most Japanese American communities. This one was held outside the Seattle Buddhist Temple in the 1960s. *Denshopd-i38-00018, Seattle Buddhist Temple Archives, Denshō.*

taught makeshift classes. Often, the teachers were recent college graduates but not accredited teachers, as education positions were generally closed to Japanese Americans before the war (James 1987a, 27–33). To combat boredom and attempt to establish as much of a sense of normality as possible under the circumstances, other activities, such as baseball leagues, were organized (Nakagawa 2001, 76–79).

From the temporary detention camps, the preponderance of our respondents report that they were moved to a permanent WRA camp (97.3%). The civilian WRA was the administrative heir of the WCCA, which was responsible for the initial phase of the incarceration. The latter agency was more oriented toward "dispatch" than to the personal and economic concerns of their charges. The WRA, on the other hand, approached their job of administering the permanent camps with a more liberal and idealistic, albeit oftentimes contradictory, perspective. They attempted to provide the schools with a progressive curriculum designed by a Stanford professor and, in the larger incarceree community, they conceded to various types of community participation and some self-government (James 1987a, 37–42; Broom and Kitsuse 1956, 18–24).

WRA "relocation centers." Virtually all of those sent to Puyallup were moved to the Minidoka, Idaho, WRA center; some 65% of Denshō respondents were "permanently" incarcerated there. Those who were initially housed in Pinedale were sent to the Tule Lake, California, WRA camp, which was a short distance south of the Oregon border near the town of Klamath Falls. About a quarter (25.1%) of the respondents were initially sent to Tule Lake.

The Minidoka WRA camp was built on sagebrush-filled desert land, part of a federal water reclamation project. The compound stretched for some two-and-a-half miles and contained approximately five hundred barracks. Temperatures sometimes soared over 110 degrees in the summer and plummeted to ten or twenty degrees below in the winter. Occasional dust storms coated the crack-ridden barrack "apartments" with fine layers of brown dust. These conditions were difficult for the Seattle-area incarcerees, who were used to much more moderate weather.

The living area of the compound consisted of some thirty-five blocks, each containing twelve barracks, a mess hall, a recreation hall, and a large building with community bathrooms, showers, and a laundry. A typical "family apartment" consisted of a single 20-by-24 foot room, which came equipped with only a potbellied stove and Army cots. As in other WRA camps, some people stole scrap lumber to build furniture for their otherwise bare rooms. Also similar to other camps, large acreage was turned into productive farmland so that the center would be, to a significant degree, self-supporting with respect to food. The food itself was low-cost and served en masse in a mess hall, frequently after the incarceree was forced to wait in a long line. Typical "memorable" items were Vienna sausages, mutton, and orange marmalade. The quality of preparation varied with the skill of the incarceree cooks in particular blocks (Burton et al. 1999, 205; Spicer, Hansen, Luomala, and Opler 1969, 108–111).

The Tule Lake WRA center was also built on a federal reclamation project. At an elevation of 4,000 feet, similar to Minidoka, it had cold winters and hot and dry summers. Its terrain was flat and treeless with sandy loam soil. The compound sprawled over 4,685 acres, 1,110 residential, 3,575 agricultural. From the start, Tule Lake was plagued with conflict, being the site of several major strikes (Burton et al. 1999, 279–83). In early 1943, the Army and the WRA attempted to determine the loyalty of individuals in all ten of the camps for the purposes of either recruiting soldiers for the newly authorized 442nd Regimental Combat Team (RCT) or so they could be relocated to areas outside of the Pacific Coast exclusion zone. This process was called registration. Ultimately, Tule Lake was chosen to become a segregation center and house the so-called "disloyals" from all of the WRA camps. Many of the "loyals" who were in Tule Lake were moved to other camps or left for the "outside" at the same time. However, many "loyals" remained at the segregation center, leading to a volatile mixture of "loyals," "disloyals," and "fence sitters" (e.g., Thomas and Nishimoto 1946, 221–36). This led to conflict in the camp both with the WRA administration and among incarcerees themselves; the level of conflict among the latter was unique in the WRA compounds. (Additional consequences of registration are discussed below.)

As there were over twenty-five thousand Nisei who were school-aged during the incarceration, educational facilities were an important feature of the "permanent" compounds. Initially, the WRA, unlike the Army and their handling of the temporary incarceration centers, felt that enlightened planning could make camp schools a progressive force substantially equivalent to education outside of the barbed-wired compounds. Unfortunately, reality turned out quite differently, given the converted barrack facilities, lack of furniture, equipment and books, and teacher attrition (James 1987a,

43–79). Further, the WRA was never able to attract sufficient numbers of qualified teachers to the harsh campsites with their primitive facilities. Hundreds of incarcerees had to serve as teaching assistants in the classrooms (Wollenberg 1976). After Tule Lake became a segregation center, and turmoil and military repression took place, the public schools were closed for half a year and Japanese language schools proliferated. In the last two years of its existence, two parallel school systems developed, the first Americanized and operated by the government, the other resistant to Americanization and run by dissident incarcerees. The latter system attempted to prepare children for their anticipated return to Japan (James 1987b).

Length of stay in WRA camps. In late 1942, as the months ground on, signs of institutionalization became visible among the incarcerees. In part, this was due to the "bureaucratic" culture within the camps, which emphasized daily routine, orderly relations, prepared activities, and responsiveness to directives (Broom and Kitsuse 1956, 25). As a consequence, the WRA began to ease the cumbersome procedures to temporarily relocate outside of the Pacific Coast exclusion zone. While a large number (48.4%) of our sample "waited out the war" in the WRA camps (and left after December 1944; see table 3.1), there were many who left earlier. About a third (33.0%) left before October 1943. The number of Denshō respondents who reported leaving before October 1943 is considerably higher than the average for all of the WRA camps combined (Thomas 1952, 114). This is probably due to a combination of two factors. Those who came from the Seattle area, as compared with the much larger number from California, faced less discrimination and were therefore somewhat more assimilated before the war (e.g., Thomas 1952, 102–20). Thus, they probably felt less apprehension about reentering society (cf. Embree 1943). Over the course of war, some 20% of our sample moved to a second WRA camp.

Registration. One event that forced some families to change camps was the ill-conceived registration program briefly discussed earlier. In the beginning of 1943, the Army and the WRA decided to attempt to determine the "loyalty" of individual incarcerees. Ironically, one of the justifications given for the mass removal of the entire ethnic group from the Pacific Coast was that it was impossible to separate the "sheep from the goats."[2] Registration, or the administration of the "loyalty questionnaire," was intended to make this distinction for two purposes. The first was to screen volunteers from the camps for the 442nd

Regimental Combat Team (RCT) that was being formed. Up until this point in the war, Nisei were generally barred from joining the military.

Second, the WRA wanted to more expeditiously release "loyal" incarcerees to areas away from the Pacific Coast exclusion zone to resettle on indefinite leave. The instrument used to determine "loyalty" was an innocuous looking questionnaire titled "Application for Leave Clearance." It included question 27, which asked the respondent about his or her willingness to serve in combat, and question 28, which inquired whether the individual would disavow loyalty to the Emperor of Japan. Answering question 28 in the negative marked one to be segregated to Tule Lake, which was converted to a segregation center in the summer of 1943 (e.g., Thomas and Nishimoto 1946, 85).

These questions, indeed the whole registration process, were fraught with ambiguity and produced a great deal of anger and resentment (e.g., Miyamoto 1989; Thomas and Nishimoto 1946, 53–83). The dual purpose of the questionnaire precipitated much speculation as to what the government's ultimate purposes were and how individuals and families should answer so as to best protect their future (e.g., Broom and Kitsuse 1956, 26–28). Ultimately, some 11 percent of the incarcerees in all of the camps taken together gave "no-no" or "disloyal" answers, qualified their answers, or simply did not register (Daniels 1993, 14). The rest, or a substantial majority, gave "yes-yes" or "loyal" answers. Most of those who answered "no-no" did so out of resentment and frustration over their continued degrading treatment rather than from what might be characterized as "disloyalty." Others did so in an attempt to keep the family together, anticipating that a "yes-yes" answer would subject Nisei males to the draft or relocation to the Midwest or East. One narrator recalled,

My father felt insulted being asked those questions 'cause he had no intention of going back to Japan or anything or he had no allegiance to Japan and here they [are] asking them questions after they take all the property away and everything, so he was bitter. And the other thing was he didn't know if—where to go home to 'cause there was nothing left so the alternative was maybe Japan. We should go back to Japan 'cause there is nothing here. So that's why he answered no. I don't think it was any loyalty to Japan or anything. (Kenge Kobayashi, denshovh-kkenge-01-0007)

Tule Lake had the highest percentage of "no-no's" (49 percent of Nisei and 42 percent of Issei) of any of the ten WRA camps. This was the reason it was selected to be the segregation center. The "disloyals" or "segregants" from the nine other camps were sent to Tule Lake, which had ten outlying blocks built to house some of them. Some six thousand "yes-yes" Tuleans moved to other camps, but four thousand "yes-yes" remained, not wanting to move for a third time in a little over a year. By the spring of 1944, Tule Lake had become the largest of the ten WRA camps, holding over eighteen thousand incarcerees. Additional six-foot-high, lighted chain fences and guard towers were built after it became the segregation center (Tule Lake Committee 2000, 47–52).

In October 1944, a worker was killed in a truck accident at Tule Lake. The administration's handling of this incident led to widespread work stoppages and eventually the declaration of martial law. In response to the unrest, twelve hundred soldiers and eight tanks were sent to the segregation center. Tule Lake became the only camp that had a stockade, a "jail within a jail." As expected, the segregation center came to house the majority of pro-Japan and resistance groups. One that was particularly active was the *Hoshi-dan*. In addition to the main organization, it had separate factions for both young men *(Hokoku)* and women and girls *(Joshi-dan)*. Besides having conflicts with the camp administration, the pro-Japan factions eventually pressured many of the "old Tulean, loyal" Nisei and Kibei to renounce their citizenship (Burton et al. 1999, 279–89; Miyamoto 1989; Thomas and Nishimoto 1946, 303–61; Tule Lake Committee 2000, 47–52).

Registration was one of the reasons, but not the most important, why some incarcerees were moved to a second WRA camp. Thirty-nine of our King County, Washington, respondents state that they moved to a second WRA camp. The largest number (46.2%) moved to Minidoka, the second largest to Heart Mountain, Wyoming (23.1%), and the third largest number to Tule Lake (15.4%; see table 3.1). Those who were from Bainbridge Island voluntarily moved to Minidoka because of conflicts with people from the isolated fishing village of Terminal Island in Manzanar.

Feelings About Incarceration: Negative and Positive

Current overall feeling about the incarceration. One of the key questions in the Denshō survey assessed our respondents' current overall feelings about their incarceration. Specifically, it asked, "If the very worst years of your life were given a score of 1 and the very best years a score of 7, what score would you give your camp years?" As can be seen in table 3.2, there was a good

Table 3.2. Overall Evaluation of Camp Years

Overall Evaluation of Camp Years[1]	%
Worst years (1)	11.5
Worst years (2)	13.7
Neither worst nor best (3)	21.3
Neither worst nor best (4)	35.5
Neither worst nor best (5)	14.2
Best years (6)	3.8
Best years (7)	0.0
Mean	3.49
SD	1.31
Number of cases	183

[1] Overall evaluation of camp years was measured with a Likert-type scale whose values ranged from 1 to 7. The labels "Worst years," "Neither worst nor best," and "Best years" were placed next to values 1, 4, and 7, respectively.

deal of variance in the responses to this question. The mean score was 3.49, a "neither best or worst years" answer, although with a slight leaning toward the negative end of the spectrum. Consistent with this, one-quarter (25.2%) of the respondents rated their camp years as the worst years of their life (response alternatives 1 and 2), while only 3.8% rated them as their best years (response alternative 6; none chose 7).[3]

Specific negative and positive recollections of the incarceration. To obtain a clearer picture of the underlying reasons why our former incarcerees felt the way they did about their incarceration, we employed open-ended questions that asked them to recall both their positive and negative experiences in camp. The first inquired, "What were the most difficult experiences you faced during your time in (respondent's camp)?" These narrative answers were subsequently coded into the most commonly used broad categories; the eight that were most frequently mentioned are listed in table 3.3. As might be expected, the majority of former incarcerees reported that the physical aspects of their camp existence were the most negative part of their camp experience. Specifically, they mentioned living conditions, weather/climate, and food, in that order. More interestingly, the next five most commonly recalled difficult experiences were of a psychological or social relational character. These five were, in order of frequency mentioned: Sense of confinement (14.1%), uncertainty (7.6%), family separation (7.1%), prejudice and

Table 3.3. Memories of Negative and Positive Experiences in WRA camps

Variable	%
Difficult experiences: %Yes	
Living conditions	52.7
Weather/climate	39.7
Food	26.1
Sense of confinement	14.1
Uncertainty	7.6
Family separation	7.1
Prejudice and discrimination	6.0
Taking care of family	2.7
Positive memories: %Yes	
Friends	51.6
Social activities	28.3
Sports	9.8
Work opportunities	8.7
Carefree routine	6.5
Arts and crafts	6.0
No positive memories	15.2
Number of cases	184

discrimination (6.0%) and taking care of the family (2.7%). Hiroshi Kashiwagi, a Nisei, recalls the feeling of confinement:

> Tule Lake . . . it was a prison; I must emphasize this fact. Physically, there were the barbed wire fence and the guard towers manned by MP's with rifles and the machine guns; many of the soldiers were veterans of the war and still quite nervous. We didn't dare go near the fence for fear of being shot at, and there were instances of that. But in addition to the physical confinement, there was the fence around our spirit, and this imprisonment of the spirit was the most ravaging part of the evacuation experience. (Tule Lake Committee 2000, 37)

Given the harsh and depressing circumstances of the incarceration, one might reasonably wonder whether our respondents have any positive memories of their years spent in the desolate compounds. This area of inquiry is particularly intriguing in that it is not at all clear what responses one might expect. In fact, when we asked respondents about their positive recollections of the WRA camps, they gave six distinct categories of responses (see table 3.3). In descending order of frequency mentioned were: Friends, social activities, sports, work opportunities, carefreeness, and arts and crafts. Surprisingly, over half (51.6%) of the respondents spontaneously mentioned that the friends they made during their camp years were an affirmative memory for them. Social activities were also remembered by many (28.3%) as a positive feature of their incarceration experience. Here a visual history narrator recalls one popular type of social activity in the camps:

> I think dancing became a big recreation, because all you needed was a record player and a few people. And so it was an activity that most of the young people got involved in. And going to a dance was a big thing. So, if you were a Romeo, you could lead a good life in camp and become famous for being a good dancer or whatever . . . there were many relationships made during those days that resulted in marriage. (Kunio Otani, denshovh-oku-nio-01-0015)

Still, the third most common response to the inquiry about positive recollections was that the former incarceree had no positive remembrances of their camp days (15.2%).

Life-Stage (Age) Effects

Overall feeling about the incarceration and life-stage. To examine age-related effects on how the former incarcerees now evaluate their camp years, we segmented our sample into four life-stage groups. These groupings, keyed on how old incarcerees were when they were first incarcerated, were childhood (5–11 years), adolescence (12–17 years), college years (18–22 years), and early adulthood (23–35 years). As can be seen in table 3.4, there were substantial and statistically reliable life-stage effects on the general question that asked respondents to compare their incarceration period with other periods of their lives. The respondents who experienced the exclusion and incarceration at an older age had a significantly more negative overall recollection of their incarceration than younger individuals ($p < .01$). Moreover, the test for linearity of the life-stage effect on this measure was significant ($p < .01$). Thus, the later the life-stage of the respondents during imprisonment, the more negative their overall feelings about the incar-

Table 3.4. Overall Evaluation of Camp Years
by Life-Stage at Incarceration and Gender

Age at Incarceration	Mean Camp Score
5–11	3.70**
12–17	3.57
18–22	3.42
23–35	2.76
Gender	
Male	3.20*
Female	3.58

Gender by Age at Incarceration	Gender	
	Males	Females
	(Mean Camp Score)	(Mean Camp Score)
Age at Incarceration		
5–11	3.64	3.80
12–17	3.31	3.82
18–22	3.11	3.76*
23–35	2.59	2.91

$^a p < .10$ $^*p < .05$ $^{**}p < .01$ level $^{***}p < .001$ (two-tailed tests)

ceration. The mean overall evaluation score for those in their childhood life-stage was 3.70; adolescence, 3.57; college years, 3.42; and early adulthood, 2.76. Those incarcerated in their early adult years had both the most negative and distinctly different overall recollection of their camp years as compared to individuals in the other life-stages.

Specific negative recollections by life-stage. When the three most frequently reported negative recollections, those focusing on the physical aspects of living conditions, weather/climate, and food, were cross tabulated with the life-stage categories of 5–11 years, 12–17 years, 18–22 years, and 23–35 years, there were no significant age-associated effects (see table 3.5). These negative memories were mentioned consistently across all age groups.

With regard to the less frequently reported complaints about the imprisonment period, specifically those of a psychological or social nature, the

Table 3.5. Memories of Incarceration Experiences
by Life-Stage and Gender

Variable	Age at Incarceration				Gender	
	5–11	12–17	18–22	23–35	Male	Female
Difficult Experiences: % Yes						
Living conditions	48.6	56.6	50.0	57.9	44.1	62.2*
Weather/climate	43.3	41.5	34.6	42.1	33.3	46.7[a]
Food	29.7	20.8	19.2	39.5	21.5	31.1
Sense of confinement	2.7	15.1	25.0	10.5*	18.3	10.0[a]
Uncertainty	2.7	9.4	11.5	5.3	5.4	10.0
Family separation	2.7	13.2	3.8	5.3	4.3	10.0
Prejudice/discrimination	0.0	7.5	9.6	5.3	10.8	1.1**
Taking care of family	2.7	0.0	3.8	5.3	1.1	4.4
Positive Memories: % Yes						
Friends	54.1	62.3	55.8	28.9**	49.5	54.4
Social activities	27.0	43.4	25.0	13.2**	23.7	33.3
Sports	18.9	18.9	1.9	0.0***	17.2	2.2***
Work opportunities	0.0	7.5	13.5	10.5	4.3	13.3*
Carefree routine	13.5	5.7	3.8	5.3	7.5	5.6
Art and crafts	10.8	1.9	3.8	10.5	3.2	8.9[a]
No positive memories	13.5	9.4	11.5	31.6*	11.8	18.9
Number of cases	37	53	52	38	93	90

[a] $p < .10$ * $p < .05$ ** $p < .01$ *** $p < .001$ (two-tailed tests)

only significant life-stage effect was on the response "sense of confinement ($p < .05$)." Twenty-five percent of the college-aged students reported that the feeling of confinement was a problem. Teenagers (12–17 years) and adults between the ages of 23–35 years were intermediate on this measure (15.1% and 10.5% respectively), and those who were young children were least likely (2.7%) to note that confinement was a problem for them. Even though the life-stage differences were not statistically reliable, uncertainty, another psychological hardship, was also spontaneously recalled slightly more often by the 18–22 year olds (11.5%) and 12–17 year olds (9.4%). It seems plausible that the college-aged were the most vigorous and impatient about their circumstances and thus felt most strongly the constraining and limiting nature of camp life. Overall, those who were young children (5–11) at the time of their incarceration were, perhaps not surprisingly, the least likely to report negative psychological or social memories.

Specific positive recollections by life-stage. When positive recollections are cross-tabulated with the same four life-stage categories that were used to examine negative memories, an interesting pattern emerges (see table 3.5). Those who experienced the incarceration during their teenage years (12–17 years) most frequently (62.3%) reported friends as a positive feature of their camp years. The least likely to report friends as a positive remembrance were those who were already in their early adult years (28.9%) and had many responsibilities with which to deal ($p < .01$). The same pattern emerges with regard to reporting social activities as a positive feature of the incarceration period. Forty-three and four tenths percent of teenagers spontaneously reported this as a positive remembrance as contrasted with 13.2% of those in their early adult years ($p < .01$).

With regard to sports, as might be expected, a greater proportion of children and teenagers remember this as an affirmative feature of their camp years (both groups at 18.9%) as contrasted with just 1.9% of the college aged. None of those who were young adults at the time mentioned sports ($p < .001$). Furthermore, it was this oldest group, the young adults, who were the most likely to make the sad commentary that they had no positive memories of their incarceration (31.6%, $p < .05$). This finding is telling given that this life-stage group, due to their greater maturity at the time, might be expected to have the most cognitively complex view of the incarceration of any of the age groups in our sample.

Gender Effects

Overall feeling about the incarceration and gender. Did male incarcerees differ from females in their overall feeling about the incarceration? As seen in table 3.4, male incarcerees were more negative about the incarceration than females ($p < .05$). In each of the four life-stage groups, and particularly among those of college age, women tended to recall the camp experience as being less noxious than men.

Specific negative recollections by gender. Given the somewhat lower negativity of women as compared with men on their overall remembrance of camp, we were interested in gender differences in specific recollections. These might explicate the nature of the gender differences in the incarceree community. With respect to specific negative memories, women incarcerees were more likely to mention the difficult living conditions than men (62.2% vs. 44.1%, $p < .05$; see table 3.5). There are many anecdotal stories of the distaste women had for the crude communal toilets and showers. Also, women tended to point out the harsh weather/climate ($p < .10$) more than men. On the other hand, males tended to have more difficulty with confinement than women (18.3% vs. 10.0%, $p < .10$). In addition, about 11% of the male former incarcerees cited prejudice and discrimination as a problem compared to only 1.1% of the women ($p < .01$). Even though the difference was not statistically significant, it is interesting to note that women were about twice as likely as men to report familial concerns (family separation and taking care of family) as difficult recollections.

Specific positive recollections by gender. Not surprisingly, sports were a much more frequently mentioned positive memory for male than female respondents (17.2% vs. 2.2%, $p < .001$). As in the prewar community, sports were a very important part of the camps' community life. The camp newspaper reported all of the latest scores and colorfully commented on the performances of local stars. All-star teams from the different camps played championship games for enthusiastic fans; a few of the games ended in fan and player brawls (Nakagawa 2001, 79–82).

Women more frequently remembered work opportunities as an uplifting facet of their incarceration than men (13.3% vs. 4.3%, $p < .05$). Because of the unusual circumstances of camp, women probably had more opportunities to try out various occupational roles as compared with their previous lives outside. Women also tended to remember fondly the opportunity to develop art and craft interests more frequently than men (8.9% vs. 3.2%, $p < .10$).

Thus, those in various life-stages and of different genders had common as well as divergent recollections of their life during incarceration (see Table 3.6). As might be expected, most respondents vividly recalled the harsh physical conditions. However, friendships brought an important and widely appreciated element of normalcy to the incarcerees' otherwise abnormal circumstances. For the young male children, sports were a highlight. The strongest memory, overall, was that the social life in camp made life tolerable for most incarcerees, particularly adolescent females. It is not surprising that the college-aged

Table 3.6. Memories of Incarceration by Life-Stage for Each Gender

Age at Incarceration	Males				Females			
	5–11	12–17	18–22	23–35	5–11	12–17	18–22	23–35
Difficult Memories: % Yes								
Living conditions	41.0	61.5	37.0	35.3	60.0	51.8	64.0	76.2
Weather/climate	31.8	30.8	37.0	35.2	60.0	51.8	32.0	47.6
Food	3.8	23.1	0.0	41.2**	26.7	18.5	40.0	38.1
Confinement	0.0	15.4	37.0	17.7**	6.7	14.8	12.0	4.8
Uncertainty	0.0	0.0	14.8	5.9[a]	6.7	18.5	8.0	4.8
Family separation	0.0	11.5	3.7	0.0	6.7	14.8	4.0	9.5
Prejudice/discrimination	0.0	11.5	18.5	11.8	0.0	3.7	0.0	0.0
Taking care of family	0.0	0.0	3.7	0.0	6.7	0.0	4.0	9.5
Positive Memories: % Yes								
Friends	54.6	57.7	48.2	29.4	53.3	66.7	64.0	28.6*
Social activities	27.3	34.6	18.5	11.8	26.7	51.8	32.0	14.3*
Sports	31.8	34.6	0.0	0.0***	0.0	3.7	4.0	0.0
Work opportunities	0.0	0.0	11.1	5.9	0.0	14.8	16.0	14.3
Carefree routine	13.6	7.7	3.7	5.9	13.3	3.7	4.0	4.8
Arts and crafts	4.6	0.0	3.7	5.9	20.0	3.7	4.0	14.3
No positive memories	9.1	11.5	7.4	23.5	20.0	7.4	16.0	38.1[a]
Number of cases	22	26	27	17	15	27	25	21

[a] $p < .10$ * $p < .05$ ** $p < .01$ *** $p < .001$ (two-tailed tests)

males, who were most likely to have been forced to put their plans for higher education on hold or to discontinue their studies, felt the confinement and prejudice most intensely (the latter was not statistically reliable). However, it was the older incarcerees of both genders (23–35 year olds) who were most likely to report the poignant fact that they had no positive memories of their camp days at all. Associated with this, and probably causally related, it was these same young adults who were the least likely to report friends and social activities as positive memories.

Prewar Family Resources

Another way that we examined specific negative and positive remembrances of respondents' incarceration was to compare respondents who had varying amounts of prewar resources, both their family's human and financial capital as well as their own personal aspirations. This was done in an attempt to gauge whether prewar resources and aspirations influenced the former incarcerees' camp remembrances.

Total Socioeconomic Index (TSEI).   In order to have a general measure of occupational attainment for the respondents, we converted their occupation (job titles) to the Total Socioeconomic Index (TSEI) (Hauser and Warren 1997, 177–98). This index, which is based on the occupational patterns of both men and women, reflects occupational education and earnings (i.e., where occupations are ranked by the percentage of people with one or more years of college education and by earnings in different occupations) as well as the prestige rankings associated with various occupations.

Prewar resources and overall evaluation of camp.   As shown in table 3.7, when we related both prewar as well as several current socioeconomic status (SES) measures to the incarcerees' overall assessment of their camp years, a number of interesting relationships were uncovered. If the respondent's father had a more prestigious occupation (above the median TSEI score), the respondent rated his or her incarceration experience more negatively (3.2 vs. 3.6, $p < .05$). Similar trends, albeit not statistically significant, were found when we used other measures of family resources, such as father's professional and self-employment status, as well as individual respondent's aspirations. Thus, those with greater prewar resources evaluated their camp experience more negatively than those who had limited resources. This finding, by itself, may suggest that the greater relative and absolute losses of the more materially comfortable as well as those who were more motivated are reflected in a more negative overall evaluation of the incarceration experience.

Prewar family resources and negative remembrances.   Next, we cross-tabulated specific difficulties that respondents experienced during the incarceration with the socioeconomic standing of their fathers (see table 3.8). Specifically, we examined whether the professional or nonprofessional status of the respondent's father was associated with differences in what the incarcerees reported they felt. In fact, if the respondent's father was a professional, there was a greater likelihood that the individual reported psychological type difficulties

Table 3.7. Overall Evaluation of Camp Experience by Resources

		Camp Score Mean *(SD)*
Prewar Resources: Family's		
TSEI of father's occupation:	Above median	3.2 (1.3)*
	At/below median	3.6 (1.3)
Father's work in professional sector:	Yes	3.3 (1.4)
	No	3.5 (1.3)
Father self–employed:	Yes	3.4 (1.3)
	No	3.6 (1.4)
Prewar Resources: Individual aspirations		
Plans for college[1]	Yes	3.2 (1.2)
	No	3.5 (1.3)
TSEI of planned occupation:	Above median	3.1 (1.2)
	At/below median	3.3 (1.3)
Planned occupation in professional sector:	Yes	3.1 (1.3)
	No	3.3 (1.3)
TSEI of job at incarceration:	Above median	2.8 (1.4)
	At/below median	3.3 (1.4)
Current Resources		
Years of college education:	No college	3.6 (1.2)*
	1–8 years	3.2 (1.4)
TSEI of last main job:	Above median	3.2 (1.4)
	At/below median	3.5 (1.2)
Annual income:	Above $50,000	3.6 (1.2)[a]
	At/below $50,000	3.3 (1.3)

[a] $p < .10$ *$p < .05$ **$p < .01$ ***$p < .001$ (two-tailed tests)
[1] Those who said they were too young to think about college were not included ($n=64$).

connected with incarceration. About 31% of respondents with professional fathers reported confinement as a difficulty. Only 7.9% of respondents with nonprofessional fathers claimed that confinement was a problem ($p < .001$). Similarly, those with professional fathers tended to more frequently note that uncertainty was a problem they experienced during their camp days

Table 3.8. Memories of Difficult Experiences
in WRA Camps by Prewar Resources (by Father's Characteristics)

	Father Works in Professional Sector[1]		Father's Occupational TSEI Score		Father Self-Employed	
	Yes	No	Above Median	At/Below Median	Yes	No
Selected difficult experiences:						
% that said "Yes" to difficulties						
Living conditions	56.3	55.4	58.5	52.2	52.3	66.7
Food	12.5	27.3[a]	20.7	27.8	21.9	45.8
Confinement	31.3	7.9***	18.3	6.7*	14.6	0.0*
Uncertainty	15.6	5.8[a]	11.0	4.4	8.6	0.0
Number of cases	32	139	82	90	151	24

	Father's Occupational TSEI	
	Above Median	*At or Below Median*
Positive memories: % Yes		
Friends	62.2	43.3**
Social activities	36.6	22.2*
Work opportunities	7.3	11.1
No positive memories	13.4	16.7
Number of cases	90	82

[a] $p < .10$ *$p < .05$ **$p < .01$ ***$p < .001$ (two-tailed tests)

[1] Professional sector includes the following: executive, admin., managerial; engineers and other professionals; health professionals; post-secondary teachers; librarians, archivists; social scientists, lawyers, and judges; writers, artists, and entertainers.

(15.6% vs. 5.8%, $p < .10$). On the other hand, there was a trend for those whose fathers were not in professional occupations to more frequently recount food as a negative memory (27.3% vs. 12.5%, $p < .10$). A father's self-employment status was similar to professional status in the effects on their offspring's reported camp difficulties.

To obtain a more precise measure of the socioeconomic standing of the respondents' fathers, we converted their job titles to the occupational socioeconomic index, the Total Socioeconomic Index (TSEI). One interpretational ambiguity associated with our usage of the TSEI for this purpose is that it has been validated with contemporary data. Thus, to the extent that occupational socioeconomic status perceptions have changed from before World War II to the present, the validity of this measure to index the respondents' fathers' status is called into question. An indication that at least one aspect of this problem may not be as serious as it could be is Hauser and Warren's (1997, 180) finding that there is little decay in the quality of occupational reports across the adult years.

When we did a median split of the respondents based upon their father's TSEI score, 18.3% of respondents with fathers above the median reported problems with confinement as contrasted with 6.7% of those below the median ($p < .05$). Respondents whose father's occupation was above the median TSEI score also tended to more frequently mention living conditions (58.5% vs. 52.2%) and uncertainty (11.0% vs. 4.4%) as negative memories.

Similarly, those respondents whose fathers were self-employed were also more likely to report that a sense of confinement was a problem in the camps (14.6% vs. 0.0%, $p < .05$). In general, these results support the interpretation that those who had more family resources, a type of social capital, while growing up, at least as indexed by the occupational socioeconomic standing of their father, now have a more articulated, "psychological" view of the negative aspects of their incarceration experience.

Prewar family resources and positive remembrances. Next, we inquired whether there were any differences in respondents' positive memories of their incarceration as related to their family's prewar resources. When we cross-tabulated positive memories by father's resources, two patterns emerged. Those whose fathers had an occupation that was above the median on the TSEI occupational index were significantly more likely to remember friends as a source of positive memories in the camps (62.2% vs. 43.3%, $p < .01$). Those whose fathers had occupations above the median on the TSEI also reported social activities more frequently as a positive memory of their camp days (36.6% vs. 22.2%, $p < .05$). These differences suggest that those who grew up in families with more prewar socioeconomic resources made a somewhat better social adjustment in camp or at least remember it that way.

Prewar Individual Resources

Prewar individual resources and negative remembrances. We were also interested in the effect of more individual resources or human capital on camp remembrances. Although a positive relationship exists between family resources and individual ones, they are not identical. Thus, we examined differences in negative memories as a function of the individual respondent's prewar human capital. Our measures of individual prewar resources were: whether the incarcerees had plans to attend college; the socioeconomic status (TSEI) of their planned occupation; whether their planned occupation was in the professional sector; and the TSEI score of the job they had (if any) at the time they were evicted and incarcerated. We used a median split of TSEI scores with the variables of planned occupation and job at exclusion, and yes–no response categories with plans for college and professional status. These crude categorizations were necessary due to the relatively small size of the sample. In addition, clearly these measures are non-independent. Thus, caution needs to be exercised when interpreting the reported levels of significance.

As can be seen in table 3.9, respondents who had higher-than-average prewar individual resources (i.e., those who were college bound, had higher-status occupational plans, had plans for a professional career, and who were in higher-status jobs at the time of exclusion) were consistently more likely than those with more limited resources to report uncertainty, living conditions, weather, and family separation as difficult camp memories. On the other hand, those with fewer prewar individual resources more frequently recalled food and prejudice/discrimination as noxious memories.

More specifically, those who intended to go to college were reliably more likely to report that uncertainty was a problem for them in camp ($p < .05$). Those respondents who had above-average occupational aspirations tended to more frequently mention the harsh living conditions (62.9% vs. 42.2%, $p < .10$) and the pain of family separation (11.4% vs. 2.2%, $p < .10$). Family separation also tended to be more frequently reported as a difficulty by those who planned to enter a professional occupation as compared with those who did not (12.5% vs. 2.1%, $p < .10$). The need to relocate away from the family to pursue a college degree was, at least partially, probably responsible for this effect. Similarly, those who were working at the time of their mass removal in jobs that had above-median TSEI scores more often reported that living conditions (63.6% vs. 34.3%, $p < .05$) and weather/climate (59.1% vs. 22.9%, $p < .01$) were negative issues with regard to their imprisonment. These latter effects were found mostly among those in the two older life-stage groups, as they were the two age groups most likely to be employed at the time. They generally had lower levels of higher education.

Table 3.9. Memories of Difficult Experiences in WRA Camps by Prewar Resources (by Respondent's Characteristics)

	Plans for College at Incarceration[1]		Planned Occupation: TSEI Score		Planned Occupation in Professional Sector[2]		Job at Incarceration: TSEI Score	
	Yes	No	Above Median	At/Below Median	Yes	No	Above Median	At/Below Median
Selected difficult experiences:								
% that said "Yes" to difficulties								
Living conditions	57.8	50.7	62.9	42.2[a]	59.4	45.8	63.6	34.3*
Uncertainty	15.6	4.0*[3]	17.1	8.9	18.8	8.3	9.1	5.7
Weather/climate	35.6	37.3	31.1	48.6	40.6	37.5	59.1	22.9**
Family separation	11.1	5.3	11.4	2.2[a]	12.5	2.1[a]	4.5	8.6
Care of family	2.2	4.0	2.9	2.2	3.1	2.1	9.1	2.9
Food	20.0	34.7[a,4]	22.9	24.4	18.8	27.1	27.3	22.9
Prejudice/ discrimination	8.9	6.7	8.6	11.1	9.4	10.4	0.0	22.9*
Sense of confinement	22.2	14.7	17.1	24.4	15.6	25.0	13.6	22.9
Number of cases	45	75	35	45	32	48	22	35

[a] $p < .10$ *$p < .05$ **$p < .01$ ***$p < .001$ (two-tailed tests)

[1] Those who said they were too young to think about college were not included ($n=64$).

[2] Professional sector includes the following: executive, admin., managerial; engineers and other professionals; health professionals; post-secondary teachers; librarians, archivists; social scientists, lawyers, and judges; writers, artists, and entertainers.

[3] Similar trends, even if not statistically significant, were found among those who were between 14–18 years of age at incarceration. 12.5% out of 16 respondents who were in college or had plans to attend college mentioned "uncertainty" compared to 0.0% of the 15 respondents who had no college plans.

[4] When the analysis was limited to only those who were between the ages of 14 and 18 at evacuation, the trend was similar even if not statistically significant because of the reduced sample sizes. 40% of the 14–18 year olds at incarceration who had no college plans ($n=16$) mentioned "food" as a difficulty compared to only 18.8% of those who were in college or had plans to attend college ($n=15$).

Younger respondents who indicated that they were not planning to attend college at the time of the exclusion were more likely to report that food was a noxious recollection (34.7% vs. 20.0%), although this difference only approached significance ($p < .10$). Finally, those who were working in lower rather than higher socioeconomic-status jobs at the time they were evicted recalled experiencing significantly more discrimination in camp (22.9% vs.

Table 3.10. Memories of Positive Experiences
in WRA Camps by Prewar Resources (by Respondent's Characteristics)

	Plans for College[1]		Planned Occupation: TSEI Score		Planned Occupation	
	Yes	No	Above Median	At/Below Median	Professional[2] Sector	Non-Professional Sector
Positive Memories: % Yes						
Friends	62.2	42.7*†	60.0	44.4	62.5	43.8[a]
Social activities	35.6	18.7*†	40.0	22.2[a]	40.6	22.9[a]
Work opportunities	17.8	10.7	5.7	17.8[a]	6.3	16.7
No positive memories	6.7	25.3**†	11.4	17.8	12.5	16.7
Number of cases	75	45	35	45	32	48

[a] $p < .10$ *$p < .05$ **$p < .01$ ***$p < .001$ (two-tailed tests)

[1] Those who said they were too young to think about college were not included ($n=64$).

[2] Professional sector includes the following: executive, admin., managerial; engineers and other professionals; health professionals; post-secondary teachers; librarians, archivists; social scientists, lawyers, and judges; writers, artists, and entertainers.

† When the analysis is limited only to those who were between 14 and 18 years of age at incarceration, the differences became nonsignificant, even though the pattern remains the same. That is, 69% of those with college plans ($n=16$) mentioned "friends" as a positive memory compared to only 60% of those with no college plans ($n=15$).

50% ($n=16$) of those with college plans mentioned "social activities" as a positive memory in contrast to 33% of those with no college plans ($n=15$).

Only 12.5% of those with plans for college ($n=16$) mentioned "no positive memories" compared to 26.7% of those with no college plans ($n=15$).

0.0, $p < .05$). Although we cannot be certain whether this reflected reality or not, it appears that those with greater human capital were better able to avoid being in situations that exposed them to discrimination.

Prewar individual resources and positive remembrances. As with family prewar resources, those who had greater individual resources (higher than average) prior to the war were more likely to mention positive memories about friends and social activities, while those with fewer resources remembered the work opportunities in camps or had no positive recollections of their camp experience (see table 3.10). For example, those who planned on attending college were significantly more likely to report that friends (62.2% vs. 42.7%, $p < .05$) and social activities (35.6% vs. 18.7%, $p < .05$) were positive memories of their camp days. Those who planned careers in higher-status jobs and/or had professional aspirations were also more likely to remember friends and social activities, although the differences were not statistically reliable.

In contrast, those with lower educational and occupational aspirations were more likely to remember the work opportunities in camp or not to have any positive memories at all. As previously alluded to, it could be that among these individuals, their lower level of human capital made it more difficult for them to accommodate to the chaotic and demoralizing situation they were thrust into. Further, those who planned to be in an occupation that was below the median TSEI score tended to more frequently mention work opportunities as a positive experience compared to those with above-median occupational aspirations (17.8% vs. 5.7%, $p < .10$). Clearly, given the nature of the jobs available in the WRA camps, those who aspired to less prestigious jobs were more likely to find positions in camp which more closely matched their aspirations. More significantly, 25.3% of the respondents who had no college plans reported having no positive memories compared to only 6.7% of the college bound ($p < .01$). Those who had higher aspirations before the war not only were probably likely to remain hopeful during the incarceration but were also able to actually cope better, for example, by having more rewarding social activities and relationships.

Individual's Current Resources

Certainly, it is also possible that respondents' present circumstances shape in some fashion their recollections and attitudes about past events, such as their wartime confinement. We therefore looked for differences in negative and positive memories of camp as a function of differences in the respondents' *current* socioeconomic status. Once again, our study's sample size and limited measures only permit a crude examination of this issue. Prewar resources are, at least to some degree, positively related to respondents' present status. Unfortunately, the determination of the strength of the relationship between prewar and postwar resources and the specific causal paths involved demands a much larger sample and more measures than are available in this study.

The partially redundant contemporary socioeconomic status measures we had available to us were the respondent's years of college education; TSEI score of the respondent's last main job; income; and whether or not the respondent's last main job was in the professional sector. Measures such as college education are ambiguous with respect to the time period with which they are associated. Some individuals obtained the majority of their higher education during World War II through, for example, the student relocation program, but most did so in the decade following their release from camp.

Individual's current resources and overall assessment of camp. On the overall measure assessing their WRA camp years, those who achieved higher levels of education were more negative about their incarceration experience (3.2 vs. 3.6, $p < .05$; see table 3.7). Similarly, those whose last main job was more prestigious tended to be more negative about the camps, although the differences were not significant. Those whose annual income was above $50,000 in 1989, on the other hand, tended to be less negative overall about their camp experience (3.6 vs. 3.3, $p < .10$).

Individual's current resources and negative remembrances. As shown in table 3.11.a, the only noxious incarceration recollection that was consistently related to our measures of current resources was whether or not the respondent experienced uncertainty. Compared to those who did not mention uncertainty as a problem, those who did so completed more years of higher education ($Ms = 3.1$ vs. 1.8, $p < .05$), tended to have higher TSEI scores for their last main job ($Ms = 47.7$ vs. 40.5, $p < .10$), and tended to have higher current income (6.5 vs. 5.0, $p < .10$; see table 3.11a). Whether the most recent job the respondent had was a professional one or not was also related to claiming that uncertainty was a problem: 13.7% of professionals reported uncertainty as a difficulty, while only 3.9% of nonprofessionals did ($p < .05$; see table 3.11c). The only other significant difference was that the nonprofessionals were more likely to note that the weather and climate in camp were difficulties (48.5% vs. 30.1%, $p < .01$; see table 3.11.c).

Individual's current resources and positive remembrances. Differences in what were remembered as positive aspects of the incarceration follow a somewhat similar pattern to those found earlier with prewar family and individual resources. Those who reported sports as a positive memory were consistently more likely to be better educated ($Ms = 3.3$ vs. 1.8, $p < .01$), have higher TSEI scores in their most recent job ($Ms = 53.0$ vs. 39.7, $p < .001$), and have higher incomes ($Ms = 6.8$ vs. 5.0, $p < .01$; see table 3.11.b). They were also more likely to

Table 3.11.a. Memories of Difficult Experiences
in WRA Camps by Current Resources

		Current SES, Mean (SD)		
		Number of Years of College Education	TSEI Score of Last Main Job	Income[1]
Difficulties in Camps: Yes = 1; No = 0				
Living conditions	Yes	1.9 (2.2)	41.9 (15.7)	5.2 (2.6)
	No	1.9 (2.4)	40.2 (14.4)	5.1 (2.5)
Uncertainty	Yes	3.1 (2.8)*	47.7 (12.2)[a]	6.5 (1.8)[a]
	No	1.8 (2.2)	40.5 (15.2)	5.0 (2.6)
Sense of confinement	Yes	2.0 (2.1)	42.6 (13.0)	4.8 (1.6)
	No	1.9 (2.3)	40.1 (15.4)	5.2 (2.7)
Food	Yes	2.1 (2.5)	41.2 (15.7)	4.9 (2.9)
	No	1.8 (2.2)	41.0 (14.9)	5.2 (2.4)
Weather/climate	Yes	1.7 (2.1)	40.7 (15.0)	5.2 (2.7)
	No	2.1 (2.4)	41.3 (15.2)	5.1 (2.7)
Family separation	Yes	1.4 (1.9)	36.0 (15.9)	5.5 (3.3)
	No	1.9 (2.3)	41.4 (15.0)	5.1 (2.5)
Prejudice and discrimination	Yes	1.3 (2.2)	37.4 (14.0)	4.0 (1.2)
	No	1.9 (2.3)	41.3 (15.1)	5.2 (2.6)
Taking care of family	Yes	2.6 (3.6)	35.2 (13.7)	4.5 (1.7)
	No	1.9 (2.3)	41.2 (15.1)	5.2 (2.6)
Number of cases		180	176	162

[a] $p < .10$ *$p < .05$ **$p < .01$ ***$p < .001$ (two-tailed tests)
[1] Income is coded in 14 categories with a range from 1–14.

have been working in the professional sector in their last main job (19.2% vs. 3.9%, $p < .001$; see table 3.11.c).

Those with fewer contemporary resources or less human capital, whether it was measured by number of years of college education, TSEI score of their last main job, income, or working in the professional sector in their last main job, were more likely to have no positive memories about their camp years. The respondents who could not summon up anything positive about their camp experience finished their careers in lower status jobs ($Ms =$

Table 3.11.b. Memories of Positive Experiences
in WRA Camps by Current Resources

		Current SES		
		Number of Years of College Education	*TSEI Score of Last Main Job*	*Income[1]*
Positive Memories: (1=Yes; 0 = No)				
Friends	Yes	2.0 (2.3)	42.9 (15.7)[a]	5.4 (2.5)
	No	1.8 (2.3)	39.1 (14.2)	4.8 (2.6)
Social activities	Yes	1.9 (2.3)	41.9 (16.3)	5.6 (3.1)
	No	1.9 (2.3)	40.7 (14.6)	5.0 (2.3)
Sports	Yes	3.3 (2.4)**	53.0 (15.1)***	6.8 (3.1)**
	No	1.8 (2.2)	39.7 (14.5)	5.0 (2.4)
Work opportunities	Yes	1.1 (1.8)	33.63 (11.0)*	4.43 (2.1)
	No	2.0 (2.3)	41.7 (15.2)	5.2 (2.6)
Carefree routine	Yes	2.9 (2.3)	47.7 (16.4)	5.6 (2.3)
	No	1.8 (2.3)	40.6 (14.9)	5.1 (2.6)
Arts and crafts	Yes	1.6 (2.1)	37.2 (17.0)	5.1(2.7)
	No	1.9 (2.3)	41.3 (15.0)	5.2 (2.6)
No positive memories	Yes	1.3 (2.1)[a]	35.7 (11.0)*	4.2 (2.5)*
	No	2.0 (2.3)	42.0 (15.5)	5.3 (2.5)
Number of cases		180	176	162

[a] $p < .10$ *$p < .05$ **$p < .01$ level   ***$p < .001$ (two-tailed tests)
[1] Income is coded in 14 categories with a range from 1–14.

35.7 vs. 42.0, $p < .05$), had lower incomes (4.2 vs. 5.3, $p < .05$), tended to have fewer years of college education (1.3 vs. 2.0, $p < .10$; see table 3.11.b), and were more likely to work in the nonprofessional sector ($p < .01$; see table 3.11.c). Two causal processes are suggested with regard to explaining this pattern of results, although we cannot choose between them with our data. It is possible that those who had a more difficult camp experience became more demoralized or experienced more disorganization in their subsequent life-course trajectory, and therefore achieved less. It might also be that those who ultimately did less well for other reasons remember their incarceration more negatively.

Table 3.11.c. Memories of Difficult
and Positive Experiences in WRA Camps by Current Resources

	Current Resource: Last Main Occupation	
	Prof. Sector[1]	*Non-Prof. Sector*
Difficulties in Camps (% Yes)		
Living conditions	52.1	53.4
Uncertainty	13.7	3.9*
Sense of confinement	19.2	10.7
Food	28.8	25.2
Weather/climate	30.1	48.5**
Family separation	4.1	7.8
Prejudice and discrimination	4.1	4.1
Taking care of family	2.7	2.9
Positive Memories (% Yes)		
Friends	60.3	45.6[a]
Social activities	32.9	25.2
Sports	19.2	3.9***
Work opportunities	4.1	10.7
Carefree routine	11.0	3.9[a]
Arts and crafts	5.5	6.8
No positive memories	6.8	21.4**
Number of cases	73	103

[a] $p < .10$ *$p < .05$ **$p < .01$ ***$p < .001$ (two-tailed tests)

[1] Professional sector includes the following: executive, admin., managerial; engineers and other professionals; health professionals; post-secondary teachers; librarians, archivists; social scientists, lawyers and judges; writers, artists, and entertainers.

Current Ethnic Resources

The Japanese American community, both historically and contemporarily, has been shown to have extensive formal and informal ethnic ties (e.g., Miyamoto 1984, xii–xx; Fugita and O'Brien 1991, 95–117). In chapter 2, where the prewar community was discussed, we reviewed a substantial amount of historical data to document the presence of dense organizational and friendship networks in the ethnic community at that time. Thus, it seemed useful to examine the possible impact that an individual's *current* ethnic ties may have had on

Table 3.12. Overall Evaluation of Camp Experience
by Current Social Networks

		Camp Score Mean (SD)
Social Networks		
Number of Japanese American friends (out of 3 closest)	0	2.6 (1.9)
	1	3.5 (1.3)
	2	3.1 (1.4)
	3	3.5 (1.2)
Number of memberships in Japanese American organizations	0	3.5 (1.2)
	1–2	3.4 (1.4)
	3–12	3.4 (1.3)
Number of memberships in non–Japanese American organizations	0	3.5 (1.2)
	1–2	3.5 (1.4)
	3–10	2.9 (1.3)

$^a p < .10$ $^* p < .05$ $^{**} p < .01$ $^{***} p < .001$ (two-tailed tests)

the nature of former incarcerees' memories of their camp experience. Involve-ment in these networks may, for example, affect the interpretation of these past events through a wide variety of social-influence processes. The number of current memberships, in Japanese American and non–Japanese American organizations, and the number of Japanese Americans included among the respondent's three closest friends, were used as measures of formal ethnic and non-ethnic resources and informal ethnic resources, respectively.

On the overall measure of their recollection of camp experience, con-temporary ethnic ties and ties to the wider, non-Japanese community did not significantly color the way respondents remembered their incarceration (see table 3.12). There were no statistically reliable differences related to the respondents' current differential involvement in the Japanese American or wider community.

As for specific positive and negative memories of camp, several interest-ing patterns can be seen with respect to the respondents' ties with the wider, non–Japanese American community (see table 3.13). Former incarcerees who reported prejudice and discrimination as a negative memory were more likely

Table 3.13. Negative and Positive Memories by Current Social Networks

		Japanese American Organizations Mean (SD)	Japanese American Friends Mean (SD)	Non-Japanese American Organizations Mean (SD)
Difficult Memories Mentioned				
Living conditions	Yes	1.8 (1.4)	2.4 (0.8)	1.3 (1.9)
	No	1.8 (2.0)	2.4 (1.0)	1.1 (1.7)
Weather/climate	Yes	1.8 (1.3)	2.5 (0.9)	0.9 (1.4)[a]
	No	1.8 (1.9)	2.4 (0.9)	1.4 (2.1)
Food	Yes	1.6 (1.1)	2.4 (1.0)	1.0 (1.9)
	No	1.9 (1.8)	2.4 (0.9)	1.2 (1.8)
Sense of confinement	Yes	2.2 (1.7)	2.5 (0.8)	1.0 (1.8)
	No	1.7 (1.7)	2.4 (0.9)	1.2 (1.8)
Uncertainty	Yes	1.1 (0.8)	2.3 (1.0)	1.1 (1.4)
	No	1.9 (1.7)	2.4 (0.9)	1.2 (1.9)
Prejudice/discrimination	Yes	1.6 (1.4)	2.6 (0.8)	2.2 (3.0)*
	No	1.8 (1.7)	2.4 (0.9)	1.1 (1.7)
Family separation	Yes	2.5 (1.6)	2.4 (1.0)	1.1 (1.4)
	No	1.8 (1.7)	2.4 (0.9)	1.2 (1.8)
Care of family	Yes	1.8 (1.6)	2.2 (0.8)	0.6 (1.3)
	No	1.8 (1.7)	2.4 (0.9)	1.2 (1.8)
Positive Memories Mentioned				
Friends	Yes	1.8 (1.3)	2.5 (0.8)*	1.2 (1.5)
	No	1.8 (2.0)	2.3 (1.0)	1.2 (2.1)
Social activities	Yes	1.7 (1.4)	2.4 (0.9)	1.3 (1.9)
	No	1.8 (1.8)	2.4 (0.9)	1.2 (1.8)
Sports	Yes	1.6 (1.1)	2.3 (0.9)	2.2 (2.5)**
	No	1.8 (1.7)	2.4 (0.9)	1.1 (1.7)
Work opportunities	Yes	1.2 (0.9)	2.5 (0.8)	0.7 (0.9)
	No	1.9 (1.7)	2.4 (0.9)	1.2 (1.9)
Carefree routine	Yes	1.3 (1.4)	2.3 (0.9)	1.3 (2.1)
	No	1.8 (1.7)	2.4 (0.9)	1.2 (1.8)
Arts and crafts	Yes	2.3 (1.1)	2.6 (0.8)	0.9 (1.0)
	No	1.8 (1.7)	2.4 (0.9)	1.2 (1.9)
No positive memories	Yes	1.5 (1.8)	2.2 (1.0)	0.6 (1.2)[a]
	No	1.9 (1.7)	2.4 (0.9)	1.3 (1.9)

[a] $p < .10$ * $p < .05$ ** $p < .01$ *** $p < .001$ (two-tailed tests)

to be organizationally involved in the wider, non-ethnic community (that is, they belonged to more non-Japanese organizations) than those who did not report this negative memory (2.2 vs. 1.1, $p < .05$). Yet, those who report having no positive recollections of camp tended to belong to fewer non-Japanese organizations (0.6 vs. 1.3, $p < .10$). With respect to positive memories, those who mentioned sports were, on average, members of one additional non–Japanese American organization as compared with those who did not mention sports (2.2 vs. 1.1, $p < .01$).

Finally, those who remembered friends as a positive feature of their camp years had a greater number of Japanese American friends in their current close friendship circle (2.5 vs. 2.3, $p < .05$). Probably the same social dispositions that led individuals to perceive that they had many Japanese American friends in camp are, in fact, related to the number of contemporary Japanese American friends that they currently report.

SUMMARY

Overall our respondents were, somewhat surprisingly, affectively mixed in their recollections of their incarceration experience, although with a clear tilt toward the negative end of the spectrum. Those former incarcerees who experienced the mass removal and imprisonment at an older age, when they had more complicated life roles, had the most negative overall evaluation about their experience. The very young at the time of their imprisonment appear to have been buffered, to a large degree, from the harsh realities of the forced removal and camp life by their families. Part of this age-related effect is probably due to the simpler developmental tasks facing young children. But it is also a testimony to the efforts of many older community members to create as normal a community and family life as possible in the abnormal environment of the camps.

While the difficult physical conditions were, not surprisingly, the most likely to be remembered, substantial numbers of respondents also emphasized memories that were psychological and social relational in nature. This was particularly true of those with more human capital. In general, women focused more on the difficult material and social relational conditions, while men were more prone to recall difficulties that were of a psychological nature. This latter effect may be partially a function of the greater educational attainment of males.

Despite the stark and oppressive surroundings, the majority of respondents warmly recalled the multitude of friendships, social functions, and sports activities with which they were involved during their camp years. Those who experienced the incarceration during their teenage years (12–17 years old) were especially likely to call attention to these positive social encounters. The least likely to report friends as a positive memory were those who were already in their early adult years. It was also members of this oldest group who were the most likely to make the poignant commentary that they had no positive memories of their camp years. Thus, our data consistently document that the life-stage at which the incarceration was experienced has a major and systematic effect on how the upheaval is remembered over fifty years later.

Prewar resources, both at the family and individual levels, also were associated with how the incarcerees recalled their camp years. The more prewar resources respondents had, the more articulated were their contemporary perspectives about camp life. Specifically, those with more extensive resources had both richer negative and positive memories of their incarceration years. In contrast, those with more limited prewar resources focused more heavily on the negative material aspects of the camps. They also reported that they experienced more discrimination. It seems likely that this was not a purely perceptual phenomenon, but that those who had more prewar resources were able to use them to cope with the exigencies of the incarceration.

As for the influence of current resources on respondents' recollections, the more educated respondents were more negative about their camp years. It seems plausible that the more educated would be better able to evaluate critically their wartime experiences.

In sum, what do these findings tell us about the effects of variations in prewar and current human and social capital on individuals' remembrances of their exclusion and incarceration? One, there was a duality to most individuals' remembrances. Those with more resources especially had a complex mix of negative and positive recollections resulting in a multihued recollection of their camp experience. Those with greater prewar human and social capital appear to have been better able to create meaningful social relationships in camp, becoming more involved in social activities and sports. They also were better able to avoid or deal with prejudicial situations during their imprisonment. Similarly, those who did better socioeconomically after the war, even though they evaluated their incarceration experience more negatively, also more often remembered the many friendships they made and the rewarding social activities they took part in. All in all, their recollections are a bittersweet mix of the harsh material and psychological realities of their incarceration and of the supportive social relationships and sense of community that they were able to create behind the guard towers and barbed-wire fences.

FOUR

Military Service and Resistance

I run into a Nisei soldier. He was completely drunk and he was cussing
Roosevelt up and down with the most vile language I ever heard. . . .
I heard that his parents, his father was arrested the day after he volun-
teered, and the mother subsequently went into somewhere, assembly
center, and from there to a relocation center somewhere. (George
Koshi, denshovh-kgeorge-01-0008)

By the eve of World War II, a significant number of older Nisei were
becoming eligible for military service. With the outbreak of hostilities
in Europe, many were drawn into the armed forces; some were drafted into
the U.S. Army, while others volunteered. A small number were accepted for
commissioning in the Army through the Reserve Officer Training Corps.
Unfortunately, this rather prosaic relationship to the military changed suddenly and dramatically for the Nisei after the shattering attack on Pearl
Harbor.

A little over one month after the attack, on January 19, 1942, the Nisei's
draft classification was changed from 4-A to 4-C, enemy alien. Some already
in the Army were discharged, and others had their weapons taken away. Still
others continued with their tour in a normal manner. As is apparent in hind-
sight, the size and complexity of the military bureaucracy initially led to
many inconsistencies in how different draft boards and commands handled
their Nisei. In the Pacific Northwest, some Nisei were even drafted during
this period. The following quote by a visual history narrator poignantly illus-
trates the confusion surrounding the treatment of the Nisei by the military.

March 1942, I was drafted. First I went to Texas, and that was the induction center for our area, so I went there. And ah, they didn't know what to do with me or with the Nisei. So I stayed there for about two months. And then in the meantime I was sent to Camp Robinson, Arkansas, for basic training. And then six months of basic training, I was sent to Cheyenne, Wyoming. And still, they didn't know what to do with Nisei. . . . So from Fort Warren, Wyoming, I was sent to Camp Savage for MIS training. (George Koshi, denshovh-kgeorge-01-0005)

The story of Japanese Americans and the military during World War II is, surprisingly, still emerging. Some parts of it are well known, for example, the much praised record of the 100th Infantry Battalion and 442nd Regimental Combat Team (RCT) in Europe. Other chapters, such as the Military Intelligence Service (MIS), are still being documented. The work of the MIS was kept confidential for many years after the end of the war, supposedly for national security reasons. The most recently spotlighted and also contested part of the story of the Nisei and the military is centered on the much smaller number of individuals who resisted the draft when it was imposed on them during the incarceration.

In this chapter, we first briefly outline the history of these distinctive groups to provide background for our analyses, which focus on their contemporary situation. We then explore the life-course consequences of having served in the military and, to a degree, of resisting the draft when it was imposed on incarcerated males in early 1944.

DECORATED SOLDIERS AND "REVILED" RESISTERS

The Purple Heart Battalion—100th Infantry Battalion

In Hawaii, many Nisei were involved in island defense activities even before the attack on Pearl Harbor. The largest numbers were members of the Hawaii National Guard, a mixture of draftees and volunteers. After Pearl Harbor, soldiers in the Guard became members of the 298th and 299th Infantry Regiments, which performed patrol and construction duties. In June 1942, most of Hawaii's Nisei soldiers, over 1,400, were shipped to Camp McCoy, Wisconsin, to begin training as the newly formed 100th Infantry Battalion. Tellingly, one of the rationales used to justify moving these men to the mainland was that if Japanese forces invaded the Hawaiian Islands, they might wear

American uniforms and thus be indistinguishable from Japanese American soldiers (Duus 1983, 20).

Camp McCoy, besides being a basic training post, was also an enemy alien camp. Ironically, one of the first duties assigned to the 100th Infantry Battalion was to guard the Issei who were interned there (Duus 1983, 24). In January 1943, after an unusually long training period of six months, the unit was transferred to Camp Shelby, Mississippi, for even more training. Here race relations in the surrounding Deep South communities sometimes befuddled the Hawaiian Nisei. They were faced with such questions as whether they should use the "colored" or white men's rooms and ride in the front or rear of the bus. In these situations, they were "white."

The reason that the Battalion's training period was much longer than ordinary was because the Army leadership was having difficulty deciding where and how to deploy the unit. The 100th Battalion finally shipped out to North Africa in August 1943. It first saw heavy fighting in Italy, particularly at the Cassino and Anzio beachheads. By the time the 442nd RCT (described below), made up mostly of Hawaiian and some mainland incarceree volunteers, caught up with the 100th Battalion in June 1944, the Battalion was already battle hardened and had acquired an enviable reputation. For the purposes of maintaining espirit de corps, the 100th Battalion was allowed to keep its unit designation when it became the first battalion of the 442nd Regimental Combat Team.

Go for Broke: The 442nd Regimental Combat Team

The decision to form a volunteer Nisei combat team was made in early 1943 after much vacillation on the part of the War Department. According to recent scholarship, one likely consideration in the government's decision to form the 442nd RCT was its propaganda value in arguing against the perception, particularly in the Far East, that the United States was a racist nation. Specifically, a visible "Japanese" combat unit in the U.S. Army could be seen as providing evidence against the idea that the United States was fighting a racial conflict (Fujitani 2001). The call for volunteers for the 442nd RCT eventually went out to both the mainland concentration camps and Hawaii. Originally, War Department officials expected more people to volunteer from the camps than from Hawaii. But while there was a huge outpouring of nearly 10,000 volunteers in the Territory of Hawaii, only some 1,256 volunteered from the camps. Ultimately, 2,686 were accepted from the Islands and approximately 800 from the camps (Chang 1991, 102–4; Crost 1994, 62–63; Niiya 2001, 163–64). This disparity in response was clearly related to the dramatic differences in the treatment of Japanese Americans both before and during the war in the two areas. Key, of course, was that there was no mass incarceration in Hawaii, as had taken place on the Pacific Coast. Daniel Inouye, who later became a senator for Hawaii, reflected the attitude of many of the Nisei youth on the Islands.

> On March 17th when the government of the United States designated Japanese as 4-C, which is a designation for enemy alien, many of us took this as a personal matter, an insult to us. We considered ourselves just as good Americans as our neighbors, and so we began petitioning Washington. We began offering ourselves to do anything, dig ditches, string barbed wire, what have you . . . and when the President of the United States issued a statement saying that, "Americanism is a matter of mind and heart, it is not and has never been a matter of race or color," and declared that if we wished we can volunteer and become part of this special combat team, and when the announcement was made, together with several of my classmates, we literally ran from the campus to the draft board. That's a couple of miles. We ran there and we signed up. (Daniel Inouye, denshov-idaniel-01-0005)

Many of the volunteers, both in Hawaii and on the mainland, realized that their actions would be critical for the future of Japanese Americans. In the words of one narrator:

> Well, initially, I was wondering, "What the hell is this?" I think those of us who did react to it positively, I think we did the right thing. And to this day—well, regardless of what people think—I think we did the right thing in volunteering after being kicked in the butt . . . because, gee, if you were going to live here, you've got to be a part of society. You've got to do what is expected of you. And I had no problem volunteering. I don't know which was worse: being locked up in camp or going off to war. (Masao Watanabe, denshovh-wmasao-01-0018)

The Army recruiters who went into the camps argued that volunteering was a way for incarcerees to demonstrate their commitment to the country. Thus, among the relatively small number who did volunteer, many did so to prove the viability of their American identity even after the assault on it which the incarceration represented.

The volunteers for the 442nd Regimental Combat Team began reporting to Camp Shelby in March 1943. Initially, there was considerable friction between the mainland "Kotonks" and the Hawaiian "Buddhaheads," who had grown up in markedly different racial contexts. Daniel Inouye recalls these early training days:

Both sides, especially the Hawaiian side, looked upon the others with some, I would say, distrust. For one thing it was easy to note that the mainland Japanese spoke a better brand of English. We, for the most part, spoke pidgin, which was absolutely foreign to the mainlanders because our pidgin was very unique and exclusive for Hawaii. It was a mixture of Hawaiian, Chinese, Japanese, Portuguese, and a combination of strange construction. And so oftentimes people like Kash might be listening in to our conversation, and they would smile because it's funny, and some of the Hawaii guys didn't take that too well: "What are you laughing at?" And bang, and fights became commonplace. It got so bad at one stage during the early days of our training, senior officers of the regiment seriously discussed the possibility of disbanding the regiment, that if we could not work together, how can we ever consider going into combat together? (Daniel Inouye, denshovhidaniel-01-0010)

Despite these initial difficulties and an exceptionally long training period of ten months, the unit, which had adopted the Hawaiian crapshooter's slogan of "Go for Broke" as its motto, shipped out for Europe in May 1944. The regiment left its first battalion at Camp Shelby to be used for replacements. After joining with the 100th Battalion in June, the 442nd RCT initially fought entrenched Germans in the Italian countryside. It experienced its heaviest fighting and most famous battles liberating the French towns of Bruyeres, Belmont, and Biffontaine. Here the 442nd rescued the surrounded Texas "Lost Battalion" in dense forest terrain. Rudy Tokiwa, a 442nd member, recalled after the campaign that included this battle:

The 36th Division commander wanted the 442nd to pass in review. And he said, "All personnel of the 442nd will pass in review." So the 442nd passes in review. And like I say, you got three battalions plus headquarters, and they don't even have a battalion out there, passing in review. So General Dahlquist turned around and he said to the colonel, "When I order everyone to pass in review, I mean the cooks and everybody will pass in review." And Chaplain Yamada said, "This is the first time I saw the colonel cry." And he said, "This is all I have left." (Rudy Tokiwa, denshovh-trudy-02-0050)

Some of the 442nd men felt that they were treated as expendable "cannon fodder" (Robinson 2001, 169) in this and other actions. In the camps, when the call for volunteers first went out, some predicted that this would be the fate of the segregated unit.

Close to the end of the war in Europe, in March 1945, the 442nd participated in the assault that cracked the Gothic Line. One 442nd narrator recalled:

> From my perspective that was one of the most crucial battles that we had, and the most successful. We breached what was an impregnable defense line in a matter of hours by the way that we climbed up this horrible mountain. And when we reached the top, all the emplacements—I'm talking about concrete emplacements—anyway, we were behind 'em . . . so all their guns were pointed the other direction. Yeah, I guess, I'm trying to imagine for them to be so unprepared for the 442 to essentially scale that mountain must have been totally unheard of by the Germans. (Masao Watanabe, denshovh-wmasao-01-0034)

During this period, the 442nd Regiment's Field Artillery Battalion, the 522nd, was separated from the unit and attached to other units. While chasing the rapidly retreating Germans, the 522nd passed through part of the elaborate system of concentration camps and sub-camps known as Dachau and aided thousands of the starving survivors (Crost 1994, 239–48; *Fire for Effect* 1998, 59–70).

> It was really shocking to see these walking skeletons come by, and even worse to see them trying to salvage food that we would throw in a mess area, garbage pits, and stuff. And it was . . . I guess, it was very hard to believe. (Susumu Ito, denshovh-isusumu-01-0025)

The Military Intelligence Service

A third major way that Japanese Americans militarily contributed to the war effort was through the Military Intelligence Service (MIS). Considerably less is known about the important work that these some six thousand men and fifty-one WACS or Women's Army Corps soldiers performed, mostly in the Pacific. Part of the reason for this is that MIS members were (until 1972) told to not reveal their activities (Ichinokuchi 1988). The MIS was made up of trained linguists who were fluent in both Japanese and English. Most were Nisei and Kibei. Interestingly, early studies showed that the Japanese language skills of the vast majority of Nisei were too weak for them to be able to function as translators.

Even before Pearl Harbor, as tensions mounted between the United States and Japan, the Army realized that it needed experts in the Japanese language. The first sixty men recruited began their rigorous training in an abandoned airplane hanger at Crissy Field in the Presidio of San Francisco in 1941. Ironically, this was a "stone's throw" from General John L. DeWitt's Western Defense Command headquarters, where the mass removal and incarceration of Japanese Americans was orchestrated.

The language school started at Crissy Field was moved to Camp Savage, Minnesota, during the period when Japanese Americans were being evicted from the West Coast in the spring of 1942. In 1944, it was moved again, this time to larger and more comfortable facilities at Fort Snelling, also in Minnesota. It was originally shifted to Minnesota because Governor Harold Stassen was the only one who agreed to accept the school; several Western governors had earlier refused (Crost 1994, 24–25).

After intensive training, the linguists were attached, in small detachments, to units throughout the Pacific and at headquarters wherever documents needed to be translated. They not only served with U.S. forces but with those of Great Britain, Canada, Australia, New Zealand, India, and China. They proved invaluable as translators, interrogators, war crime trial interpreters, and writers of propaganda. They were at every major campaign and battle in the Pacific (Crost 1994, 21). After the war ended, many acted as interpreters in Allied-occupied Japan. Ultimately, the language school developed into the world-famous Defense Language Institute at the Presidio of Monterey. Three of the buildings on the campus are named after Japanese American MIS linguists.

The Draft Resistance

Yet, alongside the successes of many Japanese Americans in the Army, a substantial resistance to the military ultimately developed in the camps. This sentiment culminated in the refusal of a few to serve.

After the turmoil surrounding the registration program, frustration and bitterness continued to build among many of the incarcerees about their humiliating and unconstitutional treatment (e.g., Emi 1989). One concrete indicator of this was the steadily increasing number of persons who applied for repatriation and expatriation to Japan (e.g., Daniels 1993, 122). In this increasingly volatile atmosphere, in January 1944, the Army decided to draft Japanese Americans out of the camps. For most incarcerees, this was simply another unfair action in a long, sorry string of unjust acts. For a minority, it was the "last straw."

> I say, "Hey, this is stupid. They kick us around and now you're going to have to go and prove that you're an American?" To me it was pure gut. . . . Volunteer to the U.S. Army? Well, no way, from my feeling. It was just totally wrong. Take us back to Seattle, get our parents and get our hotel back, and get us back into what we were. We were American. (Frank Yamasaki, denshovh-yfrank-01-0024)

Another resister in the following quote expresses a similar view.

> I thought that there would be more people thinking the way I did because of the situation, but apparently most other people felt that they were guilty and that they should prove themselves loyal. Whereas my thoughts were, I have been and I always will be, but you never trusted me and you made me an enemy alien. So until you clear me of that, I'm not gonna do anything. (Gene Akutsu, denshovh-agene-01-0028)

Thus, unlike the 442nd volunteers, many of whom were intent on proving their Americanism, the resisters insisted that their rightful, unsullied American identity must be restored first before they would act like an American. To have their rights stripped away without due process of law and then be forced to serve in a segregated combat unit was just too much for these individuals. Many, but not all, had answered "yes-yes" on the "loyalty questionnaire," and said they would serve if their rights were restored.

This perspective was most apparent in Heart Mountain, where the only organized resistance to the draft emerged, led by the "Fair Play Committee." Ultimately, seven of the "Fair Play Committee" were sentenced to four years in federal prison. Significantly, several of these leaders were themselves not eligible for the draft. With respect to the young men who received their draft notices, initially sixty-three did not report for their physicals, and they were tried at the largest mass trial in U.S. history in the District Court in Cheyenne, Wyoming. They were found guilty and sentenced to three years in either Fort Leavenworth or McNeil Island, Washington, federal penitentiaries. One resister remembered:

> At that time when we went to give our plea, we also were asked if we had a lawyer to represent me and I told him, "No sir, I don't," and so they said, "Well, we will appoint a court lawyer for you." And unfortunately, I wound up with a lawyer who was the head of the American Legion. And so, when we wound up, after the pleas were given, the attorneys came and met up with us individually and various places to talk to us privately. They gave us the court date. When I wound up with my attorney in a private office, the first thing he said was, "You're a damn fool. I'll be darned if I'm gonna help you at all. You're up on your own, boy." (Gene Akutsu, denshovh-agene-01-0016).

Ultimately, the number of resisters from all of the War Relocation Authority camps totaled 315. There were 38 from Minidoka and 27 from Tule Lake. At Tule Lake, the outcome was diametrically different from that of the Heart Mountain trial (Muller 2001, 74, 131, 141–42). Presiding Judge Louis Goodman dismissed the charges against the resisters based upon due process grounds, stating:

> It is shocking to the conscience that an American citizen can be confined on the ground of disloyalty and then, while so under duress and restraint, be compelled to serve in the armed forces or be prosecuted for not yielding to such compulsion. (Emi 1989, 47)

The 111 resisters from the Poston, Arizona, camp were fined one cent in 1946, while those in other camps received prison sentences ranging from two to five years. President Truman eventually issued a presidential pardon to all of the resisters on Christmas Eve, 1947 (Muller 2001, 216n; Niiya 2001, 152–54).

The Legacy of Japanese American Soldiers and Resisters

By the end of the war, the 442nd Regimental Combat Team was being hailed as the most decorated unit in U.S. military history for its size and length of service. In fact, soon after the 442nd RCT started to compile its brilliant record, it began to be used by the War Relocation Authority and other groups to try to make reentry of the incarcerees into society easier. Specifically, it was employed as ammunition against those who opposed resettlement, initially in the "new" locations away from the Pacific Coast. The record of the 442nd demonstrated the loyalty of Japanese Americans in a way that was incontrovertible to most Americans. Many years later, it proved to be a critical factor in the passage of redress legislation. Even today, accolades for what the units contributed continue. In June 2000, the Department of Defense completed a review of the World War II records of Asian Americans who had been awarded the Distinguished Service Cross (DSC), the second-highest Army combat medal. It upgraded nineteen 100th Infantry Battalion and 442nd Regimental Combat Team DSCs and one Silver Star to the Medal of Honor. Also, the Military Intelligence Service was awarded a Presidential Unit Citation (even though technically it was not a unit).

Reactions to the draft resisters, or resisters of conscience, as they are now called by some, have changed a great deal over the years. Nonetheless, their wartime actions continue to be controversial within the Japanese American community and largely unknown to the outside society until recently. Immediately after the war, many in the ethnic community shunned the resisters. Many Nisei confused the draft resistance with the "no-no" issue. Some who had been close "buddies" before the war would not speak to each other when they returned to Seattle. In the words of a well-known resister,

> I could take a lot of, what you call crap, from anybody, and I used to hand it right back to them. So I was very strong physically, so if somebody says something, I just turned around and give them a dirty look and they just back off. But in my mother's case, it was the Issei who constantly say, "Your son's a draft evader, coward, chicken shit," kept pressing, and cut her off, cut her off, cut her off . . . and there's no place for her to go. So she stayed in this one small dingy room and at the beginning she says, I can't go anywhere, I can't even go to church. And she sat there, and whatever she was thinking, that is what led her to committing suicide. (Jim Akutsu, denshovh-ajim-01-0023)

Over the years, a few have gradually reintegrated into the community, initially into more "tolerant" institutions such as the Buddhist church.

I started to work for a gardener and we never talked about the past. Everyone was trying to make a living back in Seattle again. And, that's all it was.
I joined the . . . well not really joined the church, but I started attending
Buddhist church again. Because at church I didn't think there would be any
direct confrontation, and there was none. And I became fairly active in church,
and that's where I stayed, mostly. Church friends. (Akio Hoshino, denshovh-
hakio-01-0013)

However, it was not until the advent of the civil rights movement and
subsequently the Asian-American political movement that the actions of the
resisters were viewed in a positive light. Their actions clearly disproved the
myth that all Japanese Americans acted "passively" to the injustice of the incarceration. Although their motives were complex and mixed, many were not
looking to "prove" their acceptability to the larger American society but
were engaging in the seemingly quintessential American act of standing up
for their constitutional rights. Some have even argued that it was the Nisei
soldiers who "acted more Japanese" by giving their unconditional loyalty
to the government.

As previously noted, the motives of the resisters as well as those who volunteered for military service were complex. After all, whether volunteer or
resister, they all faced an extraordinarily difficult situation not of their own
making (e.g., Muller 2001, 186–92). At the present time, it appears that the
majority of Japanese Americans appreciate the validity of both the Army
volunteers' and the resisters' positions in light of the difficult choices forced
upon the incarcerees during wartime. Nonetheless, the issue of Nisei World
War II draft resistance, most notably to some Japanese American veterans,
remains contested terrain in the community.

MILITARY SERVICE AND THE LIFE COURSE

The question we wish to examine now is whether military service among
Japanese Americans during World War II had long-term consequences for
their life-course trajectories and, if so, in what ways. We would have liked
to have examined this question with the resisters as well, but could not do
so except in the most cursory way because of their minuscule numbers in
our sample.

A small but growing body of sociological research has begun to examine the consequences of serving in the military for men's subsequent life-course trajectory (e.g., Elder 1986, 1987; Elder and Bailey, 1988). This is an important question because of the large number of persons who either volunteer to serve or, as in the past, were conscripted. Serving in the military has been shown to impact the timing of major life events such as marriage, educational attainment, and occupational achievement (Hogan 1981). Several rationales have been advanced for why serving should have such a long-term impact on an individual's life course.

Teachman and Call (1996) suggest that military service potentially influences subsequent attainment in three basic ways. First, veterans possess background characteristics that differ from those of non-veterans. The physical, educational, and mental-ability criteria that the armed forces utilize to screen individuals are related to success in civilian life (Eitelberg, Laurence, Waters, and Perlman 1984). Second, military socialization changes individuals in ways that influence later attainment. A number of researchers have argued that the military inculcates values and knowledge that are useful for subsequent success in mainstream organizations. These researchers describe this inculcation as serving a bridging function (e.g., Browning, Lopreato, and Poston 1973). This appears to be particularly the case for African Americans (e.g., Martindale and Poston 1979).

A more specific way that military service is likely to influence attainment is by its impact on the amount of schooling an individual receives. The military can motivate or socialize individuals in ways conducive to educational attainment or simply make it financially feasible to attend institutions of higher education. The GI Bill is a prime example of the latter effect.

The third general way that being a veteran is hypothesized to influence subsequent attainment is that if a person is a veteran, it may alter the way that others perceive the individual's abilities or, more broadly, human capital. If being a veteran increases an individual's perceived human capital, employers will probably be more likely to offer the person a job.

Historical specificity. These positive attributions notwithstanding, a number of scholars have also documented how the consequences associated with having served in the military vary based upon the particular historical period being examined. Certainly the meaning of serving during World War II was quite different from that of, for example, serving in the Vietnam conflict. For the vast majority of Americans, after the attack on Pearl Harbor there was no question about the moral correctness of our involvement. For most Japanese Americans, this was also the case, especially at the beginning of the war. However, because of continued ill treatment of Japanese Americans by the government, individuals' feelings about serving in the military evolved in different and complex ways (cf. Schonberger 1990).

We now turn to an examination of World War II involvement with the military among our previously incarcerated respondents. What detectable effects has this specific experience had on their life-course trajectories, if any?

Denshō Respondents and the Military

Twenty-three individuals or 12.6% of our Denshō sample of 183 incarcerees served in a military unit during World War II. This number excludes those who, for example, volunteered or were drafted but were not accepted. These soldiers were all men; two women volunteered but did not ultimately serve. Thus, all those we have categorized as having had military service at a minimum negotiated basic training and had some experience in a unit.

Comparison of veterans with military-age males who did not serve. How different were those who served in the military from those who did not? In an attempt to more precisely isolate the effects of military service, we created a comparison group of males between the ages of 14 and 28 in 1943 who did not serve. Although not entirely equivalent to the veterans with respect to age composition, they will nonetheless provide a comparison point. All of the following analyses use this comparison group of non-veteran males.

Prewar resources. Father's occupation-based Total Socioeconomic Index (TSEI) scores were similar for both those who served and those who did not (see table 4.1). However, those who served tended to have somewhat higher occupational aspirations before the war. The mean planned occupation TSEI score among veterans was 51.8 as compared with 41.7 for non-veterans ($p < .10$). Moreover, those who served had more Japanese best friends before the war, 2.8 out of a possible 3.0 as contrasted with 2.4 for those who did not serve ($p < .05$). Thus, veterans were more tightly integrated into the prewar ethnic community than non-veterans.

Current socioeconomic attainment. As can be seen in table 4.2, there were no statistically significant differences in final occupational attainment between

Table 4.1. Comparison of Veterans vs. Non-Veteran Males
(Aged 14–28 at Incarceration) on Prewar Resources

Variable	Veteran Status	
	Veterans	Non-Veterans
Father's occupational TSEI score		
Mean	31.8	32.7
SD	8.4	7.8
Number of cases	19	33
Father self-employed (%)	85	91
Number of cases	20	34
Respondent's occupational aspiration TSEI score		
Mean	51.8	41.7[a]
SD	17.9	16.6
Number of cases	14	24
Number of prewar Japanese American friends (out of 3 closest)		
Mean	2.8	2.4*
SD	0.4	1.0
Number of cases	23	36

[a] $p < .10$ *$p < .05$ **$p < .01$ ***$p < .001$ (two-tailed tests)

Table 4.2. Comparison of Veteran vs. Non-Veteran Males
(Aged 14–28 at Incarceration) on Current Socioeconomic Attainment

Variable	Veterans	Non-Veterans
TSEI score of last main job		
Mean	46.4	43.9
SD	15.0	17.6
Number of cases	22	36
Number of years of college education		
Mean	2.3	2.1
SD	2.1	2.5
Number of cases	23	35
Income		
Mean	5.2	4.8
SD	2.2	2.3
Number of cases	22	33

Table 4.3. Comparison of Veteran and Non-Veteran Males
(Aged 14–28 at Incarceration) on Current Community Networks

Variable	Veterans	Non-Veterans
Number of Japanese American friends (out of 3 closest)		
Mean	2.4	2.6
SD	0.8	0.6
Number of cases	23	36
Attend *kenjinkai* events in the last year? (Yes = 1, No = 0)		
Mean	0.3	0.4
SD	0.5	0.5
Number of cases	23	36
Read Japanese American newspaper? (Yes = 1, No = 0)		
Mean	0.7	0.7
SD	0.5	0.5
Number of cases	23	36
Attend Japanese American church? (Yes = 1, No = 0)		
Mean	0.4	0.2
SD	0.5	0.4
Number of cases	14	25
Number of memberships in Japanese American organizations		
Mean	2.7	1.8
SD	2.1	2.2
Number of cases	23	36
Number of memberships in non–Japanese American organizations		
Mean	1.7	1.4
SD	2.4	1.6
Number of cases	23	36

veterans and non-veterans. There were also no statistically reliable differences in current community involvement between veterans and non-veterans (see table 4.3). They had similar levels of participation in both informal friendship networks and formal organizations of the ethnic community. Veterans appear to belong to more Japanese American organizations, but this is likely to be a product of their involvement with the Nisei Veterans organization, which is still quite active in Seattle.

The veterans and non-veterans had similar scores on the variable that measured their overall view of their camp years. However, as can be seen in table 4.4, veterans were more active in the redress movement. They took 1.6 actions

Table 4.4. Comparison of Veteran vs. Non-Veteran Males
(Aged 14–28 at Incarceration) on Evaluation
of Camp Score and Redress Activities

Variable	Veterans	Non-Veterans
Evaluation of camp score		
Mean	3.2	3.0
SD	1.3	1.2
Number of cases	23	36
Number of redress activities		
Mean	1.6	1.0*
SD	1.1	1.0
Number of cases	23	36

$^a p < .10$ $^* p < .05$ $^{**} p < .01$ $^{***} p < .001$ (two-tailed tests)

such as contacting a legislator or contributing money to support the movement compared with non-veterans' 1.0 supportive behaviors ($p < .05$).

General picture of the impact of military service. Among Japanese Americans
who were in their late adolescent or early adult years during World War II,
being a veteran appears to have had only minor long-term effects. Before
the war, they tended to have higher occupational aspirations than the average non-veteran Nisei of that period. They were also more involved than
were non-veterans with the informal Japanese American community before
the war, as indicated by the number of Japanese American friends they
recalled having. Nonetheless, veterans tended to have similar postwar socioeconomic achievement profiles as non-veterans some fifty years after their
service. Veterans were, however, more active in the redress movement. This
is likely to be a product of their involvement with the Nisei Veterans organization in the Seattle area, which took an active role in the local redress campaign. Aside from this difference in involvement in the community and
redress, it appears that military service during World War II had few
detectable long-term effects, positive or negative.

This is unlike some of the positive effects of military service that Elder
(1986) found in his study of veterans. In Elder's study, veterans from disad-
vantaged family backgrounds were able to equal the long-term socioeconomic
success of non-veterans. Veterans who had substantial advantages in educa-

tion and careers when they entered the military continued their pattern of achievement in their post-military lives. In the Denshō sample of incarcerees, the veterans and non-veterans appear to be quite similar in prewar resources, as indicated by similar fathers' TSEI scores and high levels of prewar education. Thus, it seems reasonable that military service did not necessarily boost the achievement of veterans.

Resistance and Life-Course Trajectory

There were only three resistors in our sample of 183. Thus, the utility of statistical tests was, at best, minimal. However, we will present mean differences between the resisters' and veterans' samples when the differences are at least moderately large. This approach can at least provide suggestive leads for more systematic follow-up in the future. As shown in table 4.5, with respect to the mean TSEI scores of the job they planned on obtaining before the war, there was a sizeable difference between resisters and veterans. Resisters had a mean TSEI score of 34.0, and veterans had 51.8, indicating that the resisters had substantially lower occupational aspirations. The magnitude of this mean difference is quite large, larger than those previously reported between veterans and non-veterans. Compared to veterans, it appears that resisters, generally, came from families with fewer socioeconomic resources, as indicated by their fathers' lower TSEI scores and the lower likelihood of having a self-employed father (Ms = 27.8 vs. 31.8; 67% vs. 85%, respectively). Resisters also appear to have had somewhat fewer Japanese American best friends before the war than veterans (Ms = 2.3 vs. 2.9).

Current status. Over half a century later, at the time of the survey, there were no apparent differences between resisters and veterans in educational or occupational achievement, or in income as indexed by years of college, the TSEI score of the individuals' last job, and 1997 income, respectively (see table 4.6). Thus, educationally and occupationally, resisters ultimately seem to have accomplished as much by the later stages of their lives as veterans.

As for current informal involvement in the ethnic community, resisters had similar numbers of Japanese American best friends as veterans (Ms = 2.3 vs. 2.4; see table 4.7). But, as might be expected given their negative postwar treatment by the larger ethnic community, there is a substantial difference in their contemporary involvement with formal Japanese American organizations. The mean number of Japanese American organizations that

Table 4.5. Comparison of Resisters vs. Veterans on Prewar Resources

Variable	Resisters	Veterans
TSEI score of occupation to which respondent aspired		
Mean	34.0	51.8
SD	8.3	18.0
Number of cases	3	14
TSEI score of father's occupation		
Mean	27.8	31.8
SD	9.6	8.4
Number of cases	3	19
Father self-employed		
%	66.7	85.0
Number of cases	3	20
Number of prewar Japanese American friends (out of 3 closest)		
Mean	2.3	2.9
SD	1.2	0.4
Number of cases	3	23

Table 4.6. Comparison of Resisters vs. Veterans
on Current Socioeconomic Resources

	Resisters	Veterans
Number of years of college education		
Mean	2.0	2.3
SD	3.5	2.1
Number of cases	3	23
TSEI score of last main job		
Mean	44.5	46.4
SD	22.8	15.0
Number of cases	3	22
Income		
Mean	6.0	5.2
SD	1.0	2.2
Number of cases	3	22

Table 4.7. Comparison of Resisters vs. Veterans
on Current Community Networks

Variable	Resisters	Veterans
Number of Japanese American friends (out of 3 closest)		
Mean	2.3	2.4
SD	0.6	0.8
Number of cases	3	23
Attend *kenjinkai* event in the past year? (Yes = 1, No = 0)		
Mean	0.0	0.3
SD	—	0.5
Number of cases	3	23
Read Japanese American newspaper? (Yes = 1, No = 0)		
Mean	0.7	0.7
SD	0.6	0.5
Number of cases	3	23
Attend Japanese American church? (Yes = 1, No = 0)		
Mean	0.0	0.4
SD	—	0.5
Number of cases	1	23
Number of memberships in Japanese American organizations		
Mean	0.3	2.7[a]
SD	0.6	2.1
Number of cases	3	23
Number of memberships in non–Japanese American organizations		
Mean	0.7	1.7
SD	1.2	2.4
Number of cases	3	23

[a] $p < .10$ *$p < .05$ **$p < .01$ ***$p < .001$ (two-tailed tests)

veterans currently are involved with is 2.7. The mean number resisters belong to is 0.3. Among the resisters, this translates to one membership in a Japanese American organization for all three of the resisters in our sample. In addition, none of the three resisters attended *kenjinkai* (prefectural group) events or a Japanese American church, while 30% and 36% (respectively) of veterans did. Veterans were also twice as likely to belong to non–Japanese American organizations as resisters (Ms = 1.7 vs. 0.7).

Interestingly, resisters and veterans felt similarly about their incarceration

Table 4.8. Comparison of Resisters vs. Veterans
on Overall Evaluation of Camp Years and Redress

Variable	Resisters	Veterans
Evaluation of camp score		
Mean	3.7	3.2
SD	0.6	1.3
Number of cases	3	23
Number of redress activities		
Mean	0.7	1.6
SD	0.6	1.1
Number of cases	3	23

experience, as indicated by their overall evaluation of camp "score" (see table 4.8). Further, the resisters engaged in fewer redress activities than veterans (Ms = 0.7 vs. 1.6). This may be due less to motivational differences related to ideology and more to the impact of the greater involvement in Japanese American organizations among veterans.

A provisional picture of the impact of the war on resisters. The very tentative picture that emerges of the impact of the war on resisters is that they had lower occupational aspirations before their incarceration than the average veteran. However, ultimately their educational and occupational achievements by the end of their working lives, compared with those who did serve in the military, were similar. Not surprisingly, given the way they were viewed by the majority of Japanese Americans both during and after the war, they presently belong to few Japanese American organizations. Thus, our data are consistent with anecdotal reports that resisters have been, by and large, shunned by the Japanese American community and that the effects of this are still observable, even though their actions have been lauded by many in the community in recent years. Difficult choices made during their incarceration almost sixty years ago still reverberate for these incarcerees today.

FIVE

Resettlement

I remember very vividly the three of us sitting on the train, carrying my mother's ashes. And what we discussed, that all I could remember, not where we would live and what we would do, but what we were going to eat. And we were hoping that it would be breakfast so we could have waffles and ham and eggs and that kind of thing. So we went to a Japanese café on Jackson Street called Jackson Café and had our first meal as free people. (Chizuko Norton, denshovh-nchizuko-01-0030)

After months or even years of living under the abnormal social and physical conditions of the camps, how did the former incarcerees reestablish themselves in the world outside? This difficult period of returning and readapting to American society is usually labeled "resettlement." The War Relocation Authority (WRA) first used this term in 1942 when it began to encourage selected individuals to move to areas outside of the exclusion zone (Niiya 2001, 347–48). College students were the first group to be able to leave camp, attending a specific group of institutions in the Midwest and East which agreed to accept them. The National Japanese American Student Relocation Council, which was formed on May 29, 1942 in Chicago, frequently helped these students financially as well as administratively. This organization, which was originally called the National Student Relocation Council, had representatives on its board from a wide range of liberal groups, such as the American Friends Service Committee, YMCA and YWCA, church members, educators, some Nisei, and other concerned individuals (Okihiro 1999, 28–48).

A small number of incarcerees who were able to negotiate the cumbersome clearance procedures in effect at that time and had secured outside jobs were also able to leave the camps in the latter part of 1942 for areas outside of the Pacific Coast exclusion zone. By this time, the WRA realized that the camp experience was beginning to sap the vitality from many previously energetic individuals and had other corrosive effects (e.g., War Relocation Authority 1946c, 20).

In early 1943, the disastrous registration program discussed in chapter 3 was used not only to determine the "loyalty" of individuals so that the Army could recruit volunteers for the 442nd Regimental Combat Team, but also so that the WRA could more expeditiously process "loyal" incarcerees for resettlement to areas outside of the exclusion zone (e.g., Daniels 1993, 112–16). Initially, a small but steadily increasing number of Nisei left the camps on "indefinite leave," mostly for the intermountain states and the Midwest. But the majority of incarcerees chose to remain in the camps until they could return to their West Coast homes. Many felt insecure about moving to an unknown area and facing a potentially hostile reception with little in the way of economic or social resources (Embree 1943). By the time incarcerees were permitted to return to the West Coast, in January 1945, roughly 30 percent had already left the ten WRA compounds (War Relocation Authority 1946b, 143–45).

While in the camps, the imprisoned frequently heard stories, some true, some rumors, of ugly treatment that previous resettlers had received when they tried to restart their lives outside of the WRA camps. To combat this, the WRA began a campaign that portrayed, in glowing terms, the experiences of some of those who had already left. It featured reassuring photographs of smiling resettlers in their own apartments describing a comfortable lifestyle in their chosen communities, usually a city in the Midwest (Denshō 1997). Nonetheless many of the Nisei incarcerees felt, for various reasons, such as not wanting to leave their Issei parents or fearing that they would not be able to get a job, that it was more prudent to "wait out the war" within the confines of the camp. In December 1944, when the announcement was made by the WRA that all the camps would be closing and everyone would have to resettle, some incarcerees experienced severe anxiety about having to go "outside." On the other hand, some Nisei were motivated to relocate without their Issei parents because they could temporarily escape responsibility for them or from an oppressive family situation (Broom and Kitsuse 1956, 45).

A DIFFICULT AND PAINFUL REENTRY INTO THE "OUTSIDE"

As might be expected, reentering a society in which the overwhelming majority had supported the imprisonment of Japanese Americans presented many challenges to the resettlers. Some of those who left camp early as select college students felt that they were part of a diaspora into a new world. They often found themselves the only Japanese in college towns in states they had never even thought of visiting, such as Missouri, Indiana, and Ohio. The experience was in stark contrast to both the oppressive but concentrated ethnic communities they had just left and the comfortable Nihonmachis with their ethnic small businesses, organizations, and neighborhoods that they had known before the war. Now they had to face an exciting but also frightening world outside of the camps alone, under pressure as "representatives" of all Japanese Americans (James 1985).

Most of the incarcerees who left camp to pick up the threads of their work and family lives faced serious hurdles. For one, the majority had little remaining in the way of economic resources. The period was particularly humiliating for many Issei who had lost all that they had worked for, as was poignantly recalled by this visual history narrator:

> They were all having to start from scratch. I know my dad, he went back to this factory where he was a foreman for years and years, and now this little boy that he trained, the boss's son is grown and he was the one managing it. And I remember one day when he came home, his face was just like a sheet, white as a sheet. The boss, apparently, things had changed during the war time and they have a different manager and a different way of operation and I guess the boss said "Yama you stay home." . . . So then he went to one of the semi-relatives or close friends who had a restaurant and he went over there to wash dishes. I saw him. He died. He was hurt, his pride and everything else. So the pain after the war, I think is much more severe. (Frank Yamasaki, denshovh-yfrank-01-0031)

Depending upon the area they resettled in, the former incarcerees faced varying degrees of discrimination, most notably in housing. Apartments and homes were in short supply during the war due to large-scale labor migration into the cities related to defense industries and after VE Day because of returning demobilized soldiers. To help the resettlers reestablish themselves in areas new to them, first outside the exclusion zone and later within it, the WRA set up over forty resettlement offices in various cities beginning in early 1943 (Niiya 2001, 347–48).

The Loss of Community

What made reentry into society difficult for many incarcerees was the fact that the social fabric of their prewar lives had been destroyed. The ethnic, neighborhood, community, and economic networks in which they had been previously deeply embedded were either severely disrupted or destroyed. One visual history narrator recalled a feeling common among former incarcerees in the early days of resettlement in Chicago:

> You looked for friends and relatives and others who were of the same back-ground, simply as a kind of—a means, a crutch, to get over a difficult period. (S. Frank Miyamoto, denshovh-mfrank-03-0025)

Working against this adaptive process was the government's explicit pol-icy of discouraging the rebuilding of ethnic networks and neighborhoods. The WRA specifically warned resettlers against gathering in large groups and reforming the ethnic enclaves that had been such a useful "safe harbor" prior to the war (e.g., Linehan 1993; Loo 1993). The agency felt that "spread-ing out" the resettlers and having them assume a "low profile" would min-imize resistance from receiving communities (e.g., Robinson 2001, 228–29). Particularly in the early phase of resettlement, before the West Coast was reopened, the resettlers were supposed to be "invisible as possible as Japa-nese" (Nishi, 1998–99, 4). Nishi (1998–99, 3) writes the following about interactions with whites:

> Seared by wartime events into raw racial self-consciousness, each contact called for meticulous attention to cues about what was expected, so that one would not become conspicuous by not knowing what to do or by making a mistake.

Nonetheless, the issue of rebuilding the Japanese American community (both its formal institutions as well as informal networks) as contrasted with practicing what might be described as "unobtrusive assimilation" soon became an internal debate within the ethnic community itself. Many Nisei felt that they should not recreate the separate institutions they had before the war but integrate as much as possible into those of the larger society. After all, some argued, was it not their isolation and lack of integration that had contributed to the hostile reaction of the larger society?

Rebuilding Community

Yet, given the reality of the treatment they had just endured, most Nisei felt a strong need to be among those who "understood" their experiences. Here is one Nisei's recollection of his feelings about whites at the time.

> Immediately after I came back, I don't have no interface with white people, except that they were customers and every so often they would come out to see how we were doing. But it was all Japanese. Then when I started to work for the hotel, of course, initially I would be under the managing housekeeper. She was a white woman, and I felt . . . I don't know whether I would say scared, but I had very little communication with the *hakujins* and I felt a little, I guess you could say inferior. That's been my life compared with *hakujins*. But she was very friendly, and very helpful. I still remember that time when we . . . she said, she called me Tom, I always used my English name when I worked outside. "Come on Tom," she says, "I gotta go get some, order some sheets and things. Let's go up and see what they have." And she wanted to go out to the wholesaler up the street. And I had to walk along beside her and I felt so conspicuous walking with a *hakujin* woman. It was all on my part. Because she didn't make me feel that way at all. And gradually I got to learn to live more in the *hakujin* world. Where I became very good friends with the owner and the different managers that they had. Visited their homes and, got to know them pretty well. Got a little more relaxed with the *hakujin* community. (Akio Hoshino, denshovh-hakio-01-0013)

If many Nisei felt this way, how were the Issei, who were now on average in their late fifties and who at best spoke rudimentary English, going to reestablish not only their occupational but social lives without Japanese American institutions? Further, the consequences of the family and community disorganization that were a product of the uprooting and incarceration were beginning to become all too visible. In Chicago, out-of-wedlock births, gambling, prostitution, mental illness, and crime were starting to show up on the police blotter. The joint Nisei and Issei Resettlers Committee felt that ethnic community institutions had to provide social-recreational outlets for the Nisei or many would be lost (Nishi 1998–99, 7). Thus, it is not surprising that the resettlers ultimately recreated many of the informal social networks and ethnic institutions that had been so vital to their accommodation before the war. A visual history narrator remembers the situation in Los Angeles.

> We decided, whoever was there, in the JACL office, that somebody had to take care of the social aspect of the returning Niseis. And Los Angeles was known for clubs. They had clubs of ten girls or twelve girls here and eight there. They had so many clubs. So we started a club service bureau. Mary Ishikawa and Teri Kuwata and I. And it became an information bureau. Where can you hold dances? Which halls will allow you? Some places won't take Japanese. How much does it cost? What activities are going on, and at what church? We just ran the Club Service Bureau for about three, four years, and also Christmas Cheer we started, to help the people who were seeking public assistance at the LA County Bureau of Public Assistance. And they were all Japanese families at that time. (Sue Okabe, denshovh-osue-01-0010)

The specific character of these institutions changed from the prewar to postwar period as the leadership and needs of the community shifted from being Issei to Nisei oriented (e.g., Broom and Kitsuse 1956, 1–2; Spickard 1983). For example, the Issei-dominated Japanese associations never revived, but the Nisei Japanese American Citizens Leagues began to expand rapidly. In cities that attracted a significant number of resettlers, Buddhist temples and Protestant churches with exclusively Japanese American congregations were either quickly created or restarted, as were recreational groups such as softball, basketball, bowling, and golf leagues. In the words of an active Protestant minister:

> We'd gone through the same experiences, either in the service or, whether in the camps or coming back. And so we had some wonderful experiences coming together as a large group of the young Nisei couples . . . it's just something like the immigrants—as we mentioned before, how they needed to have a support group and a social group. So it was a boom time. People tell their friends, and they start coming. And the church would begin to grow. So we moved from a mission status, where we were getting help from the denomination, to becoming a self-supporting group. And that took place when I was pastor of that Evergreen Baptist Church. Yeah. And then we

developed our own constitution. Fact is, we grew so that we were able to open up another church on the west side of Los Angeles. So that was a boom time. (Rev. Paul Nagano, denshovh-npaul-01-0013)

The Issei did recreate some organizations that were geared to meet their language and other needs, such as Japanese-language church services, *kenjin-kais*, and numerous cultural and arts groups.

Discrimination, Psychological Stress, and Unexpected Help in Housing, Schools, and Jobs

With regard to housing, there was a tendency for resettlers to cluster in less desirable neighborhoods or those that were experiencing racial transition. As previously mentioned, this was partially a product of the tight rental and housing markets found in urban areas during wartime and the early post-war period. Attempting to move into "better" neighborhoods often led to humiliating episodes of discrimination.

We started looking for a house and we did suffer discrimination, housing discrimination because the north end they didn't want to show us anything and then West Seattle. They told my husband—one real estate office told my husband that they're saving the homes for veterans returning from war, returning veterans. And so he got mad and he said, "What do you think I am?" (Louise Kashino, denshovh-klouise-01-0026)

Among school-age resettlers who reentered public schools, there were almost universal reports of being bullied or taunted by their classmates. Further, some small businesses that provided personal services, for example, beauty shops and barbershops, were restarted in part because of the uncertain reception resettlers might receive in mainstream equivalents.

You know where to go eat and where to go because some weren't very friendly to you. And so, all that data was transferred between individuals. And you knew what places we were invited in, and what places we were not happy to be accommodated. So there was a lot of, scrutiny as to what kinds of activities you can engage in, where you should patronize in terms of stores and things of this nature. (Henry Miyatake, denshovh-mhenry-02-0026)

Other businesses, such as service stations, garages, grocery stores, and nurseries, were established simply because of the general need for such services, the skill sets of the resettlers, and the informal ties within the ethnic group which helped support such establishments.

When the resettlers left camp for the last time, not only did they face numerous social and economic uncertainties, but psychological ones as well. On the personal and perhaps even subconscious level, some former incarcerees felt either anguish about being powerless to resist the injustice which had been meted out to them or, on the other hand, thought that their own or the ethnic group's inadequacies were somehow responsible for their treatment (Miyamoto 1986–87; Nagata 1993, 26–35). An example of the latter is the frequently heard remark among former incarcerees that the Japanese were too cliquish or isolated, and hence the incarceration and resettlement were, in the final analysis, a good thing because it forced them to be exposed to a much wider array of experiences in the larger society.

The result of these and other unresolved feelings and uncertainties for many resettlers was a strong tendency to suppress open discussion about what they had just endured. The incarcerees, in particular, avoided talking about their wartime experiences with non-Japanese, since it might lead to insensitive if not discriminatory remarks or an awkward display of feelings that could not be verbalized. Even when the Nisei discussed the incarceration among themselves or with their own children, it raised many "unanswerable" and uncomfortable questions about their treatment and their own reactions to it (e.g., Ng 1989).

> Our experience during World War II was so painful and so humiliating that without our discussing it with each other, most of us decided to raise our children as if they were white. Don't talk about what happened during World War II. In fact, don't even talk about the Japanese culture. We could eat rice and we could go to Buddhist church and all, but tread lightly and keep all this other stuff away. So what happened was that the Nisei parents didn't talk about any of this. They worked very hard to be prosperous, to be successful, and they made it; but their children grew up not even realizing that this was something that you can't erase and that the eyes of the public see you differently from what your parents see you. The Nisei parents wanted very much not only for them to be successful, but their children to be successful. And all of you have been successful. You are successful, but the core,

the spirit of the Japanese culture as well as the pride, I think, was missing. (Chizuko Norton, denshovh-nchizuko 01-0039)

A partial resolution to these issues would have to await the larger societal transformation that emerged in the 1960s, after Japanese Americans had incontrovertibly reestablished themselves in American society.

On the other side of the ledger, individuals from the larger society sometimes went out of their way to assist the resettlers. A few whites opened their homes temporarily to returnees (e.g., Duveneck 1978, 238–44). Others helped them find jobs. The major cities frequently had volunteer resettlement committees, typically made up of a coalition of churches, civic leaders, and other concerned individuals, who tried to increase acceptance by the broader community. As noted in chapter 4, these committees, in concert with WRA resettlement offices, often fed the media positive publicity, such as the outstanding combat record of the 442nd Regimental Combat Team, and otherwise tried to create a welcoming atmosphere (Linehan 1993).

RESETTLEMENT AMONG KING COUNTY NISEI

Our survey data examined three aspects of the resettlement process among the King County Nisei sample. First we noted where they lived before they were incarcerated and tracked where they traversed after their release from their WRA camp to their settling down in the Seattle area. We also noted how long they stayed in each area and what their reasons were for moving there. Second, we compared the socioeconomic mobility of those who initially resettled elsewhere with those who returned directly to the Seattle area. Third, we inquired about the strongest memories the respondents had of their resettlement years.

The Road Back to Seattle

In order to study the resettlement patterns of our King County sample, we asked the survey respondents to indicate where they lived immediately before their incarceration and the places where they resided after their camp years. All of the respondents were living on the West Coast prior to their mass removal. Seventy-three and six tenths percent resided in King County. In order to track their postwar movement patterns from the time they were released from camp, we had them sequentially name and number all of the places they lived on a map of the United States. Further, we asked respondents to indicate the inclusive dates they resided at each location. To simplify the analyses, we present data from only the first three locations where our respondents lived. For the majority of former incarcerees, these three locations include all of the places they resided in the decade immediately following their departure from the camps.

Dispersal. Overall, it is apparent that the events associated with the exclusion and incarceration widely scattered the Japanese American population during the early postwar years. In the King County sample, only 25.4% (*n* = 46) returned directly to the same town or city they lived in before the war, wherever that might have been. Less than half (46.4%) even returned to the same state from which they were evicted when first released from the camps.[1]

If one examines where individuals resettled from a regional perspective, as shown in table 5.1, slightly more than half (55.5%) of the 182 respondents in our sample (with valid responses on the items) returned directly to one of the three Pacific Coast states when they first left the WRA camps. Over forty percent (42.9%) initially moved outside of the Pacific Coast states, mostly to the Midwest or East. A very small percentage (1.6%) expatriated, usually with their Issei parents, directly to war-torn Japan.

Length of stay where first resettled. As shown in table 5.2, a quarter (25.3%) of our sample made their first move out of the "relocation centers" directly to what was to become their permanent postwar home. The other three-quarters moved at least once more. Among those who made additional moves, they stayed at this initial place an average of 4.3 years.

Among those who moved from their first postwar location to a second area (see table 5.1), a substantial majority (73.5%) either moved to or within the general area of the Pacific Coast. Only 25.7% made a move outside of the Pacific Coast. A minuscule percentage moved abroad, 0.7%. Almost half (46.3%) of those who moved to a second postwar location permanently stayed in this location, and slightly more than half (53.7%) moved a third time (see table 5.2). The mean number of years that all of the individuals who made a second post-incarceration move stayed in the first location, before moving, was 4.3 years. Among those who made a third move, they stayed in

Table 5.1. Place Resettled After Incarceration

	Location	Percent
First location		
	Pacific Coast[1]	55.5
	Outside Pacific Coast (U.S.)	42.9
	Japan	1.6
	Other	0.0
	Number of cases	182
Second location		
	Pacific Coast	73.5
	Outside Pacific Coast (U.S.)	25.7
	Japan	0.0
	Other	0.7
	Number of cases	136
Third location		
	Pacific Coast	76.7
	Outside Pacific Coast (U.S.)	20.5
	Japan	2.7
	Other	0.0
	Number of cases	73

[1] Pacific Coast = CA, WA, OR

their second place of residence an average of 4.7 years before moving to the third location.

About 40% of our sample made a third move in the postwar period (40.1%). Of these, 76.7% moved to or within the Pacific Coast (see table 5.1). The remainder (20.5%) moved to or within a non–Pacific Coast area, again mostly to the Midwest and East. Only about 20% of our respondents made additional moves.

In general, what do these figures reveal about the postwar resettlement patterns of Japanese American incarcerees? It should be kept in mind that our sample was a contemporary one drawn from the greater Seattle area. Thus, we have no information about those who lived in the area before World War II and did not return. In addition, we have in our sample those who moved to King County after the war, but lived elsewhere before, principally in California.

Table 5.2. Resettlement Moves

	First Location	Second Location	Third Location
Stayed vs. moved (%)			
Stayed	25.3	46.3	50.0
Moved	74.7	53.7	50.0
Number of cases	182	136	72
Mean length of time lived in location (years) for those who subsequently moved			
Mean	4.3	4.7	5.8
SD	7.9	6.9	11.2
Number of cases	135	72	36

Recognizing these limitations, the following resettlement patterns emerge from our data. First, when they left the WRA compounds, the majority of individuals did not return directly to their prewar homes. In the case of those who left before January 1945, this was not possible because of the ban on returning to the exclusion zone. Among those who moved at least once more, the average length of stay in their first place was 4.3 years. Roughly comparable figures were found for resettlers' second and third moves, if they made such moves. Finally, there was a strong tendency to return to the West Coast. When an individual or family did move, three quarters of the time it was to the Pacific Coast.

Subsequent moves among those who initially returned to the Pacific Coast. As previously noted, 55.5% of incarcerees initially returned to the Pacific Coast. As shown in table 5.3, except for the small number who went to Japan directly from the camps, those who moved to a West Coast location stayed longer than those who moved to other areas. This is probably due in part to the fact that many in the sample lived in King County before the war, and thus were moving back "home" and tended to settle permanently. In order to test this, we compared the mean "stay time" among those who initially resettled in the Seattle area (King County) as contrasted with those who initially resettled outside of the area. Among those who were originally from the Seattle area before the war, if they returned directly to the area, they stayed in this location an average of 9.4 years before moving again. If they did not return to their "home" in King County, they moved again after staying in their non–Seattle location an average of 3.8 years ($F = 6.2$ [1,133] $p < .01$).

Table 5.3. Time Stayed in First Three Resettlement Locations by Region (Those Who Subsequently Moved)

	Pacific Coast	Outside Pacific Coast	Japan	Other
First location (years)				
Mean	5.2	3.4	11.3	—
SD	8.6	7.3	4.0	—
Number of cases	54	78	3	0
Second location (years)				
Mean	6.3	3.1	—	3.0
SD	8.9	3.7	—	—
Number of cases	36	35	0	1
Third location (years)				
Mean	8.3	3.3	1.5	—
SD	14.2	6.2	2.1	—
Number of cases	19	15	2	0

Movement patterns of those who moved away from the Pacific Coast. How did the experiences of those who initially moved away from the Pacific Coast after their incarceration differ from those who returned directly to the West Coast? As previously noted in table 5.1, 44.5% first moved to an area other than the Pacific Coast. Since we surveyed individuals who were living in the Seattle area, all of these individuals who initially moved outside of the Pacific Coast had to move, at a minimum, at least one more time. As can be seen in table 5.3, those who made second and third moves outside of the Pacific Coast stayed in these locations about half as long as those who moved to the Pacific Coast. Among the three respondents who left for Japan after the incarceration and came back to the United States, it took them an average of 11 years to return.

Reasons why incarcerees left the camps and resettled in specific areas. As pointed out in chapter 3, the decision to leave camp was frequently complex, pressured, conflicted, and anxiety provoking. In order to get a general picture of why, in their own minds, they left camp, we asked our respondents an open-ended question about the issue. As can be seen in table 5.4, the largest number indicated that they left because the camp was closing (34.4%). A substantial number (16.9%) said they "just wanted to get out." School (14.2%) and work

Table 5.4. Reasons for Leaving WRA Camp

| | | First Resettlement Location | |
	Total	*Pacific Coast*	*Outside Pacific Coast*
Reason (%)			
Camp closing	34.4	48.5	14.1***
Left for school	14.2	5.9	25.6
Left for work	12.0	5.9	19.2
Drafted	3.8	5.9	1.3
Volunteered for Army	3.3	3.0	3.8
Medical/ health reason	0.5	0.0	1.3
Just wanted to get out	16.9	17.8	16.7
Other	14.8	12.9	17.9
Number of cases	183	101	78

$^a p < .10$ $^* p < .05$ $^{**} p < .01$ $^{***} p < .001$ (two-tailed tests)

(12.0%) were cited by others. Military service in the form of the draft (3.8%) and volunteering (3.3%) drew a smaller number of individuals away from the camps. With respect to the intriguing question of why incarcerees went to particular locations, family was cited by 32.2%, work by 20.2%, "home" by 11.4%, school by 10.4%, and military by 6.6%.

Resettlement Location and Occupational Attainment

In his classic book *Japanese Americans: The Evolution of a Subculture* (1976), Harry H. L. Kitano presents both anecdotal and census data that suggest that those who resettled east of the Mississippi, at least initially, did better in terms of socioeconomic mobility than did those who returned directly to California. He speculates that Japanese Americans faced less discrimination away from the Pacific Coast.

The limited historical evidence relevant to this question does consistently indicate that the Midwest and East were more receptive to the resettlers than were the intermountain states and the West Coast (e.g., Caudill 1952). Moreover, cities were generally less hostile than small towns and rural areas (Daniels 1993, 159–62). One example of the difference in the economic opportunity structure is that trade unions generally would not accept Japanese Americans on the Pacific Coast but would in the Midwest and East (c.f. Daniels 1993, 161; Linehan 1993). In places such as Chicago, the resettlers quickly earned a reputation as good workers and thus were sometimes actively solicited (e.g., Caudill and DeVos 1956).

The question of whether those who left for the Midwest and East ultimately "did better" than those who returned to the West Coast directly from the camps has also occasionally been discussed and debated among the former incarcerees themselves. Many who settled in the East and Midwest feel a certain pride in having successfully established themselves in an area with few Japanese Americans. Nonetheless, most are still strongly attracted to ethnic community life on the Pacific Coast. To varying degrees, they miss the familiar foods, organizations, and community events that they had known before the war.

As previously noted, since our data were collected from respondents currently living in King County, we cannot completely answer the question of relative success, since it would require data from those who currently live in areas outside of the greater Seattle area, specifically off the West Coast. Nonetheless, we can examine the economic and occupational well-being of those who returned directly to the Pacific Coast as contrasted with those who initially lived outside of the area but ultimately returned to the area.

If one compares the average income of Japanese Americans living in different areas using U.S. Census data, as has Kitano (1976, 90–93), one has to be concerned about potentially confounding factors, such as the disparate percentage of Japanese nationals living in different cities who are in the United States for varied reasons. Those, for example, who are temporarily here as corporate executives would be expected to have relatively high levels of education and income. Other potential confounds are differences in cost of living in the different areas, and hence, income.

As discussed earlier, one of the measures on our survey instrument was the final occupation or "main job" of the respondent. Fortunately, occupations are recalled with a high degree of accuracy (Hauser and Warren 1997, 179–80). In order to get a general measure of the socioeconomic standing of these occupations, we converted (similar to what we did in chapters 3 and 4) each respondent's last job category to a current occupational socioeconomic index, the Total Socioeconomic Index (TSEI) (Hauser and Warren 1997, 177–298). This measure is related to occupational education, income, and prestige and is based on the job patterns of both men and women. As shown in table 5.5, those who initially moved outside of the West Coast ultimately achieved last

Table 5.5. Characteristics of Those
Who First Resettled in or Outside of Pacific Coast

Prewar and Current Characteristics	Total	First Resettlement Location	
		Pacific Coast	*Outside Pacific Coast*
Age at incarceration (years)			
Mean	17.5	16.4	18.9**
SD	6.6	6.7	6.2
Number of cases	177	100	77
Gender (%)			
Male (*n* = 89)	49.7	56.2	43.8
Female (*n* = 90)	50.3	56.7	43.3
Number of cases	179	—	—
TSEI of father's occupation			
Mean	31.4	30.6	32.5
SD	8.6	7.8	9.5
Number of cases	168	97	71.5
TSEI of planned occupation			
Mean	41.9	38.7	45.1[a]
SD	16.5	13.7	18.6
Number of cases	78	39	39
Number of years of college education			
Mean	1.88	1.9	1.8
SD	2.3	2.3	2.3
Number of cases	176	101	75
TSEI of last main occupation			
Mean	41.1	38.6	44.3**
SD	15.2	14.4	15.6
Number of cases	172	98	74

[a] $p < .10$ *$p < .05$ **$p < .01$ ***$p < .001$ (two-tailed tests)

"main job" TSEI scores that were significantly higher than those who first moved to the Pacific Coast (Ms = 44.3 vs. 38.6, $p < .01$).

To look into whether there were socioeconomic or resource differences in the family backgrounds of individuals who initially moved to or away from the Pacific Coast, we examined the TSEI score of the respondent's father's occupationand found no TSEI score differences between the two groups. There was also very little difference in the number of years of college that the two types of respondents had completed.

Next, we examined TSEI scores of the occupations that the respondents anticipated entering immediately before the exclusion and incarceration interrupted their plans. This measure should provide an indication of the respondents' occupational aspirations prior to the incarceration. As shown in table 5.5, those who first resettled outside of the Pacific Coast, principally in the Midwest and East, tended to have higher planned TSEI scores than those who returned directly to Washington, Oregon, or California ($Ms = 45.1$ vs. 38.7, $p < .10$). The magnitude of this difference in TSEI scores of planned occupation between those who resided in and outside of the Pacific Coast was similar to the size of the significant difference of TSEI scores of last main occupation in table 5.5, but the cell sizes in the former were considerably smaller. This was due to the fact that those who were children and young teenagers during the incarceration were not old enough to think seriously about their career plans. Thus, there was considerably less statistical power with the planned occupation analysis, which is the likely reason for the lack of significance between the means.

Taken together, these results tentatively suggest that differences in family socioeconomic resources as indexed by the TSEI score of father's occupation did not influence where the Nisei moved. Nonetheless, it should be noted that one reason why it was difficult to discriminate reliably among TSEI scores of the Issei parents was the restricted range of occupations that the Issei could occupy because of the language barrier vis-à-vis mainstream society and the discrimination they faced during the prewar era. As detailed in chapter 2, most were farmers and other small businessmen. Only a few were laborers immediately before Pearl Harbor.

Further, table 5.5 shows that those who moved outside of the Pacific Coast were significantly older on average than those who directly returned to the Pacific Coast ($Ms = 18.9$ years vs. 16.4 years, $p < .01$). Older Nisei were more likely to leave the camps for the Midwest and East before the WRA closed them. Clearly, children had to wait until their parents left. Interestingly, there were no gender differences in movement to or away from the Pacific Coast. Women were as likely to venture to new areas as were men.

Early vs. late leavers. An interesting dimension of the question of who initially resettled in or outside of the Pacific Coast is the comparative human capital of early vs. late leavers. All of those who left the camps to resettle before January 2, 1945, moved outside of the exclusion zone. One might expect that these individuals who left earlier would have more human capital than those who left later, when the Pacific Coast was reopened and the camps were closing. One factor is that many of the early leavers were students attending colleges. Further, one would anticipate that the more vigorous, acculturated, and vocationally skilled would be less intimidated by the challenges of the unknown and possibly hostile world outside of the camp gates. Also, as WRA officials recognized, the longer incarcerees stayed in camp, the more apathetic and demoralized they tended to become (Broom and Kitsuse 1956, 32, 42).

In order to limit our analyses to those who could, in principle, choose to leave the compounds if they desired, we restricted our sample in the following analyses to only those who were 18 years and older at the time of the incarceration (maximum age was 35 years). The restriction reduced our sample size (dependent upon the specific analyses) to approximately 85.

The mean TSEI score of former incarcerees who left before the exclusion zone was reopened was 39.9 ($n = 61$). Those who left after it was reopened had a mean score of 32.1 ($n = 25$), a statistically significant difference ($F = 5.5$ [1,84] $p < .05$). Those who left before the Pacific Coast was reopened had fathers who had jobs with higher TSEI scores ($Ms = 32.0$ vs. 28.8). This difference was also statistically reliable ($F = 4.2$ [1,81] $p < .05$).

There was some indication that those who left early also had higher aspirations than those who waited until the Pacific Coast reopened to resettle. Those who left before January 2, 1945, had a mean prewar planned occupation TSEI score of 42.1, and those who left after had a score of 34.2 ($F = 3.1$ [1, 56] $p < .10$). Consistent with this pattern of findings, but not statistically reliable, was the fact that those who left early had more college education at the time they were incarcerated than those who left after the reopening of the exclusion zone ($Ms = 1.7$ years vs. 1.0 years).

This set of analyses clearly document that those who left the camps early (and initially resettled outside of the Pacific Coast) had more human capital, on average, than those who left after the exclusion zone was reopened.

Why the Midwest/East effect? It is intriguing to speculate about why those who initially moved "back East" before they eventually settled in the Seattle area did better, at least with respect to occupational socioeconomic attainment, over their life course than did those who returned immediately to the Pacific Coast. Consistent with Kitano's thesis, it is probable that higher prewar human capital (which apparently survived the turmoil of the mass removal

Table 5.6. OLS Estimates of Effect of First Resettlement Location
(In or Outside of Pacific Coast) on TSEI of Last Main Job

	TSEI of Last Main Job	
	Model 1 Beta	Model 2 Beta
Moved outside Pacific Coast (1) vs. Pacific Coast (0)	0.29**	0.18*
TSEI of planned occupation before incarceration		0.31**
Number of years of college education		0.39***
Age at time of survey		-0.18*
Gender (Female = 1, Male = 0)		-0.13
Constant	37.42***	63.47***
R²	0.08	0.55
df	1, 73	5, 69
p	0.01	0.001

$^a p < .10$ $^* p < .05$ $^{**} p < .01$ $^{***} p < .001$ (two-tailed tests)

and incarceration) combined with the more open opportunity structure outside of the Pacific Coast interacted to produce higher observed occupational
socioeconomic index scores some fifty years later. Specifically, it is likely that
this human capital/context interaction produced an initial "faster start" in
getting "back on one's feet," which generated enough momentum to produce long-term effects on occupational achievement.

    In order to obtain a less confounded picture of the relationship between
some of the variables that bear on this hypothesis, we ran several OLS (ordinary least squares) multiple regression equations. The criterion variable in
this series of analyses was the TSEI score of respondent's last main job. In
the first equation, the predictor variables were whether the individual initially relocated in or outside of the Pacific Coast states; TSEI score of the
respondent's prewar planned occupation; the number of years of college
education the respondent completed; the respondent's age; and gender.
The latter four variables were viewed analytically as control variables. As
shown in model 1 of table 5.6, when final occupation TSEI score is regressed

Table 5.7. OLS Regression of TSEI
of Last Main Job by First Resettlement Location

	FIRST RESETTLED			
	On Pacific Coast		Away from Pacific Coast	
	Unstandardized Coefficient	Standardized Coefficient	Unstandardized Coefficient	Standardized Coefficient
TSEI of planned occupation at incarceration	0.05	0.05	0.46***	0.50***
Years of college education	2.92**	0.46**	1.92*	0.29*
Age at time of survey	-0.73*	-0.31*	-0.40	-0.13
Gender (Female = 1, Male = 0)	-2.57	-0.10	-5.13	-0.15
Constant	87.68**		55.12[a]	
R^2	0.46		0.61	
df	4, 33		4, 32	
p	0.001		0.001	

[a] $p < .10$ *$p < .05$ **$p < .01$ ***$p < .001$ (two-tailed tests)

on moving to or outside of the Pacific Coast by itself, the beta is positive, significant, and moderately large. When control variables are entered into the equation in model 2, significant variables are the area resettled in, prewar planned occupation TSEI score, the number of years of college education completed, and age. This finding suggests that final socioeconomic occupational attainment is positively related to initially resettling outside of the Pacific Coast, even after accounting for differences in aspirations and age. Additionally, having a higher planned prewar occupation or the aspiration it represents and number of years of college education are also positively related to respondents' final job TSEI scores. Age is negatively related. The age finding indicates that younger respondents did better with respect to ultimate socioeconomic occupational achievement. This makes sense given that the younger the individuals, the more likely they were able to exploit the increasingly open postwar opportunity structure and economic expansion.

In an attempt to gain a clearer picture of the effect of where individuals first moved during their resettlement, we split the sample based upon the location of their first move.[2] As shown in table 5.7, greater education had a similar positive effect on final occupational status regardless of where the former incarcerees resettled. But the TSEI score of their planned occupation was only significant for those who moved away from the Pacific Coast (columns 3 and 4 of table 5.7); high aspirations mattered only for individuals who moved to the new areas, usually the Midwest or East. Although the negative direction of the effect for age was similar for both geographic areas, it was significantly related to final occupation TSEI scores only among those who initially moved to the West Coast (first two columns). Thus, age held back incarcerees more among those who moved back to the Pacific Coast.

Gender differences. As previously noted, men and women relocated to areas outside of the exclusion zone at similar rates. However, once in the Midwest or East, did either gender have an advantage over the other in dealing with resettlement issues, given the constraints of their gender roles? To examine gender differences, we split the sample into males and females and reran the regression equation. When this was done, resettlement location had a stronger relationship with final TSEI scores for men than for women (see column 2 of table 5.8). Also, number of years of education and age were significant only for males (column 2). However, planned occupation TSEI was significant only for females (column 4).

Although many other variables which we did not measure are potentially involved, these results suggest that males were better able to take advantage of the more open opportunity structure outside of the Pacific Coast, particularly if they were younger. Moreover, having higher levels of education paid richer occupational dividends for males than for females. Gender restrictions in occupations, particularly in the immediate postwar period with its large number of returning military personnel, likely reduced the payoff of education for women. It is also probable that marriage and family demands played a role in dampening educational and occupational attainment. On the other hand, women with high occupational aspirations were better able to translate those hopes into reality. Aspirations were less predictive for males.

Table 5.8. OLS Regression of TSEI of Last Main Job by Gender

	Males		Females	
	Model 1 Beta[1]	Model 2 Beta	Model 1 Beta	Model 2 Beta
Moved outside Pacific Coast (1) vs. Pacific Coast (0)	0.39* (13.33)	0.22[a] (7.61)	0.22 (4.87)	0.19 (4.30)
TSEI of planned occupation before incarceration		0.20 (0.21)		0.40* (0.30)
Number of years of college education		0.47*** (3.22)		0.19 (1.16)
Age at time of survey		-0.25* (-0.88)		-0.07 (-0.14)
Constant	40.00***	92.92**	34.23***	32.29
R^2	0.14	0.63	0.05	0.27
df	1, 38	4, 35	1, 33	4, 30
p	0.05	0.001	0.21	0.05

[a] $p < .10$ * $p < .05$ ** $p < .01$ *** $p < .001$ (two-tailed tests)
[1] Unstandardized coefficients.

STRONGEST MEMORIES
OF THE EARLY YEARS OF RESETTLEMENT

To begin the process of exploring how former incarcerees themselves now recall their resettlement over half a century after they experienced it, we asked them a broad, open-ended question. This question, which allowed them to answer in their own words, asked, "What are your strongest memories of the early years of resettlement, that is, the place you moved right after camp?" We coded the responses into discrete categories. Multiple responses were permitted. As shown in table 5.9, the most frequently recalled strong memory of resettlement that former incarcerees had was facing discrimination (24.7%). Interestingly, the second most frequent strong remembrance was the lack of discrimination (21.4%). For 13.7%, the difficult living conditions of the period were most salient. Others remembered

Table 5.9. Strongest Memories of Early Years of Resettlement

Strongest Memories	Percent Who Mentioned
Discrimination	24.7
No discrimination	21.4
Difficult living conditions	13.7
Hard work	12.6
Economic hardships	12.1
Positive social life	8.2
Harsh weather	7.7
Loneliness	6.0
Other	62.1
Number of cases	182

the hard work required during the period (12.6%) and economic hardships (12.1%). The only positive memory about resettlement, mentioned by 8.2% of the respondents, was the rewarding social life of the era. Other negatives recalled were harsh weather (7.7%) and, understandably, loneliness (6.0%).

Pacific and non-Pacific-Coast differences. In order to examine how the experiences of those who initially resettled outside of the Pacific Coast compared with those who immediately returned to it, we broke down the responses in table 5.9 by the area in which the former incarceree first resettled. The results are quite striking in that on five of seven specific categories, those who moved to a locale outside of the Pacific Coast reliably reported having a better experience than those who returned to the Pacific Coast. As shown in table 5.10, not only were living conditions more frequently reported to be difficult on the West Coast, but so were social conditions (18.8% vs. 5.1%, $p < .01$; 4.0% vs. 14.1%, $p < .01$). Most importantly, a much higher percentage of those who spontaneously reported experiencing no discrimination had resettled outside of the Pacific Coast (30.8% vs. 14.9%, $p < .01$). Consistent with this, a significantly higher percentage of those who returned directly to the Pacific Coast reported strong memories of facing discrimination (30.7% vs. 17.9%, $p < .05$). The only more negative resettlement experience that those who moved to the Midwest or East mentioned, not surprisingly, was harsh weather (11.5% vs. 4.0%, $p < .05$). Clearly, resettlers who initially moved away from the Pacific Coast have more positive mem-

Table 5.10. Strongest Memories
by Resettlement Location, Age at Incarceration, and Gender

Memories (%)	Resettlement Location		Age at Incarceration				Gender	
	Pacific Coast	Out of Pacific Coast	5–11	12–17	18–22	23+	Male	Female
Harsh weather	4.0	11.5*	—	—	—	—	—	—
Difficult living conditions	18.8	5.1**	—	—	—	—	—	—
Hard work	17.8	6.4*	—	—	—	—	—	—
Loneliness	—	—	—	—	—	—	3.2	8.9[a]
Discrimination	30.7	17.9*	37.8	24.5	25.0	10.5[a]	—	—
No discrimination	14.9	30.8**	—	—	—	—	—	—
Positive social life	4.0	14.1**	—	—	—	—	—	—
Number of cases	101	78	37	53	52	38	93	90

[a] $p < .10$ *$p < .05$ **$p < .01$ ***$p < .001$ (two-tailed tests)
Note: — Differences not significant.

ories of their initial resettlement period than do those who returned directly to the Pacific Coast. These findings provide significant support for the thesis that those who initially moved outside of the Pacific Coast achieved higher occupational status because they got their start under less discriminatory circumstances.

There were no statistically reliable age or gender effects associated with moving to or outside of the Pacific Coast. There was a tendency for younger individuals to more often report discrimination and for women to mention that they suffered from loneliness more frequently than men. The former probably was due to the almost universal taunting that returning school-children experienced upon reentering public schools. Some Nisei even implicate their teachers. For those who were of school age during the early days of their resettlement, these experiences are still very salient and painfully recalled.

Prewar socioeconomic aspirations and resources. Finally, we explored whether those who had high as compared with low prewar socioeconomic aspirations had different recollections of their resettlement years. Perhaps the contrast between what they hoped to achieve and the reality of the "lost years"

Table 5.11. Selected Strongest Memories
of Early Years of Resettlement by Prewar and Current Resources

	TSEI of Planned Occupation	Plans for College	Number of College Years of Education	Annual Income In 1996
	Mean (SD)	% With	Mean (SD)	Mean (SD)
Economic hardships				
Mentioned	53.0 (15.6)**	83.3***	—	6.67 (3.4)***
Not mentioned	40.2 (15.9)	32.4		4.9 (2.4)
Harsh weather				
Mentioned	31.5 (6.8)*	—	0.6 (1.3)*	—
Not mentioned	43.5 (16.8)		2.0 (2.3)	
Loneliness				
Mentioned	—	75.0*	—	—
Not mentioned		34.8		

^{a} $p < .10$ $^*p <.05$ $^{**}p <.01$ $^{***}p < .001$ (two-tailed tests)

Note: There are no significant differences based upon father's self-employment status, ownership of house prior to evacuation, father's occupation TSEI score, and TSEI score of last main job. Also, there are no significant differences among those who mentioned discrimination, difficult living conditions, positive social life, and hard work as their strongest memories.

in camp has been more troublesome for those who had high aspirations. Table 5.11 shows that those who reported experiencing economic hardships during resettlement had significantly higher planned occupation TSEI scores ($Ms = 53.0$ vs. 40.2, $p < .01$). Also, those who cited economic hardships as a strong memory associated with the period were much more likely to report expecting to attend college before the war (83.3% vs. 32.4%, $p < .001$). In addition, those who ended up with higher levels of current income reported having experienced more economic hardships during resettlement.

These results argue that those who had higher aspirations experienced the reality of the incarceration as more negative than did those who had lower aspirations. In a similar manner, the income results suggest, in a very tentative way, that those who ultimately did better economically recall their earlier struggles more negatively. This may be due to their having higher and more exacting standards that helped them to succeed in the first place.

SUMMARY

Our survey data clearly document that the resettlement process initially widely scattered individuals and families across the country. Only one-fourth of the resettlers returned to the same town or city that they lived in before the uprooting. Less than 50 percent even directly returned to the same state from which they were evicted. However, there were strong secondary migration effects pulling individuals and families back to the Pacific Coast. When the resettlers subsequently moved from their initial resettlement location, it was very probable that they were moving to some place on the West Coast.

With respect to why resettlers moved to a particular location, the most common rationale given was that that was where their families were moving. This is not surprising given that many Nisei were still children or adolescents at the time. Moreover, those Nisei who were older had responsibilities to care for their aging Issei parents. The second most frequently cited reason for moving to a particular location was employment. Thus, for many of the young adult Nisei, starting or restarting their careers was paramount.

Perhaps the most fascinating finding is that those Nisei who initially resettled outside of the Pacific Coast ultimately achieved a higher occupational status by the end of their working lives. This was the case even though all of our sample ended or were ending their careers in the Seattle area. Significantly, the individuals who initially moved eastward had higher prewar occupational aspirations than those who returned directly to the Pacific Coast. There was no significant difference in the amount of education that the two groups attained, and thus it cannot account for the occupational attainment differences.

Contrary to what might be expected, there were no gender differences between those who moved to the Midwest and East Coast versus the Pacific Coast. Women were as "adventurous" as men in moving to the then unknown, exciting yet simultaneously frightening parts of the country. This is not to say that gender made no difference in the experience of resettlers. When we examined effects potentially related to gender more closely, the impact of where the former incarcerees resettled and of education was stronger for men than for women. Thus, women appear to have been less able than men to capitalize on their education and to take advantage of job opportunities. It seems reasonable to assume that job discrimination along with gender role constraints linked with marriage and family dampened the incarceree women's ability to exploit the more open opportunity structure outside of the Pacific Coast. On the other hand, the influence of prewar occupational aspirations was significant only for females. Therefore, high aspirations made a greater difference among women than men. Women possibly needed greater motivation, which is likely to be positively correlated with aspirations, to break through the gender barriers then in effect.

Although we do not have the measures to definitively test the following thesis, our findings strongly suggest it. Basically, there appears to be an interaction between the human capital resources of the resettlers and the constraints and opportunities of the area in which they resettled. With respect to the latter, our data document that those who initially moved away from the Pacific Coast remember where they resettled as less discriminatory and more welcoming than those who returned directly to the Pacific Coast. Further, those who left camp before the Pacific Coast was reopened had more human capital than those who left after. Thus, it seems quite plausible that the greater human capital of those who left camp early for the Midwest and East helped them take advantage of the greater opportunities in these areas and thus gain occupational "momentum." Even though these individuals eventually returned to the Pacific Coast, it appears that this initial momentum, which came, perhaps, at a critical time in their career development, was enough to boost their overall occupational life-course trajectory relative to those who returned directly to the Pacific Coast.

There was some indication that men were somewhat better able than women to deploy their human capital and convert it into occupational gains. This would be consistent with the interpretation that gender-based job discrimination as well as cultural role prescriptions worked against women's occupational achievement. Despite these probable impediments, women who aspired to higher-status occupations, compared to women who had lower aspirations, were better able to realize their prewar hopes. There was no such effect of prewar aspirations for men.

With respect to the most salient memories that the former incarcerees have of the resettlement period, the strongest recollections revolve around discrimination. Some 25% remember having to deal with it during this period. A slightly smaller percentage (21%) report that they were struck by its absence. It seems very likely that the resettlers, because of their immediately preceding uprooting and WRA camp experiences, were highly vigilant to the presence or absence of discrimination. Significantly, those who returned directly to the Pacific Coast were much more likely to report experiencing discrimination, while those who first relocated to the Midwest and East reported its absence.

In addition to the extremely burdensome individual and familial struggles that the resettlers had to deal with during the early postwar years, the ethnic community had to be rebuilt. The psychological legacy of the incarceration experience and the resettlers' scattering into environments that were frequently less than welcoming made it all the more imperative for the former incarcerees to reconnect with those with whom they felt comfortable. For the mostly Seattle-raised Nisei, who were now in their twenties, this was a process that they were well equipped to undertake. Their prewar experiences in the vibrant communities of the Pacific Northwest in the 1930s and their need for both material and social support combined to provide the social capital and motivation to accomplish this extensive undertaking.

On the other hand, other forces pushed in the direction of simply assimilating as quickly as possible into the larger society. More specifically, there were external and internal pressures to avoid clustering in ethnic neighborhoods and forming visible groups that drew attention to the resettlers' ethnicity. Understandably, most Nisei were still not socially comfortable with whites and others. This is reflected, for example, in their very low postwar intermarriage rate (Spickard 1989, 58).

The duality and tension involved in seeking out each other versus unobtrusively assimilating ultimately produced a different, less visible ethnic community than the one that existed before the war. Consistent with their high prewar aspirations, a large proportion of Nisei went on to earn college degrees. Thus, they were no longer tied almost by necessity to each other (as were their Issei parents) in economic relationships in agriculture or other types of small businesses (cf. Bonacich and Modell 1980, 47–58; Modell 1977, 94–126). Fewer formal and informal business associations were thus formed.

Nonetheless, because of their extensive prewar and camp social ties and their shared sensibilities, which were cultural as well as forged by the incarceration, the Nisei were still strongly drawn to each other. Ethnic churches were restarted or, if in a new location, started; many Japanese American Citizens League chapters were formed in areas where there were no Japanese Americans before the war, and a great variety of athletic, social, and cultural organizations were organized. With the Nisei in the majority of leadership roles, the postwar community was different in character from the prewar Issei-led one. As a geographic community, Nihonmachi was much reduced in its size and scope of activities. Nonetheless, informal social connections, frequently between different families than before the war, and the organizational life of the community persisted to a significant extent. We will further explore the evolution of this community in subsequent chapters.

SIX

Marriage and Family Formation

Life went on in camp and people fell in love, got married, and had kids. And it kind of strikes me as being a little unusual when I hear people say, "I was born in camp." To realize that those things were going on. It makes you believe that there was sort of a normal life going on during the period we were in the relocation centers. (Kunio Otani, denshovh-okunio-01-0015)

As noted in chapter 2, the family was the key social unit for members of the prewar Japanese American community. However, even before the advent of World War II, the Japanese American family was headed toward a major transformation. The primary reasons for this were the widening linguistic, cultural, and political gulfs that were becoming increasingly evident between Issei parents and their Nisei children as the latter began to reach maturity in the 1930s. For the most part, the acculturated Nisei were oriented toward careers in the larger society. When the leading edge of this geogeneration was rebuffed in its attempts to land union and professional jobs before World War II, its members only reluctantly returned to the Issei-dominated ethnic economy.

Nonetheless, the exclusion and incarceration suddenly placed new and unanticipated pressures on the family as a social and economic unit. Although the literature covering this aspect of the wartime experiences of Japanese Americans is quite limited, we briefly review what is available. Then, using Denshō survey data, we explore several previously unasked, family-related questions about the long-term consequences of the incarceration. Specifically, we examine how it potentially altered the Nisei's life course, either by accelerating or delaying the incidence and timing of marriage and childbearing.

FAMILY DYNAMICS AND THE INCARCERATION

Life-Course Analytic Perspective

The life-course perspective that we have been drawing upon assumes that the effects of exposure to traumatic events such as the incarceration are frequently expressed across the life-span of the individual and perhaps even into the next generation (e.g., Elder and Clipp 1988). Exposure to other types of massive social dislocations, such as economic depressions, war, and weather-related catastrophes, have been shown to affect the timing of pivotal family-life transitions such as marriage and childbearing (e.g., Mayer 1988; Rodgers and Thornton 1985; Winter 1985). Thus, an intriguing, albeit unexamined question about the incarceration is whether it impacted the timing and perhaps even the order of these key life transitions and, if so, in what ways. Further, personal characteristics such as gender and life-stage would be expected to influence the specific nature of these incarceration-impacted, family-related transitions.

It should be noted that it is very unlikely for either an informant or social scientist to notice the effect of events such as the incarceration on these types of life-course transitions because their detection, given the multiple determinants involved and substantial individual variation, requires a large number of systematic observations. If, for example, incarcerees married, on average, two years earlier than they normally would have because of the incarceration, this may be difficult for informants to "notice," particularly if age-related marriage norms are shifting over time.

Historical Backdrop

While we have presented the historical background to the incarceration and early resettlement in previous chapters, some relevant highlights bear repeating here to set the context for our present discussion of marital and family issues. As political tensions escalated between Japan and the United States in the 1930s, they frequently produced strains in the relationships between Issei parents and their rapidly acculturating Nisei children. Not only were their cultural orientations substantially different, but even basic communication between the two groups was frequently difficult. As noted in chapter 2, it was often problematic for the two generations to communicate their complex personal and political feelings, given the Issei's generally poor grasp of English and the Nisei's deficient mastery of Japanese. Often this language barrier produced a kind of a standoff in which important differences were left unarticulated and unresolved but "contained."

As discussed in chapter 3, the enormously disorganizing series of events that occurred in rapid succession after the attack on Pearl Harbor displaced the Issei from their positions of leadership and authority in both the family and the ethnic community. Consequently, many older Nisei were prematurely rushed into assuming responsibility for both of these institutions during "evacuation" and the first year of incarceration. Moreover, throughout the resettlement process, older Nisei were usually in the vanguard of the family's efforts to reestablish its economic and social stability, whether in unfamiliar areas of the Midwest and East or back on the Pacific Coast. They had to scramble to find their own and their family's economic and social footing in a world frequently very different from the one they had known before the war. As highlighted in chapter 5, even though they faced job and housing discrimination, particularly on the West Coast, they also encountered new opportunities that were not available to them before the war.

Change in Family and Community Leadership

One of the most widely observed consequences of the incarceration was the disruptive effect it had on families (e.g., Broom and Kitsuse 1956, 37–49; Kitano 1976, 75–77; Spicer, Hansen, Luomala, and Opler 1969, 104–8). Even though War Relocation Authority (WRA) policy was to avoid splitting families, in many ways camp life had this effect psychologically, if not physically. For one, it eroded Issei parental authority. As pointed out in chapter 2, the Issei father frequently ran a farm or small business in which the wife and children were indispensable unpaid workers. In effect, he was not only the leader of the family but also an integrated economic unit, both of which usually reinforced the other. Moreover, within the male-dominated ethnic community, the father often held a position of authority and respect, particularly if he was active in key organizations such as the Japanese Association or the Buddhist, Methodist, or Baptist church.

The attack on Pearl Harbor led to a series of events that destroyed these roles and the authority and identity they provided. Most visibly, numerous Issei community leaders were stigmatized by being detained and sent to

Department of Justice (DOJ) internment camps for enemy aliens. The following recollection is from a visual history narrator who, as a young girl, saw her Issei father picked up and detained:

> Yes, that was when I used to go home from school, and he'd wave to me through the windows, you know, of the jail. When he was in there at the beginning, it was the most difficult time because he was all by himself and I just couldn't understand why he was there. And so he would wave to me when I came back from school. And it was just, kinda, I guess you would call it embarrassment or whatever and I would just run past that window and wave to him and run. (June Takahashi, denshovh-tjune-01-0014)

With the detention of the Issei, older Nisei suddenly became responsible for their younger brothers and sisters. One narrator recalled:

> My oldest sister was just a pampered little child. And then my father is taken away and she's all of a sudden feeling she has to live up to the responsibility of being the head of the household. I think that it must have been really tough on her. So between my mom and sister—I was just a kid so I don't know much about her—but between my mom and my sister, they paid a high price. (Mako Nakagawa, denshovh-nmako-01-0011)

Those Issei who were not interned by the DOJ were not initially permitted by the WRA to occupy leadership positions. Thus, at first only Nisei could serve on camp community councils. The justification given by the agency was that the Issei would impede the creation of a "community as nearly American as possible." This process was not without its difficulties, as the stripping of the Issei of their long-held leadership roles caused considerable conflict within the imprisoned communities (Broom and Kitsuse 1956, 23–24; War Relocation Authority 1946a, 26–36).

Further, the structure of social life in the camps emphasized individual rather than family participation. Children frequently ate with peers, and recreational activities were also usually age and gender graded. The cramped barracks became a place mostly to rest and sleep. A narrator who was a child at the time reported:

> Both my parents were no longer always around as they had been, and now my brothers and I were kind of left to our own devices. I was young enough so that I could still be told to behave by the friends of my mother and father,

obasans and *ojisans.* But my oldest brother loved this freedom, and he felt that now he could do what he wanted with his cohorts, and they became kind of like a gang in camp. . . . And there were often many little gangs that sprung up, and they would have their own meetings and their own kinds of things, rituals that they would go through. But I just knew that my parents were always so upset about the way Jimmy was sticking with those bad boys, and they were making him bad, you know. And yes, he wasn't as obedient. I remember him talking back to my dad, which he never did before. (May K. Sasaki, denshovh–smay–01–0018)

Another narrator who was a teenager at the time recalled:

I didn't pay much attention to my parents 'cause for the first time, they sort of left us alone. We were not as closely supervised. They were not as, if you might, strict with us, about, "Where are you going? Who are you going to be with? How long? What are you doing?" There were no questions. So there was a great deal of freedom, sudden freedom. And any early teenager will tell you, that's something dreams are made of. (Sue Okabe, denshovh–osue–01–0006)

Finally, the economic control the Issei fathers previously had because of the authority they wielded in their small businesses was diminished, since pay in the camps was earned by individuals rather than by integrated productive units, such as a farm or hotel (Broom and Kitsuse 1956, 36–41).

It is possible that these burdens impacted incarcerees in the timing of life transitions such as marriage or childbearing, sometimes in subtle psychological ways and other times in a more observable fashion. The uncertainties and turmoil of the period may have delayed these events or in some cases accelerated them. With the Denshō survey data, we explore the timing and character of these significant life-course transitions in the lives of the Denshō former incarcerees.

MARRIAGE PATTERNS IN THE DENSHŌ SAMPLE

Current Marital Status of Respondents

The figures relevant to marriage reported in this chapter are based upon those individuals in the Denshō sample who were at least 18 years of age

Table 6.1. Marital Status at the Time of the Survey

				MALE		FEMALE	
		Gender		Age at Incarceration		Age at Incarceration	
	Total Sample	Male	Female	18–22	23–35	18–22	23–35
Panel A							
Marital status when surveyed (%)							
Married	65.6	86.4	45.7**	88.9	82.4	52.0	38.1
Widowed	25.6	9.1	41.3	3.7	17.6	32.0	52.4
Divorced	2.2	2.3	2.2	3.7	0.0	4.0	0.0
Separated	1.1	0.0	2.2	0.0	0.0	4.0	0.0
Never married	5.6	2.3	8.7	3.7	0.0	8.0	9.5
Panel B							
Ever divorced (%)	7.8	6.8	8.7	11.1	0.0	8.0	9.5
Number of cases	90	44	46	27	17	25	21

[a] $p < .10$*   *$p < .05$ **$p < .01$ ***$p < .001$ (two-tailed tests)

at the time they were evicted from their West Coast homes ($n = 90$). This restriction was put in place to limit our analyses to those who were, at the time, normatively of marriageable age. Further, to facilitate age-related comparisons, we divided these respondents into two life-stage groups, those 18–22 and 23–35 years old. At the time we interviewed this subset of respondents (1997), they ranged in age from their mid seventies to late eighties. As shown in panel A of table 6.1, 65.6% were married and 25.6% were widowed at the time they were surveyed. Given the ages of our respondents and the longer life expectancy of women, it is not surprising that women (41.3%) were much more likely to be widowed than men (9.1%). Only five (5.6%) of our respondents who were 18 years or older at incarceration never married. Of the five, four were women and one was a male in the 18–22 age range. Two of the never-married women were in the 18–22 range at the time of incarceration; the other two were in the group aged 23 and over.

Divorce. Consistent with what has been previously reported in the literature (e.g., Kitano 1976, 206; Fong 1998, 207), the divorce rate among the Nisei is very low when compared with current American averages. Only

2.2% were currently divorced, while 1.1% were currently separated (see panel A, table 6.1). Even when we considered those who were ever divorced (panel B, table 6.1), the divorce rate was only 7.8%. It is probable that our sampling procedure (registered voters) and differential refusal rates somewhat artificially lowered the divorce and separation figures. Nonetheless, even if one makes significant allowances for these potential distortions, the divorce/separation rate in this population is still very low by contemporary standards.

When did the Seattle Nisei Get Married?

With respect to when our respondents were married, the data presented in table 6.2 show that one-third (33.7%) were married prior to their incarceration. Women (43.9%) were more likely than men (23.8%) to have married before they entered camp. This is consistent with the younger normative marriage age for women. About 8% (8.4%) of the incarceree sample were married while they were in camp. The majority, 57.8%, married after they left the dreary compounds. Men were substantially more likely to marry after they left camp than women (73.8% vs. 41.5%).

Nisei Age at Marriage: Comparisons with National Norms

In order to gauge the impact that the incarceration might have had on the Seattle incarcerees' entry into marriage, we examined the average (median) age at marriage separately for males and females and, in addition, subdivided the sample into two age groupings, 18–22 and 23–35 years at incarceration. We also present data on national norms[1] for the relevant time periods to examine society-wide trends for age at marriage during the period when the Nisei were getting married. The U.S. Census Bureau collects the most reliable national data on age at marriage. As the median is the measure of central tendency used in reporting census marriage data, for the following comparisons our survey data were converted into medians rather than arithmetic means.

As can be seen in table 6.3, in 1940 the national median age at marriage was 24.3 years for males and 21.5 years for females. In addition, it should be noted that the national median age at marriage *dropped* in 1950 to 22.8 years and 20.3 years for males and females respectively (e.g., Ahlburg and De Vita 1992, 17–19; Bouvier and De Vita 1991, 2–11). The 1955 and 1960 figures for both genders are virtually identical to those for 1950.

In comparison, the median age at marriage for the Denshō respondents

Table 6.2. Percent Married Before, During, and After Incarceration

		Gender		MALE Age at Incarceration		FEMALE Age at Incarceration	
	Total Sample	*Male*	*Female*	*18–22*	*23–35*	*18–22*	*23–35*
Time Period of Marriage							
Before incarceration	33.7	23.8	43.9**	0.0	62.5***	13.6	78.9***
During incarceration	8.4	2.4	14.6	0.0	6.3	22.7	5.3
After incarceration	57.8	73.8	41.5	100.0	31.3	63.6	15.8
Number of cases	83	42	41	26	16	22	19

[a] $p < .10$ *$p < .05$ ** $p < .01$ *** $p < .001$ (two-tailed tests)

who were of marriageable age (18 years and over) at the time of incarceration was 27.0 years for males and 23.0 years for females. Overall, the Nisei incarcerees married at a considerably older age than the general U.S. population. Although it would require a much larger sample to be able to control for several potentially confounding factors to definitively answer the question of the effect of the incarceration on age of marriage, it seems quite plausible that it did, in fact, delay the marriages of the incarcerees.

In order to make the effects of the incarceration somewhat clearer, we compared those who married before the incarceration with those who did so after the incarceration for our total marriage-aged sample. This comparison controls for ethnic community marriage norms and the structural factors that delayed Nisei marriages vis-à-vis national norms. As shown in table 6.3, those who married after the incarceration were about a year (males) to two years (females) older when they entered marriage than those who married before camp. Among males aged 18–22 years, none married before or during their camp years. All married during the resettlement period at the relatively old median age of 27.5 years. It should be emphasized that during this postwar period, in the country as a whole, age at marriage was going in the opposite direction, that is, markedly decreasing.

Self-Reported Impact of the Incarceration on Marriage Plans

Do the Nisei themselves perceive that the incarceration influenced their marital plans? As previously observed, unless the link to a specific incarceration-

Table 6.3. Median Age at Marriage by Gender, Age at Incarceration, and Time Period of Marriage

Age:	INCARCERERS										U.S. POPULATION[1]				
	Total Sample				18–22			23–35							
Married:	Entire Period	Before Incarceration	During Incarceration	After	Before Incarceration	During Incarceration	After	Before Incarceration	During Incarceration	After	1930	1940	1950	1955	1960
Males															
Median age at marriage	27.0	26.5	27.0[2]	28.0	—	—	27.5	26.5	27.0[2]	31.0	24.3	24.3	22.8	22.6	22.8
Number of cases	42	10	1	31	0	0	26	10	1	5					
Females															
Median age at marriage	23.0	22.0	22.5	24.0	20.0	22.0	24.0	23.0	24.0[2]	27.0	21.3	21.5	20.3	20.2	20.3
Number of cases	40	17	6	17	3	5	14	14	1	3					

[1] Source: U.S. Bureau of the Census, *Current population reports*, P-20, no. 450 (March 1990) and P-20, no. 461 (March 1991).
[2] The age at which the one respondent in this category got married.

related event is very clear and salient, it is unlikely that individuals would attribute the timing of their marriage to the incarceration. Therefore, it is perhaps not surprising that, as seen in table 6.4, two-thirds (67.5%) of the marriage-aged respondents (at least 18 years old at incarceration) reported that the incarceration did not influence their marital plans. However, among the 32.5% who did indicate that their marriage plans were impacted by their incarceration, close to a third (30.8%) reported that they married early. As would be expected, this was particularly the case for the older cohort of men (those aged 23–35 years at the time of incarceration). Of those in this life-stage cohort who reported that the incarceration did influence their marriage plans, 83.3% said that they married earlier than planned due to the incarceration.

Reasons for accelerating marriage plans. A common explanation that older Nisei give for marrying before they had planned was that the couple did not want to be potentially split up and sent to different camps. This was a real possibility if the two families lived in different parts of a region or were otherwise geographically separated. One female narrator recalled:

> We knew we're going to be evacuated and people were going to be evacuated according to where they lived. Everybody had to be with their own families and my family was in Kingston . . . and we knew that people around Fife were going to Puyallup along with the Seattle bunch and we could foresee a separation. We had been engaged since long before the fall before, and we were going to get married when he finished law school, which was the next June. But it just meant that we could get married now or just forget it for quite a long time, we didn't know how long. . . . So I told Toru that either I go with them and we just not get married for a while, or let's get married now. (Kiyo Sakahara, denshovh-storu_g-01-0030)

Another 30.8% stated that the incarceration affected their marital plans in that they met in camp and were subsequently married.

Reasons for delay in marriages. In the "relocation centers," incarcerees were faced with a great deal of uncertainty about, for example, when they would leave the compounds, given the vagaries of the war and the WRA's resettlement program (e.g., Embree 1943). Some who might otherwise have married probably decided to wait until the future was somewhat more certain. Even when the former incarcerees were outside of the camps during reset-

Table 6.4. Percentages for Whether
and How Incarceration Affected Marriage Plans

| | | MALE | FEMALE | | | | |
| | | Gender | | Age at Incarceration | | Age at Incarceration | |
	Total	*Male*	*Female*	*18–22*	*23–35*	*18–22*	*23–35*
Marriage plans							
Affected	32.5	38.1	26.8	34.6	43.8	34.8	16.7
Not affected	67.5	61.9	73.2	65.4	56.3	65.2	83.3
Number of cases	83	42	41	26	16	23	18
How affected marriage plans?							
Married earlier	30.8	33.3	27.3	0.0	83.3**	25.0	33.3
Got closer in camp	7.7	13.3	0.0	11.1	16.7	0.0	0.0
Met in camp	30.8	26.7	36.4	44.4	0.0	37.5	33.3
Other	30.8	26.7	36.4	44.4	0.0	37.5	33.3
Number of cases	26	15	11	9	6	8	3

[a] $p < .10$ * $p < .05$ ** $p < .01$ *** $p < .001$ (two-tailed tests)

tlement, there were pressures which probably slowed down getting married. In fact, for some the initial months of resettlement turned out to be even more difficult than when they were imprisoned. Some were virtually penniless, living in a strange city isolated from a community of Japanese Americans. Many were anxious to "make up for lost time" in any way that they could. Individuals put in long hours in various types of low-wage service and manufacturing jobs or on their farms and in other types of small businesses. Among those who worked for others, there was a considerable amount of job-hopping in search of better wages (Caudill and DeVos 1956). For many, the felt responsibility to help the family "get back on its feet" probably took precedence over personal desires to find a suitable partner and get married.

Another factor that was likely to be involved in the delaying of Nisei marriages was the breakup of prewar formal and informal social networks by wartime events. When families resettled, they frequently lost touch with one another because of the geographic dispersal that took place. As pointed out in chapter 5, less than half of Nisei resettlers even returned to their home state when they first left their WRA camp. Even though there was strong motivation to do so, it took time to construct a new social infrastructure outside of the camps. Part of this involved the creation and strengthening of informal relationships among families. Frequently, families that had not been close before the war became so after they both moved to a new location. The creation of a new social infrastructure also involved the building or rebuilding of organizations within the community. This included such institutions as the churches, athletic leagues, Japanese American Citizens League chapters, and other venues such as cultural groups, which made it easier for Nisei to meet and develop bonds with one another.

Similarly, Issei social networks were also in disarray because of the diaspora created by resettlement. Thus, they were in less of a position to "engineer" mate selection for their Nisei children as they had sometimes done before the war. Consistent with Japanese tradition, the prewar unions of many Kibei and Nisei were arranged to varying degrees. Certainly, Issei parents exerted considerable influence on the selection of marital partners, as it symbolized and in some real ways involved the "joining" of families. Sometimes a *baishakunin* or "go-between," usually a trusted family friend, acted as a matchmaker. Nisei tended to downplay this arrangement even if they benefited from it to some degree because it ran counter to the American ideal of marital partner selection based upon romantic love. It was thus viewed as somewhat embarrassing and something resorted to by those unable to make their own arrangements. An extension of the arranged marriage was the occasional sending to Japan of those, particularly males, who needed mates.

Eight respondents in our total sample (which includes those who were children at the time of incarceration) never married; of the eight, seven were women. They may have been, to varying degrees, "casualties" of the same dynamics that delayed marriages for others. Considering the prevailing pro-marriage and pro-family norms of the times (Bouvier and De Vita 1991, 4–6; Ryder 1973, 61), the wartime disturbances and privations that the Nisei experienced must have been substantial to have delayed marriages to the extent that they did.

FERTILITY PATTERNS OF DENSHŌ WOMEN

Another major life event that could have been impacted by the incarceration was childbearing. It is quite conceivable that due to the uncertainties and stresses associated with the forced removal, incarceration, and resettlement, fertility was reduced. It is well documented that economic depressions, for example, are associated with lowered fertility rates (e.g., Coale and Zelnik 1963, 21–41; Easterlin 1987, 3–34; Grabill, Kiser, and Whelpton 1958, 25–50; Ryder 1973, 58–60). We were therefore interested in the childbearing patterns of the women in the Denshō sample. Since all of these women had completed their childbearing by the time they were surveyed, no age restrictions were placed on the samples used for these analyses.

With respect to fertility, table 6.5 shows that the mean number of children borne by all of our female respondents was 2.8. The ever-married women had a mean of 3.0 children. None of the seven women (which includes those of all ages at incarceration) who remained single had any children. The modal number of children for the ever-married women was also 3 (32.5%). A fifth of the women (20.5%) had 2 children and another quarter (24.1%) had 4 children. The U.S. Census total fertility rate (TFR) for the years 1960 and 1965, the approximate period when most of our respondents were completing their childbearing, was 3.7 and 2.9 children respectively (U.S. Department of Health and Human Services, National Center for Health Statistics 1985).[2] Thus, the cumulative number of children that the Denshō respondents had was slightly lower than the national figures around the peak of the baby boom in 1960 (the baby-boom period was from 1946 to 1964; e.g., Bouvier and De Vita 1991, 2). It was not until after 1965 during the post-baby-boom period that the national figures decreased to the relatively (for the time) small number of children born to the former incarcerees.

However, one might ask whether these differences are due to age variations between the Denshō sample of incarceree women and women nationally. If the incarceree women are older overall than women nationwide, that might account for some of the differences in the former's somewhat lower fertility rate. In order to control for any confounding effects of age distribution differences between our incarceree sample and the U.S. population, we compared age-specific birth rates (live births per 1,000 women in specified age groups) for the relevant time periods (see table 6.6). In the interest of clarity, only data for two prime childbearing age groups of incarcerees, 20–24 and 25–29, are included in table 6.6. Those interested in the fertility history of the full range of age groupings can find the data in table 1 of appendix D.

Inspecting the total fertility rates for U.S. women in the two age groups from 1940 to 1975 reveals the baby-boom story. From 1945 to 1950 and

Table 6.5. Mean Number of Children Born to Incarceree Women

Variable	All	Ever Married	Never Married
Number of children			
% with:			
0 Children	13.3	6.0	100.0
1	4.4	4.8	
2	18.9	20.5	
3	30.0	32.5	
4	22.2	24.1	
5	8.9	9.6	
6	1.1	1.2	
7	1.1	1.2	
Mean (SD)	2.8 (1.6)	3.0 (1.4)	0
Number of cases	90	83	7

Table 6.6. Age-Specific Birth Rates (Average) for Women
in the Incarceree Sample (20–29 Years Old) and United States

Age at the beginning of time period	20–24		25–29	
	Incarceree	U.S. (Year)	Incarceree	U.S. (Year)
1931–41	121.2	135.6 (1940)		
Number of cases	6			
1942–45	227.3	138.9 (1945)	107.3	132.2 (1945)
Births in camp	170.5		71.5	
Births after camp	56.8		35.8	
Number of cases	22		7	
1946–49	228.3	196.6 (1950)	197.5	166.1 (1950)
Number of cases	23		19	
1950–59	242.1	258.1 (1960)	181.5	197.4 (1960)
Number of cases	19		27	
1960–75	125.0	113.0 (1975)	109.4	108.2 (1975)
Number of cases	1		12	

Note: Birth rates are live births per 1,000 women in specified age group.
Source for U.S. data: U.S. Department of Health and Human Services, National Center for
Health Statistics, Vital Statistics of the United States, vol. 1, Natality (Hyattsville, Md., 2000).

1960, birth rates rose for both age groups before beginning to decline in 1964.[3] It was not until approximately 1975 that national birth rates declined below their pre–World War II levels.

The age-specific birth rates of the 20–24 age group of incarcerees during the camp (1942–45) years were substantially higher (227.3/1,000) than the national rates in 1945 (138.9/1,000). Because not all of the incarceree women of this age group were in camp throughout the 1942–45 period, we separated the births in this period into births that occurred in camp from births that occurred after the mother left camp. Three quarters (170.5) of the births among those in the 20–24 age group took place while the women were in camps. Similarly, the age-specific birth rates of the same age group in the early resettlement years (1946–49) were a little higher (228.3/1,000) than the national level in 1950 (196.6/1,000). The fertility experiences of those in the older age group of 25–29 years are similar, except during the war years when the small number of older women had a somewhat lower birth rate than U.S. women.

It was during the prime baby-boom years, 1950–59, that the birth rates of the younger group of incarcerees peaked, but at levels slightly lower than the national figures for the same time period. In contrast, during the same period the older incarcerees not only had somewhat lower age-specific birth rates (181.5/1,000) than the rates for the comparable national group (197.4/1,000), their rates also declined compared to the high of 197.5 births per 1,000 incarceree women during the early resettlement period of 1946–49. By the 1960s, the incarceree women were beginning to reduce their childbearing, similar to women in the larger society.

Given the small sample sizes in the incarceree age groupings, caution should be exercised in generalizing our findings. That said, overall, we find no evidence that the incarceration lowered the age-specific fertility of Nisei women during the years of the incarceration and early resettlement (1946–49). It is possible that the incarceration had a delayed effect that ultimately suppressed somewhat the total number of children incarceree women bore.

Timing of Children

Another potentially interesting way to look at the fertility history of incarcerated Nisei women is to examine the timing of their children's births. In table 6.7, we present data on the mother's age when she had each of her

Table 6.7. Median Age of Mother
by Live Birth Order, U.S. and Incarceree Sample

				Live Birth Order			
	1	*2*	*3*	*4*	*5*	*6–7*	*8+*
1940							
U.S.	23.2	25.6	27.4	29.0	30.9	33.1	37.7
Incarceree, married							
Before camp	24.0	27.0	32.0	34.0	—	—	—
Number of cases	16	13	9	4	0	0	0
During camp	23.0	26.0	28.0	33.0	32.5	32.0[1]	—
Number of cases	7	7	7	5	2	1	0
1950							
U.S.	22.5	25.3	27.6	29.2	30.7	32.6	36.7
Incarceree, married							
After camp	25.0	27.0	30.0	32.0	33.0	35.5	—
Number of cases	53	52	38	19	7	2	0
1960							
U.S.	21.8	24.0	26.6	28.5	29.8	31.6	35.0

Source: U.S. Department of Health and Human Services, National Center for Health Statistics,
  Vital Statistics of the United States, vol. 1, *Natality* (Hyattsville, Md., 2000).
[1] The age at which the one respondent in this category had her child.

children for both formerly incarcerated women and U.S. women generally.
When we compare the age at which women, nationally and in the incarceree sample, started their childbearing, several interesting findings emerge.[4]
In general, incarceree mothers who were married before or during camp
were approximately the same age as U.S. women when they had their first
child. For example, U.S. mothers in 1940 had their first child at a median
age of 23.2 years. The incarceree mothers who were married before they
were evicted had their first child, on average, at 24.0 years. Those who married while in camp had their first child at a median age of 23.0 years, an age
very similar to the 1940 U.S. norm.

On the other hand, Nisei women who married after the incarceration
had their first child substantially later than U.S. women generally (National
Center for Health Statistics figures, 2000). Figures for U.S. women indicate
that in 1950 the first child was born when the mothers were a median age

of 22.5 years old. In contrast, incarceree women who got married after they left camp had their first child when they were substantially older, a median age of 25.0. Generally, incarceree women who married before camp had their first child when they were slightly older than U.S. women and "spread out" their subsequent childbearing more. After the war, during resettlement, women incarcerees had their first child at a significantly older age in comparison to both Nisei women who married during the prewar period and the U.S. population.

Resources, Marriage, and Childbearing

A related area that we wanted to explore was the effect of resources on the timing of marriage and childbearing. The general literature has shown that education delays women's age at marriage and childbearing (Bianchi and Spain 1986, 70–72, 123–28; Rindfuss, Morgan, and Swicegood 1984; Rindfuss and Sweet 1977, 33–43, 65–71). Would this relationship hold for the Denshō respondents? We were also interested in whether an incarceree's family of origin's socioeconomic status (SES) would influence the timing of marriage and first birth. To examine this, we used father's Total Socioeconomic Index (TSEI) score as a proxy measure for family-of-origin socioeconomic status.

The first OLS (ordinary least squares) regression analysis was run with age at marriage as the criterion variable and TSEI of father's occupation and years of college education as the predictor variables. The second regression analysis utilized the interval between date of marriage and first birth as the criterion variable and age at marriage, father's TSEI score, and college education as predictors.

The number of years of college education completed was associated with a delaying effect on age at marriage only for women who were in the older 23–35 age group when incarcerated (Beta = 0.48; $p < .05$; see table 6.8). Similarly, college education (Beta = 0.65; $p < .05$) was related to delaying the start of childbearing only for this older group of women. Also, the older these women were at marriage, the quicker they started their childbearing (Beta = -0.58; $p < .05$), perhaps in an attempt to compensate for "lost time." There was no detectable effect for family of origin's socioeconomic status, at least as indexed by father's TSEI score. In sum, similar to patterns in the general U.S. population, the marriage and childbearing biographies of women aged 23–35 at the time of their imprisonment were affected by the

Table 6.8. OLS Regression of Age at Marriage
and First Birth Interval on Selected Independent Variables,
Incarceree Women Aged 23–35 at Incarceration

	Age at Marriage Beta (Unstandardized)	First Birth Interval Beta (Unstandardized)
Age at marriage	—	-0.58 (-0.76)*
TSEI score of father's occupation	0.08 (0.05)	0.34 (0.33)
Number of years of college education	0.48 (1.18)*	0.65 (1.96)*
R^2	0.25	0.54
df	2, 16	3, 12
p	0.10	0.05

[a] $p < .10$ *$p < .05$ **$p < .01$ ***$p < .001$ (two-tailed tests)

amount of education that they had attained. For all the incarcerees, it appears that the turmoil associated with the mass removal, incarceration, and resettlement overrode any minor socioeconomic differences.

WHAT'S IN A NAME

> Up until the time I had gone into camp, everyone referred to me with my Japanese name, which was Kimiko. So I was always Kimi-chan, Kimi-chan, and that was okay. But I began to sense that it was because I was Japanese that I was in this camp because I looked around and we're all Japanese. And I think that's when I came to this decision that whenever I get out of here, I'm not gonna be Japanese anymore. At that age, it doesn't make any sense but that's what I decided. I never said anything to anyone but I remember that near the end when we were ready to leave, when people would call me Kimi-chan, I would pretend not to hear them. I could hear them muttering and everything but I wouldn't hear them, and I figured that's the way I'm going to do it. I'm not going to be Kimiko anymore. I'm going to be May because that is my name also. And I never used my name Kimiko after. (May K. Sasaki, denshovh-smay-01-0023)

Another aspect of the family that we explored which should provide an indication of how incarcerees responded to the pressures that engulfed them was the naming of their children. The process that all parents engage in when choosing names for their offspring is, no doubt, a complex one, influenced by numerous historical, social, and psychological factors. For example, in the United States, Lieberson and Mikelson (1995) have discussed the possible influence of the civil rights epoch on the naming of African-American children. Kaul-Seidman (1999) has shown that the names of children in a modern-day Zionist settlement articulate the Jewish identity of their parents. At the same time, unusual first names, according to Levine and Willis (1994), are rated lower than more common ones.

The types of first names that the Issei gave to their Nisei offspring exhibit an interesting pattern.[5] Many Nisei were given Japanese first names, others Western or European ones, even in the same family. One can only speculate about the factors that influenced the Issei, at any particular historical moment, to choose a European instead of a Japanese name. It seems that the perceived likelihood of returning to Japan would be one such factor. This raises interesting questions about whether political events, such as the Ozawa Supreme Court decision in 1922 that reaffirmed the ban on Issei naturalization, increased the propensity of Issei parents to give their children Japanese rather than European names.

During the period when our Nisei survey respondents were having their firstborns, specifically the 1930s through the 1960s, epic changes were taking place for Japanese Americans as well as the country as a whole. The period began with the dominant racial ideology of ethnocentric "Anglo-conformity" (e.g., Gordon 1964, 85). By the 1960s, racial minorities, particularly the better educated, were taking a more self-confident, assertive stance. It might be surmised that these changes would somehow be reflected in the naming of children. Since virtually all Sansei children were given Western or European first names, we decided to examine the middle names of firstborn children. It is quite common for Sansei to have European and Japanese middle names. Thus, we attempted to detect any systematic changes in the ethnicity of these middle names over time. It was assumed that the choice of such a middle name would reflect, among other things, a desire to accentuate or downplay one's Japanese, as contrasted with American, identity.

As can be seen in table 6.9, if one divides the relevant period into three eras, prewar and incarceration (up to and including 1945), resettlement (1946–65), and "civil rights" (post-1965), there is a striking shift in the ethnicity of middle names given to firstborn Sansei children. Prior to World War II

Table 6.9. Middle Names of Firstborn by Time Periods of Birth

	Child Born		
	Pre-war/ Incarceration	Resettlement (After Camp to 1965)	Civil Rights Era Post-1965
Middle name			
Percent English (n)	20.0 (5)	70.3 (64)	40.0 (10) ***
Percent Japanese(n)	80.0 (20)	29.7 (27)	60.0 (15)
Number of cases	25	91	25

***Name differences are significant at the $p < .001$ level (two-tailed test).

and during the incarceration, 20 out of 25 (80%) of the children were given Japanese middle names. However, during the resettlement years, there was a marked shift to European names, 64 out of 91 (70.3%). Finally, there appears to be a modest swing back to a preference for Japanese names after the mid-1960s, 15 out of 25 (60%). These "period" differences were statistically reliable ($\chi^2 = 23.33$ [2 & 141], $p < .001$).

Why did these changes in name preferences occur when they did? Our interpretation is that prior to and during the war, the Nisei were clear about their Japanese identity, were less self-conscious about it, and had it more strongly reinforced by their day-to-day existence in a largely segregated ethnic community. During resettlement, after the degradation of the incarceration, it is likely that parents wanted to avoid any stigma potentially associated with a Japanese name being attached to their children. This can be seen as generally consistent with Levine and Willis's (1994) finding that unusual names are rated lower. Most Nisei parents were probably highly concerned that their children be able to "fit into" their new, oftentimes non-Japanese social world. After all, they themselves were very vigilant about the reactions of others to their "Japaneseness" during this period. The following two visual history narrators, the first a parent and the second a child during resettlement, describe their feelings during this epoch.

I really felt, and I think others have said the same, that our experience during World War II was so painful and so humiliating that without our discussing it with each other, most of us decided to raise our children as, as if they were white. Don't talk about what happened during World War II. In fact, don't even talk about Japanese culture. We could eat rice and we could go to Buddhist church and all, but tread lightly and keep all this other stuff away. (Chizuko Norton, denshovh-nchizuko-01-0039)

I know some kids had a tough time, with having their, with having their friends come over and meet their parents because they felt their parents were so different, so (they) tended not to have kids come over or, or to be embarrassed if their kids were doing something that, or if their parents are doing something that didn't seem very American. And I don't know if I ever really had that feeling, but at the same time, I know a lot of people did. But I know I had that feeling about myself that I wished I was, that I was not Japanese. (Frank Kitamoto, denshovh-kfrank-01-0029)

With the subsequent advent of the civil rights movement and its Asian-American component in the 1960s, the worldview of many Nisei parents started to shift. Many began to feel a type of ethnic pride that was difficult to imagine a little over a decade earlier, during resettlement. A new perspective evolved which emphasized preserving their seemingly rapidly dissipating Japanese American culture and community as much as possible for future generations.

SUMMARY

Overall, our data suggest that the Seattle male and to some extent the female Nisei, specifically those who were college-aged (18–22 years) at the time of their incarceration, married at a substantially older age than they would have if there had been no mass incarceration. If their marital ages are compared with national norms, the college-aged Nisei married markedly later than the general population. None of the 26 males who were in this life-stage group married before or while they were incarcerated. They also married somewhat later than the older Nisei who married before the incarceration. Moreover, if these college-aged Nisei were being influenced by the prevailing societal trend of earlier marriages during the baby-boom era, then these young Nisei should have married sooner, not later, than the older Nisei cohort.

The fact that the median age at marriage of the young Nisei was so old after the war suggests that their marriage plans were delayed by the turmoil

of the incarceration and resettlement. It is likely that the burden of reestab-
lishing their and their family's economic and social stability fell heavily on
this initially unmarried group during the resettlement. The Issei fathers of
these young adult men were in a very weak position to spearhead the family's economic and social recovery, given that their ethnic social networks
were either disorganized or otherwise weakened and their language skills
were inadequate for most well-paying, mainstream jobs.

The college-aged Nisei women also faced similar marriage delays, albeit
not as long as the males. The disruption of the community networks that
had previously aided in finding suitable matches and the need to care for
their Issei parents were likely burdens for these women. Consistent with this,
if a college-aged (at incarceration) Nisei woman was not married when she
left camp, she married when she was older and started her childbearing some
two and a half years later than the average U.S. woman. Thus, overall, for
both the younger male and female Nisei, the wartime experience delayed
their marriages and the start of their childbearing period.

The sharp increase in giving their firstborn children European instead of
Japanese middle names during the resettlement period strongly suggests that
the Nisei wanted to strengthen the American identity of their Sansei children.
Further, it was probably seen as useful in helping their children unobtrusively
meld into the larger society. This sentiment was likely the product of the Nisei's
own struggle during resettlement not to draw attention to themselves and to
the perceived differences that had caused them so much hardship in the immediately preceding war years. Nonetheless, within two decades, most Nisei had
achieved economic stability and were, to a large degree, comfortably assimilated into mainstream American society. Thus, with the rise of the civil rights
and Asian American movements, there was a shift back to giving Japanese
middle names to the Sansei, this time in an apparent attempt to preserve what
was perceived as a weakening cultural identity among Japanese Americans.

SEVEN

Occupational Patterns

I don't think people got up in the morning and said, "Gee, what am I gonna do to hold down the Japs?" But some way they told you in so many unwritten ways that, "Just stay in your place, just do your thing, and don't make waves, and you'll be okay." And by and large the majority of the Nikkei said, "Well, okay, and that's fine." (Tomio Moriguchi, denshovh-mtomio-01-0016)

As we have seen in previous chapters, the momentous events associated with the mass removal and its aftermath created major discontinuities in the life-course trajectories of our Seattle-area Nisei respondents. In this chapter we explore how these shifts may have impacted the former incarcerees with respect to a key lifestyle determinant in advanced capitalist societies, that of occupational attainment (e.g., Blau and Duncan 1967). We also examine how incarcerees, now approaching the end of their lives, make sense of the impact of wartime events on their career trajectories.

As with any major social upheaval, the incarceration had different consequences for individuals depending upon a person's specific location in the social structure (e.g., Rosow 1978). For example, if one examines the impact of World War II generally, most people were negatively affected, as would be expected. However, the range of outcomes individuals experienced was very wide (e.g., Mayer 1988; Rosow 1978). Some Americans, such as those who worked in industries essential to the war effort, did well. For instance, since foodstuffs were critical for the war effort, many Puget Sound agricultural interests profited from the forced sale of Japanese American farms and crops in the spring of 1942 (cf. Daniels 1993, 47–48; Commission on Wartime Relocation and Internment of Civilians 1997, 69). Another example of an occupational sector that benefited would be construction firms, such as Del Webb and Morrison-Knudsen, that made large sums building the War Relocation Authority (WRA) camps on a cost-plus basis for the federal government (Burton et al. 1999, 205; Finnerty 1991, 40–43). In the specific case of Japanese Americans and the incarceration, since there were few wealthy individuals before the war and the incarceration experience itself was quite similar for most individuals, their range of outcomes was "flattened."

CHALLENGES AND OPPORTUNITIES

Economic Dislocation

As discussed in chapter 3, one unsurprising consequence of the mass removal and incarceration was that the families of our Nisei respondents generally experienced major economic setbacks. If they were old enough to own a store or small farm, they had to sell their equipment, merchandise, and crops for whatever the market would bear. Those who decided to keep their real property ran the risk of vandalism as well as losing it due to forfeiture for unpaid taxes.

If Nisei were still students, not only were their Issei parents and therefore their own resources damaged, but also their education was, at a minimum, temporarily disrupted. Certainly, the quality of instruction in the "assembly centers" was subpar, as it was provided by the incarcerees themselves using very makeshift facilities. Even in the "permanent" WRA camps, the facilities were generally crude, and equipment, such as that needed for chemistry classes, was nonexistent. The instructors varied widely in quality. Sometimes they were not even certified teachers but fellow incarcerees who were trying to fill in as best as possible. Thus, for those respondents who had significant prewar resources, the incarceration was a major setback. For those still in school, their education was interrupted and the quality of their educational experience significantly degraded in many instances.

Economic Opportunities

Occasionally one hears the following rather different perspective expressed in the contemporary Japanese American community. As noted in chapter 5, some former incarcerees credit the events of World War II with forcing them out of their "isolated and cliquish" ethnic communities and exposing them to a much wider array of opportunities in the larger society. One narrator stated:

> The evacuation forced some of the Japanese populations in the three states of Washington, Oregon and California to seek an opportunity to go elsewhere after they were released from camp. For those people that wanted to go elsewhere, or for those that didn't want to come back for various personal reasons. And it gave the people of the United States, other citizens, a chance to find out, some part of what happened, and gave us opportunities to explore other fields of work besides farming and fruit stands, and gardening. So, in that respect I think it was a great opportunity to explore bigger and better horizons. (Toshio Ito, denshovh-htokio_g-01-0046)

Thus, for some, forced exposure to different job opportunities combined with unprecedented postwar economic expansion produced the perception that the net effect of wartime events was, at least occupationally, positive.

OCCUPATIONAL TRAJECTORIES OF DENSHŌ NISEI

Current Socioeconomic Characteristics of Former Incarcerees

Consistent with what has been frequently observed about the postwar "success" of Japanese Americans, our Seattle-area Nisei respondents scored quite high on current socioeconomic measures. With regard to education, some 34.4% have completed four or more years of college (see table 7.1). Men were three times more likely than women to have earned a college degree. For both genders combined, 41.5% were professionals. Among men, 55.4% were professionals, and among women, 26.2% were professionals. As would be expected given the difference in educational attainment, men were over twice as likely to hold prestigious jobs, such as executive or engineer.

For a summary quantitative measure of the socioeconomic status of respondents' occupations, we again employed the Total Socioeconomic Index score (TSEI; Hauser and Warren 1997). Given the greater educational attain-

Table 7.1. Socioeconomic Characteristics of Respondents

Socioeconomic Characteristics	All Respondents	Gender	
		Males	*Females*
Years of college education completed (%)			
None	51.1	37.8	64.4***
1–3 years	14.4	13.3	15.6
4 years	20.0	30.0	10.0
5+ years	14.4	18.9	10.0
Number of cases	180	90	90
Occupational sector of last main occupation (%)			
Exec., admin., management	15.3	22.8	7.1***
Engineers and other	8.0	15.2	0.0
Health professionals	6.3	6.5	6.0
Teachers, post-secondary	7.4	6.5	8.3
Librarians, archivists	1.1	0.0	2.4
Social scientists, lawyers	1.7	2.2	1.2
Writers, artists, entertainers	1.7	2.2	1.2
Health technicians	2.8	5.4	0.0
Sales occupations	14.2	12.0	16.7
Admin. support occup., clerical	18.2	2.2	35.7
Protective and other	5.1	4.3	6.6
Farming related	8.9	7.6	8.3
Manual laborers	10.2	13.0	7.1
Number of cases	176	92	84
Socioeconomic Index Score (TSEI) of last main job			
Mean	41.1	46.4	35.2***
SD	15.1	16.1	11.3
Number of cases	176	92	84

[a]$p < .10$ *$p < .05$ **$p < .01$ ***$p < .001$ (two-tailed tests)

ment and higher-prestige jobs that men held, the finding that men had significantly higher TSEI scores ($M = 46.4$) in their last main job than did women ($M = 35.2$, $p < .001$) would be expected. The most common occupations for men were executive and engineer. Women, on the other hand, were most likely to have worked in administrative support or clerical jobs. This latter finding is consistent with those reported for industrial countries in general (Roos 1985).

How Far Have the Former Incarcerees Come?
Intergenerational and Intragenerational Mobility
and Transmission of Resources

Intergenerational mobility. In order to examine patterns of intergenerational mobility in socioeconomic occupational status, we compared the TSEI scores of the respondent's father's job with both the respondent's planned (immediately before World War II) as well as current (or immediately before retirement) jobs. As might be expected, over this particular historical and sociopolitical period, there was substantial upward intergenerational mobility (see table 7.2). Not only did the Nisei respondents expect to go beyond what their fathers had attained occupationally (*M* positive difference = 10.8), they actually, in fact, did achieve more (*M* positive difference = 9.9). Men, relative to their fathers, expected to increase their occupational prestige somewhat more than women, although this effect was not statistically significant. More importantly, when their own achieved contemporary TSEI score is compared with their father's, male former incarcerees increased their score (*M* = 15.4) significantly more than females (*M* = 4.3; *p* < .001). However, it should be noted that we did not have an equivalent measure of the mother's TSEI score. It has been shown that the mother's occupation is more important than the father's in predicting a daughter's attainment (Rosenfeld 1978; Stevens and Boyd 1980). However, during the historical period in which the Nisei grew up, the father's TSEI score was, no doubt, a better predictor of the family's resources than the mother's.

Intragenerational mobility. An interesting intragenerational comparison is whether the former incarcerees' actual career trajectories exceeded or fell short of the aspirations they themselves held at the outbreak of World War II. To answer this question, we compared TSEI scores of the occupations that respondents anticipated they would enter in 1941 (before incarceration) with the scores of their current job (or the job they held immediately before retirement). Somewhat surprisingly, the mean occupational prestige of the job respondents actually attained was similar to that of their planned occupation (see table 7.2). Thus, our respondents, as a group, ultimately attained an occupational level similar to that which they had anticipated before their incarceration. As discussed in chapter 2, the data showed that they were surprisingly optimistic about their ultimate educational and occupational attainment given the discriminatory barriers they faced at the time.

Table 7.2. Intergenerational and Intragenerational Occupational Mobility

Mobility Measures	All Respondents	Gender	
		Males	*Females*
Difference between fathers' TSEI scores and planned occupation TSEI scores			
Mean	10.8	13.1	8.4
SD	16.1	16.1	15.9
Number of cases	76	39	37
Difference between main job TSEI scores and fathers' jobs TSEI scores			
Mean	9.9	15.4	4.3***
SD	16.2	16.6	13.8
Number of cases	165	83	82
Difference between main and planned job TSEI scores			
Mean	0.1	1.7	–1.9
SD	15.0	15.6	14.2
Number of cases	78	43	35

[a] $p < .10$ *$p < .05$ **$p < .01$ ***$p < .001$ (two-tailed tests)

Intergenerational transmission of resources. While the respondents, similar to the U.S. population as a whole during this era, surpassed their fathers in occupational achievements, it is instructive to ask whether there was intergenerational transmission of resources such that those Nisei who came from families with more resources were more upwardly mobile than those from families with fewer resources. That is, did those progeny who had access to more human, social, and financial capital in the family, as indexed by the proxy measure of their father's TSEI score, do better than those who had access to less?

To begin examining this question, we first did a median split on respondents based on their fathers' TSEI score. We then looked at mean differences in respondents' occupational aspirations as indicated by the job they anticipated entering before World War II. The results shown in table 7.3 indicate that there is a trend toward positive intergenerational transmission of aspirations (cf. Blau and Duncan 1967; Hodge 1981; Sewell and Hauser 1976). Respondents whose fathers had higher socioeconomic occupational status (at or above the median split) tended to aspire to higher-status jobs before

Table 7.3. Prewar Resources (Father's Occupational TSEI score)
and TSEI Score of Planned and Realized Jobs

	Mean (SD) Occupational TSEI Score	
	Planned Job	*Main Job*
Father's TSEI		
Above median (median = 27.6)	45.2 (16.2)[a]	43.4 (15.6)[a]
Number of cases	40	77
At or below median	38.8 (15.9)	39.0 (14.4)
Number of cases	36	88

[a] $p < .10$ *$p < .05$ **$p < .01$ ***$p < .001$ (two-tailed tests)

the war (*M* score = 45.2) when compared to those whose fathers were below
the median (*M* = 38.8, $p < .10$). Moreover, those from families that had
more human, social, and financial capital (at or above the median) did, in
fact, tend to achieve jobs that had higher TSEI scores (*M* = 43.4) than those
with less (below the median) (*M* = 39.0, $p < .10$).

Another way to examine intergenerational mobility is to compare the
specific occupational sectors in which Issei fathers worked with their Nisei
children's actual or "main" job TSEI score. We divided father's occupation
into five categories that ranged from a high of professions to a low of manual labor. As can be seen in table 7.4, in all categories, there was upward
mobility, the strongest being in the service and manual labor sectors ($p < .05$).
Similar to Blau and Duncan (1967), respondents whose fathers were in these
lower-status and farming sectors made the largest relative strides in intergenerational mobility. But, as can be seen by comparing table 7.5 with table
7.6, this pattern of upward mobility is largely limited to men. If one compares the overall gain of women to men, it is strikingly smaller for women,
the mean gain in TSEI score from father to daughter being 4.2. Sons, on the
other hand, had a much larger mean gain of 15.4 ($p < .001$; table 7.2). Moreover, men had fairly uniform gains across the occupational spectrum.
Women, on the other hand, with professional fathers were actually "down-
wardly mobile." Only the four women who were in the manual labor category made substantial gains vis-á-vis their fathers. In studies of the general
population, daughters have been shown to be less likely to "inherit" the
father's occupation than sons (Roos 1985).

Table 7.4. Intergenerational Occupational Mobility (TSEI Score Differences Between Respondent's Realized Job and Father's Job): All Respondents

	Mean[1]	SD	Cases
Father's occupation			
Professional	4.2*	16.4	31
Sales	7.9	17.4	34
Services	16.2	17.9	19
Farming, forestry	9.9	14.1	68
Manual labor	19.6	16.7	12
Entire sample	9.9	16.3	164

[a] $p < .10$ *$p < .05$ **$p < .01$ ***$p < .001$ (two-tailed tests)
[1] Positive sign indicates that respondent's last realized job's TSEI score surpassed father's job TSEI score. Negative sign indicates that the TSEI score of the respondent's last realized job fell short of the TSEI score of father's job.

Table 7.5. Intergenerational Occupational Mobility (Differences in TSEI Scores Between Respondent's Realized Job and Father's Job): Male Respondents

	Mean[1]	SD	Cases
Father's occupation			
Professional	12.5	10.7	15
Sales	11.1	19.2	20
Service	25.2	18.9	9
Farming, forestry	15.8	16.8	31
Manual labor	18.7	13.7	8
Entire sample	15.4	16.6	83

[a] $p < .10$ *$p < .05$ **$p < .01$ ***$p < .001$ (two-tailed tests)
[1] Positive sign indicates that respondent's last realized job TSEI score surpassed father's job TSEI score. Negative sign indicates that the TSEI score of the respondent's last realized job fell short of the TSEI score of the father's job.

Table 7.6. Intergenerational Occupational Mobility (Differences in TSEI Scores Between Respondent's Realized Job and Father's Job): Female Respondents

	Mean[1]	SD	Cases
Father's occupation			
Professional	-3.7**	17.2	16
Sales	3.4	13.9	14
Service	8.1	12.8	10
Farming, forestry	5.1	9.1	37
Manual labor	21.5	23.9	4
Entire sample	4.2	13.9	81

[a] $p < .10$ [*] $p < .05$ [**] $p < .01$ [***] $p < .001$ (two-tailed tests)

[1] Positive sign indicates that respondent's last realized job TSEI score surpassed father's job TSEI score. Negative sign indicates that the TSEI score of the respondent's last realized job fell short of the TSEI score of the father's job.

Table 7.7. Differences Between Occupational Aspirations and Achievement (Differences in TSEI Scores Between Realized and Planned Jobs): All Respondents

	Mean[1]	SD	Cases
Planned job			
Professional	-9.0***	13.7	30
Sales	3.2	11.7	23
Service	7.2	11.7	7
Farming, forestry	3.9	14.3	12
Manual labor	18.2	11.2	6
Entire sample	0.11	15.0	78

[a] $p < .10$ [*] $p < .05$ [**] $p < .01$ [***] $p < .001$ (two-tailed tests)

[1] Positive sign indicates that respondent's last main job TSEI score surpassed respondent's planned job TSEI score. Negative sign indicates that the TSEI score of the respondent's realized job fell short of the TSEI score of the respondent's planned job.

Planned vs. actual attainment. Given that there was a substantial gender difference in intergenerational occupational mobility, we examined whether there was differential mobility for females and males based upon differences in prewar occupational aspirations. Once again, we divided the planned occupation variable into five categories. These ranged from a high of the professions to a low of manual labor (see table 7.7). There was a significant effect such that, for both genders combined, those who had the highest prewar aspirations, namely those who hoped to be professionals, achieved *relatively* less with respect to their final occupational status ($p < .001$). In fact, professional status aspirants did not gain, relatively, as much as did those lower in socioeconomic occupational aspirations. Those who had low aspirations, specifically manual laborers, made the greatest gains from their prewar aspirations to their final attained occupations. This effect was similar for both females and males.

Specific cases. In table 1 in appendix E, we present a detailed list of the planned and actual main jobs of all of our respondents so that the reader can get a sense of what actually happened to specific individuals. Male and female data are presented separately in tables 2 and 3 of appendix E, respectively. Those who aspired to be managers, accountants, chemical engineers, registered nurses, or lawyers did end up in the jobs they had planned. However, among those who entertained high aspirations there were many more who experienced a downward slide. Cases in point are the two respondents who hoped to become electrical engineers but who ended up becoming electric technicians or communications equipment operators, jobs that have substantially lower TSEI scores.

On the other hand, factors such as the dispersion associated with resettlement in conjunction with the postwar economic expansion appear to have provided relatively better opportunities for those who had somewhat more modest occupational aspirations. For example, there were ten individuals who wanted to be in occupations related to sales. Two ended up with sales supervisor jobs in the later stages of their careers; two others became managers of marketing or food and lodging establishments; one finished her career as a special education teacher; the rest went into occupations such as library clerk, bookkeeper, or hairdresser.

Given the family farming background of many former incarcerees, we were especially interested in examining the career paths of the twelve respondents who planned on farming careers before the war. Only two remained in farming. One became an aerospace engineer, while the others went into occupations such as food or lodging manager and sales. The respondent who wanted to be a gardener found work as a sales supervisor. All of these jobs have higher TSEI scores than those of the earlier planned jobs in agriculture.

The upwardly mobile trajectories of those who planned to be skilled laborers is even more striking. Of the two who planned on becoming auto mechanics, one became a manager in the medicine and health sector while the other finished his career as a supervisor in the motor vehicle business. The aircraft mechanic-to-be capped his career as an aerospace engineer. The aspiring heavy equipment mechanic became a trade/industrial teacher, and the dressmaker became a telephone installer. Only the stock handler aspirant actually ended up in his planned calling.

From an overall perspective, one interpretation of these findings is that the incarceration had a leveling effect, lowering the career trajectories of those who had high prewar aspirations and raising the trajectories of those with low aspirations. Almost certainly, the disruptive nature of the event made it more difficult for some of the highly motivated to actualize their goals. This was particularly true for older as compared with younger individuals, as their higher education plans were frequently put on hold. In the case of those who had the lowest aspirations, the disruption and dispersal during resettlement probably served to expose many of them to greater opportunities than they foresaw immediately before the war. During this period, the only jobs that were definitely available were limited to either the small businesses of Japantowns or farming. The high discriminatory barriers that were in place that caused this containment fell quite rapidly during the period beginning with the initial years of resettlement through the era of the civil rights movement.

Gender. We have already seen that women could not capitalize on their family's prewar resources (as indexed by father's TSEI score) as well as men. To further explore potential gender variations in how the incarceration differentially affected males and females, we examined differences in their occupational plans as compared with actual attainment. That is, were there prewar differences in women's as compared with men's aspiration level, and if so, how were they related to their actual occupational attainment over the life course?

Our data again strongly suggest that women were more negatively affected than men with regard to occupational attainment (see tables 7.8 and 7.9). Women with the highest prewar aspirations experienced the largest drop in their "final" TSEI job scores. For example, the 10 women who planned to

Table 7.8. Differences Between Occupational Aspirations
and Achievement (Differences in TSEI Scores Between
Realized and Planned Jobs): Male Respondents

	Mean[1]	SD	Cases
Planned job			
Professional	−5.8*	13.1	20
Sales	7.5	15.6	7
Service	5.7	—	1
Farming, forestry	4.4	15.7	10
Manual labor	17.6	12.4	5
Entire sample	1.7	15.6	43

[a] $p < .10$ *$p < .05$ **$p < .01$ ***$p < .001$ (two-tailed tests)
[1] Positive sign indicates that respondent's last main job TSEI score surpassed respondent's planned job TSEI score. Negative sign indicates that the TSEI score of the respondent's last realized job fell short of the TSEI score of the respondent's planned job.

Table 7.9. Differences Between Occupational Aspirations
and Achievement (Differences in TSEI Scores Between
Realized and Planned Jobs): Female Respondents

	Mean[1]	SD	Cases
Planned job			
Professional	−15.4***	13.2	10
Sales	1.3	9.5	16
Service	7.4	12.8	6
Farming, forestry	1.2	1.7	2
Manual labor	21.5	—	1
Entire sample	−1.9	14.2	35

[a] $p < .10$ *$p < .05$ **$p < .01$ ***$p < .001$ (two-tailed tests)
[1] Positive sign indicates that respondent's last main job TSEI score surpassed respondent's planned job TSEI score. Negative sign indicates that the TSEI score of the respondent's last main job fell short of the TSEI score of the respondent's planned job.

be professionals (table 7.9) experienced a 15.4 point drop from their planned as contrasted with their final, actual TSEI job scores. In the words of one female narrator who had high prewar aspirations:

> First I wanted to go into pre-med and I did take a lot of science courses. . . . And as I said, a lot of GI's came back and it was very difficult at that time to find a slot. Well, they wouldn't accept me and probably if I had stayed on and taken another year—'cause this was after three years I applied— possibly I would have gotten into a medical school, but I think that it would have meant another four years for my parents too, not only me, but my parents. And I thought with the education that I did have, that I could convert it to a teaching degree, so I did. I got a liberal arts degree in three years, which was not worth much, and then finished up in education. (Rae Takekawa, denshovh-trae-01-0034)

In contrast, there was only a 5.8 point drop for men with similar high aspirations (see table 7.8).

Of the five women who wanted to become registered nurses, only one was able to realize her specific plan (see appendix E, table 3); the others went into occupations such as elementary school teacher, sales worker, and precision production supervisor. The gender difference in the aspirations-achievement discrepancy was less pronounced in the sales sector, even though men still surpassed their aspirations (7.5) more than the women (1.3). It is only in the lower-status sectors, namely service and manual labor, that women did better than men vis-á-vis their aspirations. The six women who ended up becoming secretaries had plans to be in that field (see appendix E, table 3). Two women aspired to be nursing aides. Instead, one became a kindergarten teacher and the second, a hairdresser. The woman who planned to be a maid ended up being a kindergarten teacher. Another example of a somewhat upwardly mobile woman who had low prewar aspirations is the one who planned on becoming a dressmaker but instead became a telephone installer.

RESPONDENTS' PERCEPTIONS OF THE IMPACT OF THE INCARCERATION ON THEIR CAREER PATH

A question that was a major focus of this study is how former incarcerees now assess the impact of the incarceration on their careers. To measure

Table 7.10. Perceptions of Effect of Incarceration on Career Path

	All Respondents	Males	Females
Has incarceration affected career path? (%)			
Increased	19.1	22.6	15.6
Made no difference	41.5	37.6	45.6
Lowered	21.9	20.4	23.3
Can't say/don't know	13.7	12.9	14.4
Other	3.8	6.5	1.1
Number of cases	183	93	90
Describe effect on career path (%)			
Reduced self-confidence	2.0	1.8	2.3
Reduced educational ambitions	1.0	1.8	0.0
Disrupted education	18.8	15.8	22.7
Slowed career	11.9	14.0	9.1
Broadened perspectives	1.0	1.8	0.0
Opened up opportunities	23.8	28.1	18.2
Changed career	12.9	10.5	15.9
Other	28.7	26.3	31.8
Number of cases	101	57	44

whether respondents felt that the incarceration accelerated, made no difference on, or depressed their occupational career trajectory, we designed a closed-ended question that asked, "Now I would like you to specifically think about the career path you possibly would have taken if there had been no World War II and internment. Compare that to the career path that you actually took or experienced. Do you think internment ultimately helped the progression of your career, made no difference, or hindered it?" As seen in table 7.10, perhaps somewhat surprisingly, the largest number of respondents felt that the incarceration made no difference (41.5%). This is probably related in part to the sizable number of respondents who were children and adolescents at the time. Smaller but similar percentages thought it either boosted (19.1%) or depressed (21.9%) their career path. Consistent with the finding of greater occupational mobility among men, a larger percentage of men than women saw the incarceration as having a positive impact on their career trajectory (22.6% vs. 15.6%). Likewise, slightly more women than men felt that the incarceration hurt their career path (23.3% vs. 20.4%).

In order to better understand the rationale behind respondents' feelings

Table 7.11. Perceived Impact of Incarceration
on Career Path by Level of Socioeconomic Index

	Planned Occupation TSEI Score	
	At/below median	*Above median*
Has incarceration affected career path (%)		
Helped	25.6	11.8
Made no difference	51.2	58.8
Hindered	23.3	29.4
Number of cases	37	38

Note: There were no differences in perceived impact by father's self-employment, by median
split on father's occupational TSEI score, by plans for college at the time of incarceration,
and by whether served in the Army or not.

about the effect of the incarceration, we followed up this closed-ended question with an open-ended one. This question asked the respondents to describe the impact of the incarceration on their career path in their own words. We then coded the resultant responses into the eight most frequently mentioned categories (see table 7.10). Overall, on this qualitative measure also, the incarceration had a more negative effect on women's perceptions. Women more often reported that it disrupted their education (22.7% vs. 15.8% for men) and that it changed their career (15.9% vs. 10.5% for men). One female narrator recalled:

> The effect of camp in the long range afterwards, was the fact that it totally interrupted my going to any college for years. Then it was, after that, getting married and raising a family and trying to survive and having to work and so forth. So if it hadn't been for camp, I think I would have gone on to the university and that would have changed my so-called career. It was just merely jobs to earn a salary. So, that's where I feel it affected me most. (Cherry Kinoshita, denshovh-kcherry-01-0011)

Men were also more likely to say that the incarceration opened up opportunities (28.1% vs. 18.2%) but also slowed their careers (14.0% vs. 9.1%).

There was some indication, albeit not statistically reliable, that those who had low prewar occupational aspirations perceived the incarceration as helpful to their careers, while those who had high aspirations viewed it as hindering their careers (see table 7.11). Specifically, more of those who planned on a job at or below the median TSEI score saw the incarceration as helpful compared with those who had planned on a TSEI occupation above the median (25.6% vs. 11.8%). Similarly, a larger percentage of those above the median on planned occupation reported that the incarceration hindered their careers compared with those at or below the median (29.4% vs. 23.3%). Thus, the perceptions of the consequences of the incarceration were largely consistent with the actual gender and occupational aspirations outcomes. These data also confirm that the recall of aspirations was not completely colored by later occupational achievements.

SUMMARY

These findings about occupational choice and mobility add another important chapter to the story of the Seattle Denshō respondents. As shown in chapter 2, prior to the incarceration, youthful Nisei were optimistic about their educational and occupational futures, particularly in light of the barriers they faced at the time. In fact, similar to the general U.S. labor force after World War II (cf. Brodkin 2001), the Nisei experienced upward intergenerational mobility, men significantly more than women. Further, families that had higher prewar levels of financial, human, and social capital had offspring, primarily sons, who subsequently achieved higher levels of socioeconomic occupational status relative to those with fewer resources.

When we examined intragenerational mobility expectations and patterns, particularly comparing prewar aspirations with actual life-course occupational achievements, we found that the incarceration period and its aftermath were associated with more negative effects for two groups of incarcerees. Those who had aspirations for high-status jobs before the incarceration were less likely to be able to actualize their plans in comparison to those who "aimed low." Consistent with this, there was some indication that those who "aimed high" before the war and subsequently did not reach their goal perceived that the incarceration hindered their occupational achievement. Likewise, those who "aimed low" and did somewhat better were more likely to say that the incarceration helped their careers.

Women incarcerees were the second group that appears to have experienced more negative occupation-related effects over their life course. They achieved less for a given level of financial and social resources in their family of origin than men. Further, the positive differences between their pre-war aspirations and their actual postwar occupational achievements were much smaller than for men. Not surprisingly, more women than men reported that the incarceration had negative consequences for their lifetime career trajectory.

What are some plausible explanations for these findings? It is probable that some of the gender differences are due to the fact that Nisei women were more likely to have sacrificed educational goals to either help their aging parents after the war, or in the case of those in the early stages of raising a family, to bear a disproportionate share of the child-rearing burden. Perhaps an indication of this was the not uncommon practice of married men leaving camp initially alone to get established before calling for their wives and children. Although this pattern was consistent with gender role expectations in the larger American society, particularly during this historical period, it was likely to have been reinforced by Japanese gender ideology that the Issei passed on, to varying degrees, to their Nisei offspring (Matsumoto 1984).

EIGHT

Religion and Making Sense of the Incarceration

We put out a little chorus book. We called it 101 Choruses. And we called our little group, "His Majesty's Envoys." And we had these little books printed—not the music, but just the words—and 101 of them. We circulated to all of the churches and then eventually into the camps. But they're all these little choruses that they sang—"Oh, Wonderful Love," "The Love of God for Me," "It Is Spring Time in My Heart"— these hymns of assurance and joy. Choruses, so they can remember them. And you can just sing them one after the other, you know. And even in the cars, the train that going over to one of these concentration camps, they didn't know what was befalling them. But we would have a good sing-fest in the coach. And it was very therapeutic. I thought it meant so much, just for them to have that very naive and simple faith in God in a time of [an] uneasy, unknown future. (Rev. Paul Nagano, desnhovh-npaul-01-0006)

Since religious beliefs and practices are often invoked during stressful events, we were interested in whether they played a role in how the Denshō respondents reacted to the incarceration. In this chapter, we explore the effects that the two major, broad religious orientations found in the Japanese American community, Buddhism and Protestantism, may have had on how our Nisei respondents responded to, and now recall, their wartime experiences.[1] A caveat is warranted before we proceed. We recognize that there is a great deal of variability in religious beliefs and practices within these categories. However, the Denshō survey instrument only permitted respondents to identify their current, self-identified religious category. It did not inquire about specific religious attitudes and behaviors. Thus, we will be able to examine only the most overarching potential distinctions between the two religious orientations.

JAPANESE AMERICAN RELIGIOUS ORIENTATIONS

The literature on Japanese American religious life is quite modest. A small number of monographs and articles discuss the history and social organization of the major Japanese Buddhist and Christian denominations (e.g., Becker 1990; Bloom 1990; Kashima 1977; Kashima, Miyamoto, and Fugita 2002; Prebish 1979; Prebish and Tanaka 1998; Tuck 1987; Yoo 2000). Thomas (1952) and Thomas and Nishimoto (1946), as part of the Japanese American Evacuation and Resettlement Study (JERS), analyzed behavioral correlates of self-reported religious preferences. Lester Suzuki (1979), a minister who himself preached in the camps, has written one of the only books solely devoted to religion in the camps.

Religious institutions continue to be quite vital in the Japanese American community. In fact, of the many organizations currently found in this ethnic group, churches appear to be the most robust. More Japanese Americans attend ethnic churches than any other formal organizational venue in the community (Fugita and O'Brien 1991, 109). Moreover, similar to many other American religious institutions, Japanese American churches serve a multitude of functions in addition to religious ones. Most provide a wide range of services such as sponsoring and in other ways supporting cultural, youth, athletic, and recreational activities. Consequently, churches are probably the most important institution with respect to maintaining ethnic cohesiveness.

The two major religious denominations in the Japanese American community have always been Buddhism and Protestantism. The majority of the Issei were Jodo Shinshu sect Buddhists (Pure Land) in their native country, although a few brought Christianity with them because of their contact with missionaries (Bloom 1998). Further, a substantial number converted to Christianity, particularly Protestantism, after arriving in the United States. Several Christian denominations actively reached out to the new immigrants and helped them cope with the exigencies of living in a foreign and frequently hostile environment (Kitano 1993). One narrator, who is also a sociologist who has extensively studied Seattle-area Japanese Americans, recalled:

The Christian church . . . was always evangelical in the sense of trying to do missionary work among those who needed it. . . . They do the kind of things, which the Japanese immigrants needed immediately. Namely, they not only save souls, but they save people physically. They would do things for them so that they would be cared for if they got sick. They created Sunday organizations whose groups of people could gather and feel a sense of friendship and intimacy and social support which they were otherwise lacking and particularly, they would create employment opportunities. They had a name for some of these young men who were sent out to do house-work, they were called "mission boys," and they got started from the missions or churches and were sent for housework from there and there-fore, they were the mission boys who got started working in that fashion. They also taught English, of course. And in the case of women, they, they would teach them sewing and American customs and cooking and what-not. So the Japanese, or the Christian churches functioned to fill a gap, a vacuum, which was created by the fact that the Japanese immigrants didn't have the kind of support group that they were so familiar with back in their own villages and native land. (S. Frank Miyamoto, denshovh-mfrank-01-0014)

With regard to the overall proportion of Buddhists as compared with Protestants, even though determining the precise number is problematic, over one-half of the community were Buddhist at the beginning of World War II (Hayashi 1995, 154; Kashima 1977, 53–54; Thomas 1952, 67–71). The largest number of Japanese American Christians were Methodists (Broom and Kitsuse 1956, 8).

Historical Experiences of Buddhists and Protestants

Before World War II, Buddhists were clearly more marginalized than Protes-tants (Yoo 2000). They were seen by the larger society as "foreign" and more closely tied to Japan. Moreover, Buddhism was often confused with state Shintoism, which was being used by the Japanese government to instill nationalism in its citizens during the 1930s (Bloom 1998; Duncan 1999). With the attack on Pearl Harbor, Buddhist priests, even in Hawaii where there was no mass incarceration, were immediately rounded up and interned. This was not the case with Christian ministers, the majority of who were not singled out for removal by government authorities but were subsequently excluded from the West Coast several months later, together with their parishioners.

Overall, Christian churches were the most important agencies mediating between the incarcerees and the larger white society (Broom and Kitsuse 1956, 2). Most of their headquarters were supportive of their Japanese American members, although they did not strongly protest the incarceration. In Terminal Island near Los Angeles, the first area that Japanese Americans were forced to vacate, the Baptist Church was active in aiding community members who were given only a panic-producing forty-eight hours to pack up and leave (Yamamoto 1998). More generally, when an area was vacated, both Buddhist temples and Christian churches served as warehouses for household goods and other possessions left behind. Most West Coast Buddhist temples and some Christian churches suffered from vandalism and theft during the incarceration period.

While in the camps, Christians generally had access to their religious leaders, unlike Buddhists. There were over a hundred Christian ministers spread throughout the ten War Relocation Authority (WRA) camps. Buddhists priests, on the other hand, were usually able to rejoin their parishioners only after the latter had been in camp for several months. Some were never able to leave the Department of Justice internment camps and reunite with their former temple members. Moreover, WRA officials more actively scrutinized Buddhist activities (Seigel 1999). In marked contrast, Christian ministers frequently received supplies and other support from their white allies outside of barbed-wire-surrounded compounds.

> For the ministers in camp, books were given, Christmas gifts were given. Even one piano was brought in and things like that. The denomination was always helping, hymnals, whatever you needed. And they were actually paying [for] it. You know, in camp the professional people were supposed to be paid by, so much. But the denomination said, "Don't take that money. We'll pay you." So they were getting a pretty good salary. But the ministers were saying, "We can't receive this kind of money when others are just receiving only so much." So they limited their salary to whatever the other professionals were getting in camp. But these are some of the ways in which the denomination wanted to say, "No, we're with you. We want to support you every way we can." (Rev. Paul Nagano, denshovh-npaul-01-0010)

Unlike the headquarters of Christian churches, which were essentially unaffected by the war, the Buddhist Mission of North America headquarters was restricted to the Topaz (Utah) "relocation" center, where the majority of Japanese Americans living in San Francisco were sent and where the headquarters of the Buddhist Mission was relocated. Thus, temple board members could only be drawn from those held captive in this particular camp. In 1944, the Buddhist Mission changed its name to the more "American sounding" Buddhist Churches of America.

The work of Dorothy Swaine Thomas and her colleagues in the Japanese American Evacuation and Resettlement Study (Miyamoto 1989; Thomas 1952; Thomas and Nishimoto 1946), which examines religion from a social demographic perspective, points out the differential behavior of Buddhists and Christians during incarceration. Thomas presents quantitative data that relates religion to crucial choices the incarcerees made. One of these was how individuals answered the two so-called "loyalty" questions given during registration. As discussed in chapter 3, these questions in the "Application for Leave Clearance" asked about the respondent's willingness to serve in combat (yes or no) and whether the individual would disavow loyalty to the Emperor of Japan (yes or no).

At Minidoka, the percentage that answered "no-no" to the "loyalty" questions was higher among the Buddhists than Christians and secular individuals (Thomas 1952, 623; Thomas and Nishimoto 1946, 106). This religion-associated difference in percentage of "no-no's" was substantial (over two to one) among Kibei and Issei, but negligible among the rest of the Nisei (Thomas 1952, 623). As noted in chapter 2, many Issei and Kibei were not only more sympathetic to Japan because of their earlier socialization there but also because of the greater difficulty they experienced being accepted by the larger American society. Additionally, the marginalization that the Kibei experienced at the hands of their more Americanized Nisei peers probably made it easier for them to take what was generally seen as an unpopular and "unpatriotic" stance. Thus, Buddhism appears to have had a different relationship to wartime political protest among the Issei and Kibei than among the more assimilated Nisei. One narrator notes:

The Kibei in the rest of the Japanese American community weren't exactly seen upon with kind eyes. And so they were really kind of floating around out there in this society, and society at that point, their own community didn't necessarily trust them, certainly the outside world didn't trust them. And I'm not quite sure what their response would have been going back to Japan because my assumption would be they would come back and they don't have any stake in Japan at that point, they don't have any place to go, and they're, for all intents and purposes, American from their point of view. So I would think that the Kibei were under tremendous pressure just to find where they fit in all of this. (Hiroshi Nakano, denshovh-nyaeko-g-01-0011)

Religion was also related to the manner in which Japanese Americans were treated in the military. The Army did not validate Buddhism as it did Christianity. For example, in the widely praised 100th Infantry Battalion and 442nd Regimental Combat Team, there were no Buddhist chaplains who served with the unit in Europe, even though Buddhism was the religion of the majority of the soldiers. The graves of Buddhist soldiers were generally marked with Christian crosses. It was not until 1989 that Buddhist services were finally held for these men in France (Bloom 1990).

Even after they left the camps, Buddhists, as compared with Christians, frequently had a different experience. When several thousand Nisei college students relocated out of the camps to the Midwest and East to continue their education, money was, not surprisingly, a major concern of many. However, since the bulk of scholarship funds came from thirteen Christian churches, the majority of the scholarships (74 percent) went to Christian students (Seigel 1999). Even during the resettlement period, Buddhists in "new" areas such as Chicago tried to make their religious activities as inconspicuous as possible, as they felt scrutinized by government authorities and the larger community (Kashima 1977, 63; Saiki and Takemoto 1999). On the other hand, many of the community-based committees formed to help the resettlers adjust to their new homes in the Midwest and East were made up of Christian church representatives. Thus, the majority of evidence suggests that Buddhists had a more difficult experience prior to World War II, during the incarceration, and in the period immediately after they left the camps.

Acculturation and Assimilation Differences Associated with Religion

Thomas (1952) and Miyamoto (1989) argue that Christian Japanese Americans were more acculturated and assimilated than Buddhists, at least through the incarceration period. As pointed out earlier in this chapter in the quotation by S. Frank Miyamoto, when the Issei immigrants arrived in the United

States, many Protestant churches provided helpful social welfare services; previously, family and village had provided these in Japan. Although the Japanese Christian churches had ethnic congregations, they continued to have contact with European Americans, given that the Issei churches were embedded in larger white institutions. Further, unlike Buddhists, the Japanese Christians were exposed in their everyday church activities to prominent cultural elements of the larger society, such as the celebration of Christmas and Easter. One Protestant minister who preached in Seattle noted:

> There were two things I think, particularly, that were responsible for many of the Buddhists becoming Christians. One is they associated Christianity with the West, or Christianity with the dominant society. So they felt that to become Americanized, it'd be to their advantage to become Christian. The other was the fact that they're in a new land, and in order to assimilate with the people, they felt that the study of [the] Bible as an English language would be the best entrance. And with the study of the Bible, which is initiated by the Protestant churches mostly, they naturally became part of the church and became Christians. (Rev. Paul Nagano, denshovh-npaul-01-0001)

Another Nisei narrator recalled the early outreach activities of the Baptist Church:

> I remember when we were still living on Seventh Avenue South, one day a white lady came. Well, I had never seen one because we lived among the Japanese only, in the middle of Japantown at that time. And here appeared a white lady that said, "Do you have any children here who'd like to go to day school?"—you know, nursery school, or kindergarten. So my mother was so happy because she had five of us at that time. The Japanese Baptist Church was just kitty-corner then on Washington Street, between our place and the Nippon Kan. And this lady turned out to be a graduate of the Baptist Missionary Training School in Chicago. And her first missionary field was with the Japanese. So she was going to start this nursery school. And we all went. And I remember, too, holding onto her hand while she went up and down Japantown, way down to Jackson Street, to King Street. There were people still living on Dearborn, way down on Dearborn. She gathered up these children, and we'd take all of them to the nursery school. So that's how, despite the fact that my mother was a Zen Buddhist priest's daughter and a Buddhist, so was my father, they were very happy that the Japanese

Baptist Church was going to take care of their children. . . . So that's how I became a Baptist. (Shigeko Uno, denshovh-ushigeko-01-0003)

In marked contrast to the substantial number of Japanese who converted to Protestantism, very few European Americans ever stepped into a Buddhist temple during the pre–World War II era.

These factors likely increased the identification of Christians (as compared to Buddhists) with American society. As a consequence, Thomas (1952) suggests that Christians and secularists were more "outside oriented" (to American society at large) during the period when they were incarcerated. However, a complicating issue is whether this stronger assimilation is more appropriately conceptualized as an "independent or intervening variable" with respect to the relationship between religion and accommodative behavior. Over the years, did those who became Christians do so because they wanted to assimilate, or were they drawn into Christian churches because of, for example, the instrumental help and social support offered, and subsequently exposed to assimilation pressures? The answer is probably that some combination of the two processes was operative, one stronger for certain individuals than others. Nonetheless, if the net result is that Christians (at least as compared with Buddhists) more tenaciously identified with the larger society and its political ideology regarding civil liberties, then they may have more keenly felt the injustice and rejection that the incarceration represented.

Different Interpretive Frameworks of Buddhists and Christians

Perhaps a third general way that religiosity has influenced Japanese Americans' feelings about their "camp experience" is through its functioning as an interpretive frame which subtly shapes the meaning of the experience. Given the impossibility of even cursorily discussing Buddhist/Christian differences along these lines due to the heterogeneity and inherent complexities in the two religious denominations, the following is intended to be suggestive only. Further, it might be argued that some of the variations discussed more broadly reflect Eastern as compared with Western perspectives rather than Buddhist/Christian differences.

A number of writers have suggested that Buddhism relative to Christianity is more subjective and inward looking (e.g., Kramer and Tanaka 1990). Groth-Marnat (1992) states that "Buddhism, probably more than any other belief system, emphasizes that people are responsible for their condition"

(p. 276) and "Buddhist cultures teach a sense of internal control, detachment, and acceptance of life events, including death itself" (p. 278). According to the Buddhist tradition, it is when the ego attempts to prevent change and clings to transient periods of happiness that suffering occurs. This suffering can be stopped through nonattachment, a state that requires commitment and discipline to achieve.

> There's a concept, a teaching in Buddhism called non-attachment. It is that bad things happen, and often they happen to me and my loved ones. But to be attached to it, get angry, want revenge or, or something to right it, many—even many years later, is quite self-defeating, because in a way you're causing your own suffering by attaching to it. And instead, look back to the present, live in the present and move on. (Tuck 1987, 244)

On the other hand, Protestantism, viewed broadly, places a greater emphasis on faith and divine force. A personal savior who determines the individual's existence in the present life and in a believed-in future life after death guides the ego. The following are illustrative quotes from two Protestant Japanese American ministers. The first comments about his faith during his exclusion from Terminal Island, and the second speaks about the Christian incarcerees' situation in the WRA camps.

> After listening to the Gospel message for several Sundays, I came to the realization that I needed this Savior and Guide to pilot my life through the treacherous days ahead. (Baba 1998, 10)

> Surprisingly, from the depths of our quagmire our resurrection followed through the grace of God and our faith in Jesus Christ. (Asai 1998, 5)

Protestants and Buddhists appear to emphasize different processes to explain the human condition. Musick (1996) points out that negative outcomes are often viewed as punishment for sin in Protestantism, at least in its conservative denominations. Brock (1996) describes the Protestant paradigm thusly:

> The human condition is defined as a state of sin, which is a state of rebellion against the will of an all-powerful and all good personal divine being. Humans are to blame for this condition because we are born to it and continually succumb consciously to its force. The penalty for this condition is

to be judged by God and to face punishment for our evil. The threat of punishment is alleviated by God's love through which salvation is offered to those who accept it. The sequence goes sin-blame-judgment-punishment-grace-salvation. (183–84)

On the other hand, she describes Buddhism and more generally the Asian religious paradigm as follows:

The human condition is suffering which arises because of ignorance. Ignorance causes us to fix on reality as static when it is actually a ceaseless interdependent process of mutual co-creation. Ignorance can be overcome through concerted efforts by spiritual seekers in a community dedicated to overcoming it through insight and wisdom. Through wisdom, compassion for suffering arises in the seeker. Wisdom and compassion help to relieve suffering. Hence, the sequence is ignorance-suffering-effort-insight-compassion-wisdom. (184)

Thus, both Buddhism and Protestantism broadly assert that the individual has responsibility for the human condition. Protestants understand the human condition in relation to a personal God, while Buddhists see themselves as more conditioned by the multitude of forces in the world and thus experience their responsibility for it in a more diffuse and indirect way (Becker 1990).

Perhaps of particular importance for an understanding of attitudes toward the incarceration is the Buddhist paradigm's suggestion that an individual's claim to fairness must be judged relative to the greater good viewed in the context of the interconnectedness and interdependencies found in the world. Specifically, Jodo Shinshu Buddhism de-emphasizes the self and stresses a more transitory, interconnected existential ethos (Kramer and Tanaka 1990). This might suggest less perseveration about those situations where one's individual rights have been violated. It also tends to encourage acceptance of life as it is and the compassionate acceptance of oneself and others (Imamura 1998).

On the other hand, Protestantism stresses more the importance of working in the world to realize the "kingdom of God." For example, African American religion, beginning with the time of slavery and the abolitionist movement and continuing into the era of the civil rights movement and Martin Luther King, used Christian theological language and the social gospel to deal with unjust suffering (Baer and Singer 1992). In the view of one writer,

Protestants deal with adversity by "forging what they perceive as dynamic, problem-solving partnerships with a divine other" (Ellison 1993, 1031).

DENSHŌ SURVEY DATA ON RELIGION

Methodological Issues

Religion. Religion, the primary independent variable in the present analysis, was indexed with a self-report measure of current affiliation. It is probable that some respondents changed religious identification, most likely from Buddhism to Christianity, during the postwar period. Nonetheless, since we are most interested in current reconstructions of the incarceration experience, present religious orientation is the most relevant measure. This is not to argue that, among those who changed religions, their earlier religion has no effect on their present views. For the most part, though, to the extent that some changed their religious affiliation, it would probably reduce the likelihood of finding statistical differences between the two groups. We focused on Buddhists and Protestants; the small number of Catholics and those other than Buddhists and Protestants were eliminated from the analysis.[2]

Of the 183 respondents interviewed, 120 (66%) self-identified as either Buddhists or Protestants. In this subsample, the 66 Protestants (55%) slightly outnumbered the 54 Buddhists (45%; see table 8.1). The remainder of the analyses in this chapter is based on these 120 Protestants and Buddhists.

Ethnic community involvement and assimilation. Two measures of current embeddedness in the ethnic community, similar to those previously employed (e.g., Fugita and O'Brien 1991, 104–16), were used as additional independent variables. They were the number of Japanese American organizations to which the respondent belonged (range 0–12) and the number of Japanese Americans among the respondent's three closest friends (range 0–3). Also, two indicators of current assimilation, the first a proxy, were used. They were education and formal organizational ties with the wider community. Education, although likely to have complex effects, was generally expected to socialize individuals into mainstream norms. It was operationalized as the respondents' total number of years of college education (range 0–8). Current ties with the wider community were indexed by the number of memberships in non-Japanese organizations (range 0–10).

As has been demonstrated in earlier chapters, these Seattle-area Nisei

Table 8.1. Descriptive Statistics of Buddhists and Protestant Incarcerees

| | | Religion | |
| | | | |
Variables	Total	Buddhists	Protestants
Religion (%)			
Buddhists	45.0		
Protestants	55.0		
Number of cases	120		
Demographic Characteristics			
Gender (%)			
Female	47.5	53.7	42.4
Male	52.5	46.3	57.6
Number of cases	120	54	66
Age at incarceration (%)			
5-11	21.4	24.5	18.8
12-17	26.5	26.4	26.6
18-22	28.2	26.4	29.7
23-35	23.9	22.6	25.0
Number of cases	117	53	64
Community Ties—Japanese			
Number of Japanese friends			
Mean *(SD)*	2.5 (0.9)	2.6 (0.8)	2.4 (0.9)
Range	0–3	0–3	0–3
Number of cases	120	54	66
Number of memberships in Japanese– American organizations			
Mean *(SD)*	2.0 (1.8)	2.0 (1.4)	2.1 (2.1)
Range	0–12	0–7	0–12
Number of cases	119	54	65
Current Assimilation			
Number of years of college education			
Mean *(SD)*	2.1 (2.4)	1.4 (2.0)	2.6 (2.5)**
Range	0–8	0–6	0–8
Number of cases	119	54	65
Number of memberships in non-Japanese American organizations			
Mean *(SD)*	1.3 (1.9)	0.8 (1.3)	1.7 (2.2)**
Range	0–10	0–6	0–9
Number of cases	119	54	65

[a] $p < .10$ *$p < .05$ **$p < .01$ ***$p < .001$ (two-tailed tests)

had dense ties to the Japanese American community. One question asked how many Japanese Americans were among the respondent's three closest friends, and the mean on this was 2.5. In addition, the former incarcerees belonged to, on average, approximately two Japanese American organizations. In contrast, the typical respondent belonged to only one non-Japanese organization. Also, they had two years of college education on average (see table 8.1).

On our two indicators of current assimilation, the Protestant respondents were more assimilated than Buddhists. Protestants were better educated ($M =$ 2.6 years of college education) than Buddhists ($M = 1.4$ years, $p < .01$). The average Protestant also belonged to one additional non-Japanese American organization ($M = 1.7$) than the average Buddhist ($M = 0.8$, $p < .01$). However, the two religious groups did not differ with respect to their membership in specific types of Japanese American or non–Japanese American organizations (political, economic, veterans, civic, or social). The exception was church membership. One hundred percent of the Buddhists belonged to a Japanese American church, as compared with 71.4% of the Protestants. There was a slightly larger percentage of females among the Buddhists; males somewhat outnumbered females among the Protestants. Protestants were slightly older, on average, than Buddhists. Both groups had a similar number of informal and formal ties to the Japanese American community.

Age and gender. The demographic variables of age when incarcerated and gender (males = 52.5%; females = 47.5%) were examined because of their likely association with different wartime experiences and perspectives. The four life-stage age groupings that were employed in previous chapters and shown to be related to numerous outcomes were utilized: Children between 5 and 11 years of age (21.4%); those who were adolescents between 12 and 17 years (26.5%); those of college age between 18 and 22 years (28.2%); and those who were young adults 23 to 35 years of age (23.9%).

Responses to incarceration. We utilized three dependent variables that measured different aspects of our respondents' current reactions to and perceptions of their incarceration. These three have been previously employed to examine other issues, particularly in chapter 3. The first was the measure of respondent's overall evaluation of their years in camp, which was a Likert scale whose values ranged from 1 to 7, with higher scores representing a more positive evaluation. Specifically, the question asked, "If the very worst years of your life were given a score of 1 and the very best years a score of 7, what score would you give your camp years?"

Two other dependent measures were used that were intended to help better understand our respondents' particular perspectives of the incarceration. The first was an item previously employed in the UCLA-based Japanese American Research Project (Levine and Rhodes 1981). It asked which of two types of camp leaders respondents *now* feel employed the better of two approaches. Respondents could indicate a preference for a leader who "worked to make evacuation and incarceration as orderly and comfortable as possible," or for a leader who "protested the injustice of the relocation and tried to have it declared unconstitutional." Responses to this question were intended to measure whether individuals currently feel that accommodating to the hardships associated with the incarceration was more important than protesting the injustice of it, or the reverse.

For the sample of Buddhists and Protestants, the respondents had a mean score of 3.3 on the evaluation of camp experience measure (range 1–6; see table 8.2). Taken as a whole, these respondents were thus currently neither strongly positive nor strongly negative about their camp experience, similar to the entire sample. However, Buddhists recalled their incarceration experience substantially less negatively ($M = 3.9$) than Protestants ($M = 2.9$, $p < .001$).

On the question that asked which leadership style respondents *now* feel was the most appropriate for a camp leader, overall 50.8% of the former incarcerees preferred the "orderly and comfortable" leader, 30.0% gave a neutral, ambivalent, or "don't know" response, and 19.2% chose the protest-oriented leader. When preferred leadership style was cross-tabulated with religious orientation, 57.4% of Buddhists preferred the "orderly" leader as contrasted with 45.5% of Protestants ($p < .001$). Thirty-seven percent of Buddhists selected the neutral, ambivalent, or "don't know" category as compared with 24.2% of Protestants. Most interestingly, only 5.6% of Buddhists chose the "protest" leader as compared with 30.3% of Protestants ($p < .01$).

The third dependent, behaviorally oriented variable asked respondents to indicate whether they had participated in the redress movement that resulted in the passage of the Civil Liberties Act of 1988. Specifically, we asked our Seattle-area Nisei how many of six types of redress activities they had engaged in (contributed money; wrote, telephoned, or telegraphed a politician; visited a politician; joined a redress organization; contacted media;

Table 8.2. Perspectives on Incarceration

| | Total | Religion | |
		Buddhists	Protestants
Evaluation of camp years			
Mean (SD)	3.3 (1.3)	3.9 (1.1)	2.9 (1.3)***
Range	1–6	1–6	1–6
Number of cases	120	54	66
Better camp leadership style? (%)			
Orderly	50.8	57.4	45.5**
Neutral/both	30.0	37.0	24.2
Protest	19.2	5.6	30.3
Number of cases	120	54	66
Number of redress activities (%)			
None	35.0	44.4	27.3*
One activity	35.8	37.0	34.8
2–5 activities	29.2	18.5	37.9
Number of cases	120	54	66

[a] $p < .10$ *$p < .05$ **$p < .01$ ***$p < .001$ (two-tailed tests)

something else). This measure was meant to provide some indication of the individual's desire, at the time of the movement, to redress their incarceration and was likely to be influenced by the respondent's involvement in the Japanese American community, particularly its formal organizations. Those who were involved in such networks are more likely to have been exposed to information about redress activities and to have been in contact with individuals favorable to the passage of redress legislation. As can be seen in table 8.2, Protestants were significantly more active than Buddhists. Forty-four and four-tenths percent of Buddhists did not actively support the redress movement as compared with 27.3% of Protestants ($p < .05$). Further, among those who were the most active (engaged in 2–5 redress activities), Protestants were substantially better represented than Buddhists (37.9% vs. 18.5%).

Regression analyses of incarceration experience. In order to assess, in a less confounded manner, Buddhists' and Protestants' evaluation of their camp experience, an OLS (ordinary least squares) regression analysis was conducted. The criterion variable was the evaluation of camp experience score, and the

Table 8.3. OLS Regression Analyses of Camp Evaluation Score

	Camp Evaluation Score	
Variable	*Model 1*	*Model 2*
Religion:		
Buddhist or Protestant	0.39/1.03***	0.33/0.88***
Age at incarceration		
5–11 versus other		0.38/1.23***
12–17 versus other		0.33/1.00***
18–22 versus other		0.25/0.74**
Gender: Female or male		0.11/0.28
Years of college education		-0.22/-0.12*
Number of memberships in non–Japanese American organizations		0.21/0.15*
Number of Japanese American friends		0.13/0.20
Number of memberships in Japanese American organizations		0.03/0.02
Constant	2.86***	1.60***
R^2	0.15	0.32
df	1, 116	9, 108
p	0.001	0.001

[a] $p < .10$ *$p < .05$ **$p < .01$ ***$p < .001$ (two-tailed tests)

Notes: OLS regression estimates: Standardized Beta/Unstandardized coefficient.

Camp score: Evaluation of camp experience on a scale of 1 (worst years) to 7 (best years).

Religion: Buddhists (coded 1) and Protestants (coded = 0).

Age at incarceration: Three dummy variables: 5–11, 12–17, 18–22, with 23–35 as the reference category.

Gender: Female (coded 1) and male (coded = 0).

primary predictor variable was whether the respondents were Buddhist or Protestant. As can be seen in model 1 of table 8.3, when the religion variable was entered by itself, the resultant Beta of .39 ($p < .001$), was consistent with the finding reported earlier, that Buddhists evaluated their camp experience significantly less negatively than Protestants.

To test for assimilation effects, we entered the two assimilation measures along with the demographic variables, age and gender, in model 2. If the difference between Buddhists and Protestants in their evaluation of their camp experience became nonsignificant after the current assimilation indicators are entered, the significance of assimilation in explaining the differences in attitude toward their incarceration would be supported. A second possibility is that, even after the assimilation and demographic factors are entered into the equation and therefore statistically controlled to some degree, Buddhists would still remember the incarceration less negatively than Protestants. This outcome would lend support to the argument that religious orientation is an important determinant of current perceptions of the incarceration.

Several patterns are worth noting in model 2. First, while the Beta for religion drops (from .39, $p < .001$ in model 1 to .33, $p < .001$ in model 2), Protestants continue to be significantly more negative in their recollection of their camp experience than Buddhists, even when the assimilation measures are entered into the equation. Our two assimilation measures, the college education proxy and membership in non–Japanese American organizations, as well as age at evacuation, were significantly associated with the camp experience score. The more years of education a respondent had, the more negatively the camp experience was perceived (Beta = $-.22$, $p < .05$). Education, no doubt, has complex effects: it probably increases acculturation and contact with non-Japanese and at the same time makes injustices such as the incarceration more salient. On the other hand, membership in non–Japanese American organizations was associated with a less negative evaluation of the camp experience (Beta = .21, $p < .05$). That is, the greater the number of non-Japanese organizations a person currently belonged to, the less negative was their view of their incarceration experience.

The two measures of Japanese American community ties (number of Japanese American friends and membership in Japanese American organizations) had no significant effects on respondents' evaluation of their camp experience. This demonstrates that involvement in ethnic social networks is not a key factor in influencing attitudes about the camp experience.

Age at incarceration was linearly related to the individual's evaluation of their camp experience. Thus, with this sample of only Buddhists and Protestants, we obtained the same results as reported in chapter 3 with the entire sample. The younger the respondents were when they were incarcerated, the less negative was their evaluation of their camp experience. The Beta for the 5–11 age group compared to the three older groups was 0.38 ($p <$

Table 8.4. Logistic Regression Analysis
of Preferred Camp Leadership Style

| | Preferred Camp Leadership Style |
Variable	Model 1
Religion	
Buddhist or Protestant	7.39/2.00**
Age at incarceration	
5–11 versus other	0.21/-1.56[a]
12–17 versus other	0.67/−0.39
18–22 versus other	0.42/−0.86
Gender	
Female or Male	1.09/0.09
Years of college education	1.03/0.03
Number of memberships in non–Japanese American organizations	0.81/-0.22
Number of Japanese American friends	0.85/-0.16
Number of memberships in Japanese American organizations	0.84/-0.18
Number of cases	82
-2 Log Likelihood	78.43
Chi-square	16.95*

[a] $p < .10$ *$p < .05$ **$p < .01$ ***$p < .001$ (two-tailed tests)
Notes: Logistic regression estimates: Exponent of regression coefficient/regression coefficient.
Preferred camp leadership style: Orderly (1) and protest (0).
See Table 8.3 for measurement of independent variables.

.001; model 2). The corresponding Betas for the 12–17 age group were 0.33 ($p < .001$), and for the 18–22 group 0.25 ($p < .01$). The oldest respondents (those in the comparison group) were the most negative.

Regression analysis of preferred leadership style. To further examine the relationship of religion to the respondents' current view about what type of camp leader they now prefer, a logistic regression was run controlling for age, gender, education, membership in non–Japanese American organizations, number of Japanese American friends, and membership in Japanese American organizations. As can be seen in table 8.4, Protestants were seven times more

Table 8.5. OLS Regression Analyses of Redress Activities

| Variable | Redress Activities | |
	Model 1	Model 2
Religion:		
Buddhist or Protestant	-0.21/-0.44*	-0.15/-0.32[a]
Age at incarceration		
5–11 versus other		0.22/0.54*
12–17 versus other		0.26/0.62**
18–22 versus other		0.15 /0.34
Gender:		
Female or Male		-0.10/-0.20
Years of college education		0.13/0.06
Number of memberships in non–Japanese American organizations		0.13/0.07
Number of Japanese American friends		0.08/0.10
Number of memberships in Japanese American organizations		0.19/0.11*
Constant	1.23***	0.23
R^2	0.05	0.22
df	1, 116	9, 108
p	0.05	0.001

[a] $p < .10$ *$p < .05$ **$p < .01$ ***$p < .001$ (two-tailed tests)

Notes: OLS regression estimates. Standardized Beta/unstandardized coefficient.

Redress activities: Number of redress activities ranged from 0 to 5. Activities included: contributed money; wrote, telephoned, or telegraphed a politician; visited a politician; joined a redress organization; and contacted media.

See Table 8.3 for measurement of independent variables.

likely than Buddhists ($p < .01$) to prefer the protest-oriented leader, even after controlling for age, gender, assimilation, and ethnic community involvement.

Regression analyses of redress activities. As shown in table 8.5, the religious affiliation differences noted in model 1 ($p < .05$) in involvement in the redress campaign became marginally significant after we introduced the same set of controls as were used in the two previous regression analyses. Specifically, controlling for age and number of memberships in Japanese American organizations reduced the previously significant difference between Buddhists and Protestants in the number of redress activities in which they had participated to a nonsignificant trend ($p < .10$). The two youngest age groups (Beta for the 5–11 age group = .22, $p < .05$; Beta for the 12–17 age group = .26, $p < .01$) were more involved in redress activities than the 18–22 and the 23–35 age groups. This is probably the result of the more vigorous societal involvement of the younger cohorts in the redress movement (who were in their mid-fifties to mid-sixties in the 1980s, when the majority of Japanese Americans became involved). The significant effect for memberships in Japanese American organizations (Beta = .19, $p < .05$) suggests that involvement in formal ethnic social networks supported the mobilization of individuals in the redress movement.[3]

SUMMARY

Our findings clearly suggest that the contemporary religious orientation of former Japanese American incarcerees is related to differing retrospective views of their World War II incarceration. Specifically, even though the Buddhists were more marginalized by the larger society than were Protestants before, during, and immediately after the war, they remember their incarceration as a significantly less negative period in their lives than do Protestants. Moreover, they have a more accommodative and less protest-oriented perspective toward the experience, as indicated by the type of camp leader they currently favor. Finally, Buddhists were somewhat less active than Protestants in the social movement to redress the injustice of their wartime treatment.

The Protestants' more negative feeling about their incarceration initially appears to be consistent with the Thomas thesis that they are still more "outside-oriented" or identified with American society and thus feel more aggrieved about their unconstitutional treatment. But the fact that significant religious differences remain even after taking into account the proxy assimilation measures of college education and involvement in non-Japanese American organizations suggests that variations in assimilation do not fully explain the contemporary differences between Buddhists and Protestants on this dimension.

The findings on the type of camp leader preferred and redress activity measures might also be interpreted as consistent with the expectation that Protestants remain more assimilation-oriented and strongly identified with

American ideology. Protestants had a greater preference for camp leaders who protested the injustice of the incarceration than did Buddhists. Moreover, the greater number of redress activities engaged in by Protestants is consistent with the view that they felt a stronger need than Buddhists to redress the failures in the political system that victimized them. However, similar to the findings about the negativity of their recollection of their camp experience, controlling for the assimilation measures did not eliminate the religion-based differences in camp leader preferences and redress activities. Overall, assimilation differences thus do not seem to be able to entirely account for the differences between Protestants and Buddhists. Given the "mainstreaming" of Buddhism that has taken place after the war, it seems likely that the acculturation and assimilation differences that previously existed between Buddhists and Protestants have now become quite small or nonexistent.

There were strong ethnic friendship as well as organizational ties among both the Protestant and Buddhist respondents. Given the restriction of range in the two variables, it is not surprising that these measures of ethnic community involvement did not mediate religious differences in perspectives about the incarceration.

While these findings are intriguing, several caveats bear repeating. Our index of religious orientation, a single, self-report measure of current affiliation, should be expanded with other measures to begin to more fully elucidate the heterogeneity and complex dynamics of religion. Additional indicators of the nature and depth of individuals' religious commitment as well as other measures of the impact of the incarceration that index different consequences are needed.

Although there are other plausible interpretations that we are not able to rule out because of the limitations of our measures, we conclude that the findings are most consistent with the view that the nature of the Buddhist interpretive framework produces a greater retrospective acceptance of the incarceration or at least a less negative view of it. Buddhists may recall their incarceration experiences less negatively because they more strongly emphasize a life-as-it-is perspective and a compassionate acceptance of the role of others and themselves in the World War II tragedy. The fact that Buddhists were less active in the redress movement and more strongly endorsed camp leaders who worked to make camp life more orderly and comfortable rather than protested the injustice of it appears consistent with this perspective.

NINE

Looking Back

Our examination of the lives of Seattle-area Nisei who were the vic-
tims of the most serious violation of constitutional rights in modern
U.S. history has taken us down numerous paths. Some of the study's findings
provide the first systematic evidence that substantiate anecdotal observations
frequently made by the former incarcerees themselves. Others shed new light
on the less visible, long-term sequelae of the exclusion, detainment, and
resettlement. A substantial number of the latter have neither been widely
discussed in the ethnic community nor reported in the scholarly literature.
In this final chapter, we highlight the most important of these empirical
findings and explore their broader analytic implications.

COMMUNITY

As we looked back over our study's findings, one of the themes that continually emerged as central to understanding the lives of the former incarcerees was that of community. When we began this research, we approached
our task as an investigation of how a calamitous event may have altered the
life courses and worldviews of members of a specific ethnic group. But,
regardless of whether we reviewed the efforts of the Issei pioneers attempting to cope with the New World or the recent drive to secure redress for
the incarceration, we were struck by the significance of the ethnic community in the lives of the majority of the respondents.

Certainly, the nature of the Japanese American community has changed markedly over the several historical periods that the Denshō respondents' lives have traversed. Its dominant characteristics and functions have necessarily been transformed as new social, political, and economic challenges have confronted Japanese Americans. One notable shift is that our respondents' generation, the Nisei, became the dominant force in the community at the beginning of World War II. Not surprisingly, their much greater level of acculturation, as compared to the Issei, led to fundamental changes in the community and its relationship to the larger society. More specifically, their particular prewar and wartime experiences have shaped the kind of community that they rebuilt during resettlement and have subsequently maintained. The Nisei have now reached the point in their collective life courses where their numbers have begun to dwindle and their influence in the community is less all-encompassing. Nonetheless, the World War II incarceration, which is such a pivotal experience in their lives, still casts a long shadow over them and, to a lesser degree, the younger members of the ethnic community.

In order to more clearly comprehend how the lives of the respondents have been impacted by the incarceration, we need to appreciate the changing dynamics of the ethnic community in which they were immersed. To guide us in this process, we propose the following five-phase model of the development of the Japanese American community. This model builds upon the work of Miyamoto (1984, 9–15) and others and is generally supported by our survey findings as well as the broader historical record.

Five stages in the evolution of the community. The first stage of community development began when male laborers from Japan started to immigrate to the mainland United States around 1890. They created bachelor-dominated, frontier-type ethnic enclaves in many Pacific Coast cities and agricultural towns. Due to pressure from the states in which these were located to choke off this immigration, the federal government entered into a "gentlemen's agreement" with Japan in 1907–8 that excluded male laborers but inadvertently allowed an influx of "picture brides." This produced a much more balanced gender ratio in the ethnic enclaves, which changed the character of the community. It signaled the beginning of the second phase of community development. This phase, which started in the early 1920s and extended through the 1930s, was much more settled and family-oriented.

Critically, as discussed in chapter 2, additional female and subsequent child labor made profitable many marginal farms and small businesses, which became the economic backbone of the community. Further, many of these small enterprises became linked to form an ethnic economy (e.g., Miyamoto 1984, 16–28; Modell 1977, 94–126) such that their collective interests were enhanced.

The outbreak of World War II marked the beginning of the third phase in the development of the community. The sudden uprooting and incarceration destroyed the extensive social and economic organizations that the Issei had developed. New social arrangements tentatively emerged during the mass removal and incarceration; some were transitory, and others were more permanent. An example of the latter is the previously noted abrupt and awkward shift in leadership from the Issei to the young, inexperienced Nisei.

The fourth phase of the community began with the release of the incarcerees during the latter stages of the war and in the years that immediately followed, i.e., the so-called resettlement period. Here, the community faced yet another set of structural, social, and psychological pressures. Not only did the government authorities discourage the re-creation of prewar informal and formal ethnic community institutions, but because of their wartime treatment, initially there was also doubt among many Japanese Americans themselves about whether such institutions should be encouraged. The Nisei's predominant orientation was to keep a "low profile" and draw as little attention to their ethnicity as possible as they concentrated on rebuilding their lives. Nonetheless, the Nisei ultimately reestablished the community for a number of compelling reasons, albeit it was in many ways a different one from that created by their Issei parents.

The fifth and last conceptually distinct phase of community development was signified by the rise of the civil rights movement and its Asian-American corollary and the push for redress. For most Japanese Americans, this era started in the late 1960s. The central characteristics of this period were a more assertive political posture, enduring community networks, continuing assimilation, and upward socioeconomic mobility.

Our labels for these periods and their approximate boundary years are: (1) Bachelor Frontier: 1890–1910; (2) Family and Community Development: 1910–42; (3) Expulsion and Incarceration: 1942–45; (4) Resettlement and Rebuilding: 1945–65; (5) Redress and Asian-American Politics: 1965 to the present.

NISEI BEFORE THE WAR:
FAMILY AND COMMUNITY DEVELOPMENT

High Aspirations. The central focus of our study has been on the Nisei who experienced the upheaval of the incarceration. Their biographies began during the Family and Community Development period of Japanese American history (1910–42). Our survey data documented that the Nisei youth growing up during this period had very high educational and occupational aspirations prior to their incarceration. Before the exclusion, among those who were 14–18 years of age when they were incarcerated, a substantial proportion (35%) planned on attending college (46% of males and 25% of females). Only 20% had decided to work or not attend college. Forty-six percent in this age group said that they were either too young to have made a decision about attending college or had not been able to make a decision by the outbreak of the war. Thus, among those who had made a decision about attending college, almost twice as many were planning on attending an institution of higher education as compared with those who had decided against it.

When the entire Denshō sample was queried about their prewar occupational plans, there was again evidence of high aspirations. Overall, more than a third (35%) reported that they had professional aspirations. The health professions were the preferred occupation among women, and engineering among men. Given the virtually impenetrable barriers that Japanese Americans generally confronted in attempting to land these kinds of "better" jobs in the larger society at the time, these findings suggest that they were optimistic and somewhat insulated from certain realities by the ethnic community. We believe that two major factors were at work to produce these hopeful perspectives.

The first factor that supported the inculcation of high educational and occupational aspirations in the Nisei was their socialization in a cohesive ethnic community that promoted educational and occupational achievement, particularly for males (e.g., Wada 1986–87; Yoo 2000, 17–23). As products of the Meiji restoration and its requirement for universal education, the Issei were advocates of educational achievement. Moreover, the extensive social and institutional networks that characterized the prewar Seattle community reinforced the family's emphasis on education and, in general, protected individuals from the more corrosive effects of discrimination. These networks created social capital by teaching individuals to interact in kin-like fashion and to be able to form and maintain ethnically based interest groups. These skills were to prove invaluable after the war when individuals were required to piece their lives together and rebuild much of the community to deal with new exigencies.

Within this highly prescribed social context, parents put pressure on young Nisei to succeed not only as individuals but also as representatives of the family. Their achievements and proper behavior, or lack thereof, affected the standing of the entire family in the community. In fact, Nisei youth were sometimes quietly or not so quietly admonished not to tarnish the reputation of the entire ethnic group (e.g., Kitano 1976, 44–45: Wada 1986–87). As Caudill and DeVos (1956) have noted, if one uses a simile to compare the "achievement paths" of a prototypical white, middle-class American to that of a young Nisei, the Nisei's was narrower and straighter, with more people on the sidelines evaluating the individual's behavior.

Second, an overwhelming majority (86%) of Seattle Nisei respondents grew up in petite bourgeoisie or small capitalist families. The typical forms of small business that these families toiled in were agriculture or some type of shopkeeping. Previous studies have shown that small capitalist families emphasize education for their children (Bland, Elliot, and Bechofer 1978; Goldscheider and Kobrin 1980). Education was seen by the Issei as the key to unlocking occupational opportunities for their children. Further, the small businesses that the Nisei worked in as they were growing up taught them to appreciate the virtues of hard work and thrift.

Since they themselves labored within the ethnic economy, many Issei were unfamiliar with the specifics of "better" jobs in the larger society. Thus, they were not in a position to provide their Nisei offspring with strategies to deal with the discrimination found in these occupational sectors. Nonetheless, many Nisei youth were much more strongly attracted to "clean" mainstream jobs than to a career working in their parents' labor-intensive farm, fruit stand, hotel, or other similar business. Thus, even though the young Nisei were aware of the de jure and de facto discrimination surrounding them, they apparently were not seriously demoralized about their occupational opportunities in the larger society before the war.

A LIFE-COURSE TURNING POINT: EXPULSION AND THE INCARCERATION

Life-stage at exclusion. Although the sudden mass removal from their Pacific Coast homes and their detention in inland camps disrupted all incarcerees' life-course trajectories, our data suggest that there was great variation in the eventual impact of this disruption. One of the major factors that mediated the incarceration's ultimate legacy was the age or life-stage at which individuals were uprooted. By and large, the younger the age at which the Nisei experienced the incarceration, the less the disorder and negative consequences. Although stressed and not functioning as well as they might have, the family and community generally buffered children and adolescents from the full force of the disruption and attack on their self-concepts. Thus, for many individuals in these age groups, the incarceration was not taxing in ways that left observable, lasting negative legacies. Older Nisei who had started their educational, occupational, and family careers paid the highest price. Not only did the uprooting and displacement force them to cope with onerous economic, social, and psychological challenges as individuals, but they also frequently had to shoulder the additional burden of responsibility for their families and, in many cases, the community at large.

Social ties. One feature of the way the Army evicted families supported the maintenance of community. Families living in various geographic areas were usually evicted together and sent to the same "assembly center" and War Relocation Authority (WRA) camp. Thus, it was easier for individuals to obtain social support and to be able to access other forms of previously developed social capital than if families from a given area had been scattered to different camps.

Moreover, familiar institutions, such as churches that ministered to spiritual needs and baseball leagues that provided adolescent socialization and recreation, were rapidly reorganized, although usually in somewhat altered forms. Evidence from our survey of the importance of these institutions in the lives of incarcerees was the widespread fond recollections of friendships and social activities that the younger respondents reported. Overall, over half of all the Nisei in the sample spontaneously reported that they had positive memories of the friendships they had in camp. Among teenagers this figure rose to almost two-thirds of the respondents. In contrast, only a third of those who were aged twenty-three to thirty-five reported positive recollections of camp friendships. Individuals in this older group also had the highest proportion of individuals (one-third) who said that they had no positive memories of their camp days.

Gender and human capital. On the whole, men were somewhat more negative about their camp years than were women. Specifically, men reported
more psychological difficulties, whereas women were more affected by the
material and social-relational conditions of camp. For both genders, greater
amounts of prewar human capital were associated with more positive social
recollections, such as friendships and social activities. Higher levels of human
capital were positively correlated with higher levels of social capital and, ultimately, with higher levels of socioeconomic attainment.

Nonetheless, those who, at the time of the interview, had achieved higher
levels of education and occupational prestige were also more negative in their
evaluation of their camp years. Apparently, education and socioeconomic
success increased the ability of Seattle-area former incarcerees to critically
evaluate their wartime experiences.

QUIET STRUGGLES: RESETTLEMENT AND REBUILDING

The reentry of Japanese Americans back into the society that had so abruptly
ejected them is clearly a neglected chapter of the incarceration story. It lacks
the drama of political decisions being made by a powerful government determining the fate of a vulnerable minority group. Thus, this period has received
scant attention by historians and social scientists. Nonetheless, in human terms,
our data document that this period posed major challenges for many of the
Denshō respondents.

The resettlement period was very difficult for a number of reasons that
are often not fully appreciated. Not only did the former incarcerees face
obvious economic and career uncertainties, but in many cases they also had
to rebuild their communities, which were critical for their social and emotional adjustment, against opposition on several fronts. In the early days of
resettlement, bureaucratic opposition came from organizations such as the
WRA and well-meaning resettlement committees. Uncertainties created by
extreme racial self-consciousness, a by-product of the incarcerees' wartime
treatment, were also sometimes problematic within the group. Thus, many
resettlers did not want to engage in activities that visibly drew attention to
their ethnicity and the stigma that was associated with the incarceration (e.g.,
Nishi 1998–99).

Most resettlers simply hoped to forget the incarceration and "get on with
their lives." They tacitly agreed not to probe their feelings about the ordeal

they recently experienced, usually going no deeper than mentioning the incredulous or humorous. Kashima (1980) has labeled this group phenomenon to suppress the incarceration experience "social amnesia."

Even though many individuals wanted to meld unobtrusively into the larger society, this was frequently not possible. Although discrimination was markedly reduced from the prewar and wartime periods, it was still prevalent, particularly in its more subtle forms. Finding housing and employment was frequently problematic. Moreover, not only did the Nisei retain their unique interpersonal style (Fugita, Miyamoto, and Kashima 2002; Fugita, Kashima, and Miyamoto 2002; Miyamoto 1986–87), but only other Japanese Americans could relate to the unique complexities of their life experiences. These factors made the rebuilding of the community, along with individual lives, a necessity. Soon after individuals got their families settled and began to stabilize economically, they started to reorganize the athletic leagues, the churches, and the social clubs, and rapidly expanded the number of Japanese American Citizens League (JACL) chapters.

The dispersal. Another direct consequence of the incarceration was the scattering of Japanese Americans geographically. Initially, less than half of the Denshō respondents returned to the state from which they were evicted. More than 40 percent initially resettled outside of the Pacific Coast area. Only a quarter moved directly to where they eventually resettled permanently. When Denshō families subsequently moved, they generally relocated back to the Pacific Coast not only because of the postwar growth of the area, but also because our sample was drawn entirely from the Seattle area. With respect to why people first resettled to particular areas, the two most common rationales given were family (32 percent) and work (20 percent).

"Go east young man, go east." Intriguingly, those who initially moved away from the Pacific Coast when they first left the camps, even though they eventually returned, ultimately attained higher socioeconomic levels than those who returned directly to the Pacific Coast states. It is probable that two processes acted in concert to produce this outcome. First, lower levels of discrimination in the Midwest and East allowed those who initially settled in these regions to secure better jobs than those who returned immediately to the Pacific Coast. Second, we also found that those who had to go to the Midwest or East (very few former incarcerees were attracted to the South) before the West Coast area was reopened at the beginning of 1945

had higher levels of human capital. Thus, those with more resources were more likely to leave camp early and initially resettle in geographic regions where the opportunity structure allowed them to make the most of their human capital.

Women more negatively impacted occupationally. When we examined gender differences, women were overall less able to capitalize on their education to obtain better jobs after the war. They could not take advantage of the more open opportunity structure outside of the Pacific Coast as well as men. Nonetheless, women's prewar aspirations were a better predictor of their ultimate occupational achievement than were men's. Possibly, women who had high aspirations and were strongly achievement-motivated were ultimately able to break through the constraints that held down less motivated women.

Consistent with what actually happened, a greater percentage of women than men saw the incarceration as hurting rather than helping their career. Specifically, women were more likely to report that the incarceration disrupted their education and forced them to change their career. A lower percentage of women than men thought that events associated with the incarceration and resettlement opened up opportunities for them.

Marriage and family. We found strong effects in marriage and family formation that were almost certainly produced by the mass removal and detention. Those who were college-aged at the time they were incarcerated married at an older age. Male incarcerees in this age grouping married substantially later than the national norms and, more significantly, approximately one year later than Nisei males who married before the war. Similarly, college-aged women married substantially later after the war than Nisei women who married before camp. This shift toward delayed marriages took place while national age-at-marriage norms were becoming substantially younger.

Consistent with delayed marriages, women who married after the incarceration started their childbearing a year later than those who married before the incarceration. These delays in two of life's major transitions, marriage and parenthood, were likely produced by the disorderliness and uncertainties created by the incarceration and the subsequent pressing need to become economically and occupationally reestablished during resettlement. Perhaps another factor was that the Nisei's social and the Issei's "go-between" networks, which facilitated establishing social and marital relationships, were disrupted and thus could not aid the process until they were rebuilt.

Strongest memories of resettlement. When we asked respondents what their strongest memories were of the early years of resettlement, the most widespread response was that of facing discrimination (25 percent). Somewhat surprisingly, the second most frequent response was the lack of discrimination (21 percent). Initially these two findings taken together seemed incongruous. The explanation is related to where the former incarcerees first resettled. Upon examining the data more closely, it became apparent that those who initially resettled away from the Pacific Coast states not only were much more likely to report less discrimination, but better living and social conditions as well. The opposite was true for those who returned directly to the Pacific Coast.

The fact that the presence or absence of discrimination was such a salient memory of resettlement suggests that, at the time, the former incarcerees were "hyper vigilant" about their racial identity and acceptance by the larger society. Although ultimately mitigated by their subsequent socioeconomic mobility and generally favorable reception by society, this "sensitivity" probably left an enduring mark on them as well as their children, who were born and raised during this era. When many of these Sansei children matured, they felt a strong need to better understand the incarceration and its effect on their family, as their parents were reluctant to talk about it when they were growing up (e.g., Nagata 1993, 75–102). Some groups, such as the Sansei Legacy Project in the San Francisco area, were specifically formed by the children of former incarcerees to explore the effects of the incarceration on the Sansei generation.

CONTEMPORARY LEGACIES: REDRESS AND ASIAN–AMERICAN POLITICS

By the 1960s, the former incarcerees had generally established broadly middle-class lifestyles and numerous active communities. Some cities, such as Gardena, Los Angeles, San Francisco, and San Jose, even had visible Japantowns or ethnic neighborhoods, albeit much smaller than those before the war, with the exception of Gardena. Japanese Americans also began to break into politics in cities such as Gardena where, from a political perspective, they had significant numbers.

The Nisei, now mostly in their thirties and forties, had children who were starting to come of age. The leading edge of the Sansei generation were in colleges and universities. Individuals in this latter generation obtained higher education in even greater numbers than did their Nisei parents, but generally with the same orientation, to acquire the skills to land a "good" job. However, some, particularly on West Coast campuses and at elite Ivy League schools, became part of a concerted push to create a more politically assertive pan-Asian identity. The social ferment of the civil rights and anti–Vietnam War movements energized these young Asian Americans to not only create a new identity, but also to pressure institutions such as universities to become more relevant to their communities. These initiatives, similar to those put forth by other groups of color, led to the creation of Asian American Studies programs on many West Coast campuses (e.g., Umemoto 1989).

Middle names and identity. Our finding of the change in the types of middle names that former incarcerees gave their first-born children reflects the changing nature of Japanese American identity. There was a clear shift from giving first-born children Japanese middle names before and during World War II to English names during resettlement, and a partial return to Japanese middle names during the civil rights era. This pattern suggests that the Nisei had a stronger Japanese identity before and during the war and an abrupt conversion to a more "low profile, attention avoiding" orientation during resettlement. The return to a preference for Japanese middle names during the 1960s and 1970s parallels the shift to a more self-confident, assertive ethnic identity that took place in many American ethnic groups during the era.

The long push for redress. During the early 1970s, a small number of progressive Nisei began pursuing reparations for their losses during the incarceration (e.g., Maki, Kitano, and Berthold 1999, 64–84; Shimabukuro 2001, 15–40). Initially there was substantial resistance from many quarters of the community to attempting to make the very government that had incarcerated them admit wrongdoing. Many were afraid of a backlash, given the recency and tenuousness of their acceptance by the larger society. Others felt that seeking monetary compensation "cheapened" their wartime sacrifices.

There was also conflict over how to seek redress, for example, whether legal or political channels should be pursued (e.g., Hohri 1988, 43–50; Maki, Kitano, and Berthold 1999, 85–91; Tateishi 1991, 191–95). Several broad-based, active grassroots and JACL-related groups emerged. Those in West Coast urban areas, particularly in the earlier years of the effort, were, not surprisingly, much more active and supportive of redress than those in rural areas.

Our analysis of religion showed that Protestants were more active in the redress movement and had a much stronger preference for a protest-oriented camp leader than did Buddhists, at least in the Seattle area. This would seem consistent with our finding that, overall, Buddhists look back at the incarceration less negatively than do Protestants. It may be that this latter finding is attributable to differences in how these faiths interpret negative life events. Additional research that specifically focuses on the many complex social and theological aspects of religion and relates them to the incarceration is needed.

On balance, the process of seeking redress, which involved almost two decades of political work, had a healing effect on the community. It counteracted the stigma many associated with their incarceration by identifying and making salient the relevant political circumstances. It also demonstrated that there was considerable support from numerous segments of the larger society to at least partially rectify what had happened to the incarcerees. The redress effort provided an avenue for individual and collective catharsis. From a political-movement perspective, its ultimate triumph was a major achievement, given the small size of the ethnic group and the fact that it cost the government over $1.25 billion during a time when a major deficit occurred in the federal budget. President Ronald Reagan signed the Civil Liberties Act of 1988, and the first letter of apology was presented and payment made in 1990.

Recent concerns. A current unresolved incarceration controversy within the Japanese American community nationwide centers on the actions of the draft resisters during World War II. The stand that the resisters took, especially the organized resistance at Heart Mountain, continues to stir deep emotions in many because the issues raised by it bear on the very difficult choices the incarcerees made during their incarceration. The resisters' actions pose complex challenges to the way some understand and remember the period. That said, perhaps the most poignant aspect of the story of the small number of draft resisters in the Seattle-area sample is their relationship to the postwar ethnic community. They appeared to have slightly fewer Japanese American best friends, but most strikingly, they belonged to almost no Japanese American organizations. Thus, besides the prison time that many served, they paid a high price for their wartime stand, given their subsequent exclusion from the ethnic community.

THE INCARCERATION, NISEI GENERATION, AND COMMUNITY: SOME FINAL THOUGHTS

Even though the Nisei respondents had their lives severely disrupted by a cataclysmic and stigmatizing event that lasted some three years, by the time they reached retirement age approximately sixty years after the incarceration, many of them had, somewhat amazingly, achieved most of their prewar goals. For both genders combined, approximately one-third had completed a college degree. Men somewhat exceeded their prewar expectations in the area of higher education; women fell somewhat short of their prewar hopes. Overall, the Nisei did very well in the area of educational attainment compared to national norms for their cohort.

With regard to occupational achievement, some 40 percent ultimately achieved professional status (53 percent of men and 25 percent of women). These percentages are also quite similar to their prewar professional aspirations. Not surprisingly, those with more initial human capital tended to achieve more than those with less. However, this effect was largely limited to men, thus suggesting gender biases which probably reflected the then operative social structures and norms of the ethnic community as well as the larger society.

In many ways, the Nisei were well equipped to rebuild their ethnic communities after the war because of their prewar experiences. Their earlier socialization and experiences in vibrant communities gave them a "template" that they could readily employ to form voluntary organizations and create and maintain dense, "quasi-kin" social networks (Miyamoto, Fugita, and Kashima 2002). In many ways the incarceration experience further strengthened the Nisei's prewar bonds with each other by providing a strong, emblematic shared experience. Given the wartime attack on their racial self-concept and resultant "hyper-sensitivity," postwar ethnic institutions provided a needed respite from the demands of dealing with more integrated occupational settings and neighborhoods and acted, similar to before the war, as arenas for personal validation. With minimal discrimination, increased intimate social contact with non-Japanese, and the concomitant escalating "respectability" associated with their rising socioeconomic status, the Nisei have had in recent times many more options with regard to social and community involvement. Nonetheless, as shown by our friendship and ethnic organizational involvement data, the Seattle Nisei are still strongly tied to their fellow Nisei and their Japanese American organizations.

Since the war, Japanese Americans have to a substantial degree been able to assimilate into the larger society while maintaining their ethnic group cohesiveness, unlike most European ethnic groups (Fugita and O'Brien 1991, 178–85). This characteristic has facilitated their rapid postwar socioeconomic mobility by allowing them to draw upon ethnic community resources to help them cope with the larger society. Nonetheless, it is apparent that with the even greater acculturation and structural assimilation of the Sansei and Yonsei (fourth generation), which involves the continuing loss of their Japanese-derived interpersonal style as well as numerous shared experiences, maintaining ethnic cohesiveness in the future will be a serious challenge (cf. Fugita, Miyamoto, and Kashima 2002).

Some speculations about psychological legacies. In the first chapter of this book we stated that we were interested in tracing the socioeconomic and, to the extent possible given the data available to us, the psychological consequences of the incarceration, which are more difficult to capture. Although some of the Denshō survey is relevant to the latter issue, we feel that if we use a somewhat wider lens than we have with the socioeconomic data, some additional insights may emerge. Adopting this approach, among the older Nisei it appears that postwar emotional healing has followed a somewhat different and possibly slower path to recovery than the socioeconomic phenomena we have examined.

In our estimation, the most important root cause of the psychological damage associated with the expulsion and incarceration was the attack on the American identity of the Nisei (e.g., Mass 1991; S. F. Miyamoto, personal communication, June 16, 2002). At the time of exclusion, most Nisei had no effective way to defend against the assault on their self-concept that it represented. Their young leaders did not, and in many ways probably could not, provide a satisfactory symbolic position for them to embrace. After several months of having to adapt to the physical and emotional degradation produced by the incarceration, they again faced another crisis, registration, which crudely thrust the identity issue at them again.

The minority who volunteered for the 442nd Regimental Combat Team and the Military Intelligence Service chose a "head-on" way to cope with this attack on their American identity. They were asserting it in one of the strongest ways possible: wearing the American uniform into combat. Others chose different ways to accommodate or resist. Some of the draft resisters insisted upon the return of their undamaged American identity before they would serve. Still others, such as some of the renunciants (those who renounced their U.S. citizenship), ultimately rejected, in anger and despair, their American identity altogether.

As previously noted, the long-fought battle for redress that ultimately forced the government to admit its wrongdoing was cathartic and cleansing for many. Nonetheless, there are still contemporary signs that the insidious psychological damage has not been completely repaired. The recent heated controversy over the placement of a modified Masaoka quote from the hyper-nationalistic JACL creed written in 1941 on the Japanese American Memorial to Patriotism in Washington, D.C., reflects unresolved tension in the community over the contested meaning of various responses to the incarceration. Likewise, the longstanding but recently much more visible and acerbic struggle between some veterans and draft resisters over the resisters' defiance in 1944 suggests a similar strain. These and other controversies reveal that underneath the surface of their seeming acceptance of Japanese America's responses to government oppression during World War II, there remains, among the Nisei, considerable unresolved tension.

THE FUTURE

Looking beyond the Nisei to the Sansei and Yonsei, it is apparent that more individualistically oriented career and family concerns continue to exert centrifugal pressures on individuals, drawing them away from the ethnic community. Given the much-reduced level of discrimination that the Sansei have experienced along with their more integrated socialization, most of them do not have the same "need" for community as the Nisei.

The resultant decline in participation in such long-standing organizations as the Japanese American Citizens League, some churches, and other community institutions continually causes concern in the community. As the Nisei reach the twilight of their lives, they and those Sansei who grew up enmeshed in rich postwar community networks and institutions are experiencing some angst about the future. As evidence of this, in 1998 and 2000, major conferences to discuss and plan for the future of the Japanese American community were held in Los Angeles ("Ties That Bind") and San Francisco ("Nikkei 2000"). They both attracted several hundred participants.

Given this pattern of change in the community, the ethnic identity and commitment to the community of future generations of Japanese Americans are likely to be based upon narrower political, historical, and cultural preservation interests. For instance, most moderate and large-sized communities (relatively speaking) have historical groups that mount exhibits and collect oral histories about the Nikkei (Japanese descent) experience. These organizations have substantial Sansei involvement. Other examples are groups that come together to socialize the next generation. In many Japanese American communities on the Pacific Coast, there are children's summer cultural groups, organized and supported by the Sansei and Yonsei, which try to pass on Japanese American culture and history. Nonetheless, these later generations' social involvements are less characterized by the dense web of intimate ethnic friendships, extensive family ties, and other quasi-kin relationships, which are characteristic of the Nisei.

Other pressures are transforming the community. Some Nikkei, consistent with Asian American political perspectives that were originally developed during the civil rights era, have become active in broader Asian and Pacific Islander organizations and coalitions (e.g., Espiritu 1992). This has been an effective stratagem to leverage influence, particularly in the political arena. However, due to the recency of immigration (post-1965) of many of the members of these Asian groups and the diversity of interests that they represent, there are limits to which Japanese Americans' needs for community can be merged into the broader Asian American agenda. For most Nisei, community is more about a shared interpersonal style, social sensibilities, cultural practices, and a common experiential history.

Not surprisingly, these various crosscurrents sometimes produce controversial interfaces with other groups. Given the well-organized and supported nature of some Japanese American activities (for example, youth sports leagues), members of both mainstream and other ethnic groups frequently wish to participate in these activities. This has led to a variety of contested policies being generated about who is Japanese American and thus can participate. Two areas where this has been almost universally contested, albeit sometimes in a semi-covert manner, are baseball and basketball leagues and beauty queen contests. King (2002) and Okamura (2002) have shown that both on the mainland and in Hawaii, many community members prefer that these organizations remain predominantly Japanese American. The reasons for this are difficult to articulate and document. The fact that a person can usually participate in these events (but not always) if one is of partial Japanese extraction but not "pure," e.g., Chinese American, suggests that there are limits to the pan-ethnic or Asian American model of community transformation, at least in more "intimate" social contexts.

As previously noted, both inside and outside commentators on the Japanese American community have been concerned about its demise. In some ways, this concern is well placed. Intermarriage continues at a high rate, somewhere in the vicinity of half of all new marriages (e.g., Shinagawa 1994; Lee and Fernandez 1998). On average, out-marriage has been shown to be associated with a reduction in Japanese Americans' involvement in the organizational life of the community (Fugita and O'Brien 1991, 133–36). Although changes in methodology make comparisons difficult, one interpretation of relevant 2000 census data is that the number of people who self-identify as "single-race" Japanese Americans has dropped since 1990. However, this figure does not take into account the many multiracial individuals who claim partial Japanese ancestry.

Unlike other major Asian groups, the influx of Japanese immigrants continues to be a trickle, approximately five thousand per year. The number of Japantowns has dwindled from around forty at the turn of the century to three, all in California. Moreover, the character of the Japantowns or Nihonmachis has been transformed from neighborhoods where people worked and played and spent most of their living time to something more akin to tourist destinations and places to occasionally shop for ethnic goods or to attend an ethnic organization meeting or festival.

In response to these changes, there is currently a thrust to revitalize the community by more broadly conceptualizing and rearticulating who is "Japanese American" (e.g., *Nikkei 2000 Conference: Summary and Analysis* 2001). These newer conceptions of Japanese American are more inclusive and reach out to underrepresented groups (e.g., *hapa* or multiracial persons; *shin* Issei [postwar immigrants]; lesbian, gay, bisexual, transgender, and young Japanese American groups) as a way to stay relevant to contemporary needs yet preserve key institutions and cultural values. If this approach is successful, the Japanese American community will persist well into the twenty-first century, but with a more variegated quality and less of the primary group character of the Nisei community. More specifically, the Japanese American community of the future may consist of a large number of interest groups who are less characterized by the deeply personal and semi-obligatory web of relationships that were the hallmark of the Nisei. Instead, there will likely be more loosely linked ethnic voluntary associations distinguished by specialized interests in which individuals actively choose to participate.

Methodology

General. As noted in chapter 1, the data reported in this book are part of an ongoing effort of Denshō: The Japanese American Legacy Project. This community-based project had its beginning in 1997. As one of its first major efforts, it designed and administered this survey to systematically document the experiences, perceptions, and status of former incarcerees. All of the data were collected in 1997. Denshō has also, as of 2001, videotaped over 110 visual histories and collected over 1,500 historic photographs. These visual histories and photographs, along with a wide variety of other material on the incarceration, have been digitized and made available on the Web site at <www.densho.org>.

Sampling. The site of the study, King County, Washington, has a significant and established Japanese American population. Many of the current residents or their families lived in the county before World War II and returned to the area after the war. According to the 1990 census, there were 21,167 Japanese Americans living in the county at that time.

The first step taken to develop the study's sampling frame was to create a dictionary of Japanese Americans surnames. This was done by obtaining War Relocation Authority records so that a list of all persons incarcerated could be compiled. All duplicate and non-Japanese names were then removed. Next, this name dictionary was used to select all Japanese surnamed individuals from the most current King County voter registration file, maintained by a local political polling firm in Bellevue, Washington, Labels and Lists. The resultant sampling frame consisted of 4,850 Japanese surnamed individuals who were registered voters and were born in 1937 or earlier. The year of birth restriction was placed on the selection of respondents so that only those who were at least five years of age at the time they were incarcerated were drawn. This was done to increase the likelihood that respondents would have at least some memories of the incarceration. A random sample was drawn from this list. As the majority of incarcerees were Nisei who have a low intermarriage rate (approximately 10 percent), the problem of not reaching the out-married, particularly women with non-Japanese surnames, was not as serious as it would have been if younger Japanese Americans were being surveyed.

A known source of error in using voter registries to generate samples is that not all eligible persons register. In studies of the general U.S. population, persons more likely to be registered are better educated, have a higher income, and are more residentially stable (e.g., Teixeira 1992, 33–37). Given the higher socioeconomic status of Japanese Americans compared to the population at large, it is likely that a higher percentage of them will be registered than the general populace.

In order to increase cooperation, a general description of the study was published in local Japanese American vernacular newspapers and organizational newsletters. The selected potential respondents were then sent a letter describing the study and soliciting their cooperation. A telephone coordinator then contacted them, screened them for eligibility and, if the individual was willing to participate, they were scheduled to be administered a survey. The refusal rate was 28 percent. Respondents were individually interviewed in their homes or at the Denshō office near Seattle's International District. The final sample consisted of 183 former incarcerees.

Survey instrument. The survey instrument contained sixty-three questions, many with multiple sections. Both closed and open-ended question formats were utilized. The average administration time was a little over one hour, although there was considerable variation.

Moves During Resettlement

Appendix B (1). First Moved to the Pacific Coast

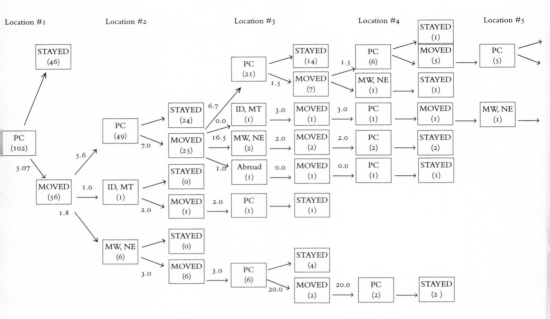

Note: Numbers in the boxes are number of respondents; numbers on the arrows are mean number of years respondents stayed in location before moving (presented up to location 4 due to
the small number of cases in later moves).
PC = Pacific Coast; MW, NE = Midwest or Northeast; ID, MT = Idaho or Montana;
Abroad = Japan, Korea, or Vietnam.

Appendix B (1). First Moved to the Pacific Coast *(cont'd)*

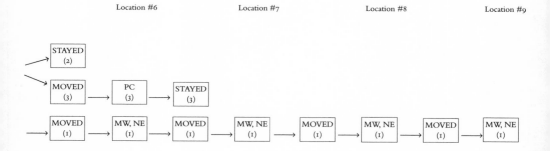

Appendix B (2). First Moved to the Midwest/Northeast after War

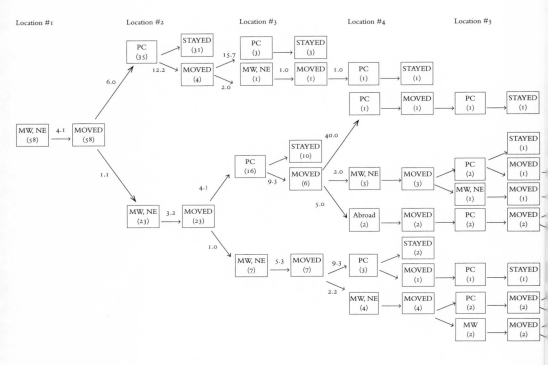

Note: Numbers in the boxes are number of respondents; numbers on the arrows are mean
number of years respondents stayed in location before moving (presented up to location 4
due to the small number of cases in later moves).
PC = Pacific Coast; MW, NE = Midwest or Northeast; ID, MT = Idaho or Montana;
Abroad = Japan, Korea, or Vietnam.

Appendix B (2). First Moved to the Midwest/Northeast after War *(cont'd)*

Location #6   Location #7   Location #8   Location #9

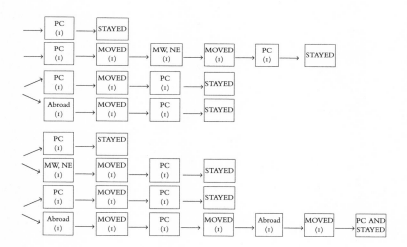

Appendix B (3). First Moved to Idaho/Montana

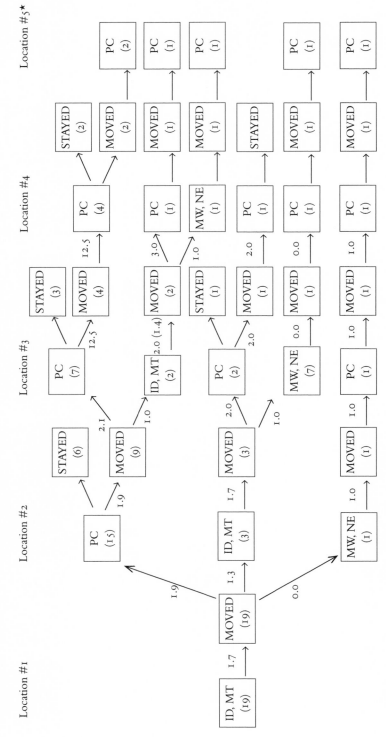

Note: Numbers in the boxes are the number of respondents; numbers on the arrows are mean number of years respondents stayed in location before moving (presented up to location 4 due to the small number of cases in later moves).

PC=Pacific Coast; MW, NE=Midwest or Northeast; ID, MT=Idaho or Montana

★After arriving at the fifth location, 2 out of 6 respondents stayed in the PC, the other 4 moved within the PC, except for 1 who moved to the Midwest in the ninth move.

Appendix B (4). First Moved Abroad (Japan, Korea, Vietnam)

Location #1   Location #2   Location #3   Location #4   Location #5   Location #6

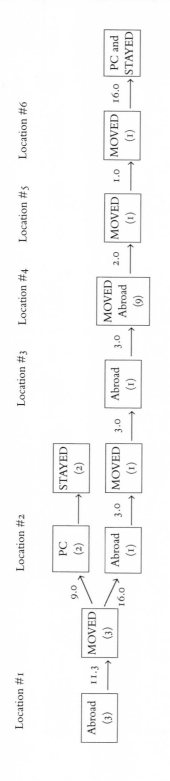

Note: Numbers in the boxes are the number of respondents; numbers on the arrows are mean number of years respondents stayed in location before moving. Abroad = Japan, Korea, or Vietnam.

Technical Note
on Fertility Rate Computations

The dates for the different life events of Denshō respondents were recorded using two formats: (a) the date format in SPSS (day/month/year, which SPSS internally represents as indicating the number of seconds from the fixed date of October 14, 1582, the start of the Gregorian calendar); (b) a numerical value for the year (1942 or 42). When a date is stored using the date format, it is possible to extract the year, month, or day from a particular date using the xdate.year (or xdate.month or xdate.mday respectively) function. In the instances when two dates were stored in the year format (for example, as 1942), we used the years as recorded.

The following examples are provided for illustrative purposes. To compute whether a child was born before, during, or after the mother left camp (table 6.6), we used the dates the mother entered and left camp and the year each child was born. The dates of entry into and departure from camp were recorded using the date function, while children's birth dates were recorded in years. To make the two sets of camp-related dates comparable to the children's birth dates, we extracted the year from the camp dates. Each child was then categorized as having been born before camp if the child's birth year came prior to the year the mother entered camp. Children categorized as being born while the mother was in camp were born between the mother's entry into camp and departure from camp. Dates when the mothers left camp were used as the marker for children coded as being born after camp.

Another example is the calculation of age-specific fertility rates for the different time periods. As noted in table 6.6, age-specific birth rates are the number of births in a given time period per 1,000 women in specified age groups. Using their age at the time of the interview, we estimated how old the women would have been if they were living in, say, 1942. This enabled us to count the number of women who were, for example, 20–24 years old in 1942. Next, we counted the number of births (using the children's birth years) during 1942–45 to women who were 20–24 in 1942. The age-specific fertility rate of the 20–24 age group for 1942–45 is then expressed as the ratio of the number of births in 1942–45 to women in the 20–24 age group divided by the number of women in that age group. In order to make the data comparable to the national age-specific rates that are presented for individual years, we averaged the Denshō rate over the relevant time periods.

A final example is the age of the mother when she had her first child and computation of birth intervals. Subtracting the mother's birth year (recorded as the actual year) from the year in which child x was born (recorded as actual year) produces the age of the mother at the birth of child x. This computation was repeated for each child. The interval between marriage and first birth was computed as the difference between year of marriage (extracted from the marriage date stored in the date format) and the year of birth of the first child. The spacing between subsequent children (e.g., the first and second child) is represented by the difference in years between the year of birth of each set of subsequent children.

APPENDIX D

Table 1. Age-Specific Birth Rates for Women
in the Incarceree Sample and United States

Age	15–19	20–24	25–29	30–34	35–39	40–44	45–49
Incarceree Women							
1931–41	75.8	121.2					
Number of cases	6	6					
1942–45	32.5	227.3	107.3	0.0	250.0		
Births in camp	NA[a]	170.5	71.5	0.0	250.0		
Births after camp	NA	56.8	35.8	0.0	0.0		
Number of cases	23	22	7	6	1		
1946–49	31.3	228.3	197.5	83.3	41.8		
Number of cases	16	23	19	6	6		
1950–59	125.0	242.1	181.5	83.3	16.7	20.0	
Number of cases	12	19	27	12	6	5	
1960–75	—	125.0	109.4	36.2	4.6	5.2	0.0
Number of cases	0	1	12	19	27	12	6
U.S. Women							
1940	54.1	135.6	122.8	83.4	46.3	15.6	1.9
1945	51.1	138.9	132.2	100.2	56.9	16.6	1.6
1950	81.6	196.6	166.1	103.7	52.9	15.1	1.2
1955	90.3	241.6	190.2	116.0	58.6	16.1	1.0
1960	89.1	258.1	197.4	112.7	56.2	15.5	0.9
1964	73.1	217.5	178.7	103.4	49.9	13.8	0.8
1965	70.5	195.3	161.6	94.4	46.2	12.8	0.8
1970	68.3	167.8	145.1	73.3	31.7	8.1	0.5
1975	55.6	113.0	108.2	52.3	19.5	4.6	0.3

Source for U.S. Data: U.S. Department of Health and Human Services, National Center for
Health Statistics, *Vital Statistics of the United States,* vol. 1, *Natality* (Hyattsville, Md., 2000).
Note: Birth rates are live births per 1,000 women in specified age group.
[a] The three children born to 15–19 age group during 1942–45 had missing data on dates of
birth needed to calculate timing of birth.

Table 1. Planned Job
in 1941 and Last Main Job: All Respondents

Planned Job	Last Main Job
1. *Executive, Administrative, and Managerial Occupations*	
(33.82/17[a]) Managers, food serving and lodging estabs. ($n = 1$)	(47.60/22) Managers and administrators
(53.79/23) Accountant and auditors ($n = 1$)	(45.83/21) Managers, service organizations
(43.33/33) Purchasing agents and buyers, n.e.c.[b] ($n = 1$)	(49.99/413) Supervisor, firefighting and prevention
2. *Engineers, Architects, and Other Professionals*	
(69.92/48) Chemical engineer ($n = 1$)	(69.92/48) Chemical engineer
(66.55/55) Electrical and electronic engineer ($n = 2$)	(46.84/213) Electric technician
	(34.39/353) Communications equipment operator
(62.42/57) Mechanical engineer ($n = 1$)	(47.60/22) Managers and administrators
(64.56/59) Engineer, n.e.c. ($n = 5$)	(50.77/5) Administrators, public administration
	(62.25/43) Architect
	(71.48/44) Aeorospace engineer
	(64.09/157) Teacher, secondary school
	(46.84/213) Electrical and electronic technician
(80.53/84) Physician ($n = 1$)	(71.48/44) Aerospace engineer
3. *Health-related professionals*	
(61.07/95) Registered nurse ($n = 5$)	(61.07/95) Registered nurse
	(60.08/156) Teacher, elementary school
	(31.16/268) Sales worker, hardware and building supplies

(continued)

223

Table 1. *(continued)*

Planned Job	Last Main Job
	(36.11/268) Supervisor, precision production occupations
	(NA/909) Not employed since 1984
(65.06/96) Pharmacist (*n* = 3)	(65.06/96) Pharmacists (*n* = 2)
	(30.30/313) Secretary
(39.65/97) Dietician (*n* = 1)	(NA/909) Not employed since 1984
4. *Teachers, post-secondary*	
(61.80/125) Sociology teacher (*n* =1)	(61.80/125) Sociology teacher
(64.09/157) Teacher, secondary school (*n* = 2)	(47.60/22) Manager and administrators, *n.e.c.*
	(38.51/243) Supervisor, sales occupations
(47.04/159) Teachers, *n.e.c.* (*n* = 1)	(65.06/96) Pharmacist
5. *Librarians and archivists*	
6. *Social scientists, lawyers, judges*	
(48.34/174) Social worker (*n* = 1)	(43.51/4) Chief executive and general admin., public admin.
(80.26/178) Lawyer (*n* = 1)	(80.26/178) Lawyer
7. *Writers, artists, entertainers*	
(44.39/188) Painter (*n* = 1)	(27.60/473) Farmer, except horticultural
(43.35/194) Artist (*n* = 1)	(19.29/725) Metal/plastic machine operator
(54.79/195) Editor, reporter (*n* = 2)	(56.49/184) Technical writer
	(33.99/476) Manager, horticultural specialty farms
8. *Health technologists and technicians*	
(38.51/207) Licensed practical nurse (*n* = 1)	(26.73/264) Sales, apparel
(48.40/214) Industrial engineering technician (*n* = 1)	(54.06/148) Trade/industrial teacher
9. *Sales occupations*	
(38.51/243) Supervisor, sales (*n* = 7)	(55.18/13) Manager, marketing
	(33.82/17) Manager, food and lodging
	(50.01/158) Teacher, special education
	(38.51/243) Supervisor, sales (*n* = 2)
	(31.47/329) Library clerk
	(33.01/456) Supervisor, personal service
(45.47/257) Sales occup., other business services (*n* =1)	(38.51/243) Supervisor, sales
(24.87/275) Sales counter clerks (*n* = 1)	(31.06/337) Bookkeeper, accounting clerk
(34.90/277) Street and door-to-door sales workers (*n* =1)	(26.02/458) Hairdresser, cosmetologist
10. *Admin. support, clerical*	
(30.30/313) Secretary (*n* = 9)	(61.07/95) Registered nurse

(30.30/313) Secretary (*n* = 6)
(26.10/469) Personal service occ., *n.e.c.*
(20.30/666) Dressmaker
(42.61/314) Stenographer (*n* = 1) (44.40/185) Designer
(31.06/337) Bookkeeper, accounting (50.77/5) Administrator, public admin.
  clerk (*n* = 3)

(64.09/157) Teacher, secondary school
(31.06/337) Bookkeeper, accounting clerk

11. *Private household service*

12. *Protective and other services*
(24.29/447) Nursing aide (*n* = 2) (36.03/155) Teacher, kindergarten
(26.02/458) Hairdresser and cosmetologist
(13.85/449) Maids and housemen (*n* = 1) (36.03/155) Teacher, kindergarten
(26.02/458) Hairdresser (*n* = 2) (27.07/365) Stock clerk
(45.47/257) Sales, other business

13. *Farming related*
(27.60/473) Farmer, except horticultural (33.82/17) Manager, food and lodging
  (*n* = 10)
(71.48/44) Aerospace engineer
(29.96/274) Sales worker
(27.60/473) Farmer, except horticultural
  (*n* = 3)
(21.30/486) Groundskeeper, gardener (*n* = 2)
(19.41/688) Food batchmaker
(25.27/804) Truck driver
(33.99/476) Manager, horticultural farm (33.99/476) Manager, horticultural farm
  (*n* = 1)
(21.30/486) Groundskeeper, gardener (38.51/243) Supervisor, sales
  (*n* =1)

14. *Forestry and logging*

15. *Fishers, hunters, and trappers*

16. *Manual labor*
(26.16/505) Auto mechanic (*n* = 2) (47.90/15) Manager, medicine and health
(36.66/803) Supervisor, motor vehicle
  operator
(39.72/515) Aircraft mechanic (*n* = 1) (71.48/44) Aerospace engineer
(30.10/516) Heavy equipment mechanic (54.06/148) Trade/industrial teacher
  (*n* = 1)
(20.30/666) Dressmaker (*n* = 1) (41.80/529) Telephone installer, repair
(20.00/877) Stock handler, bagger (*n* = 1) (20.00/877) Stock handler, bagger

17. *Military*
(905) Military, rank not specified (NA/909) Not employed since 1984

---

[a] 1990 TSEI score/U.S. Census code.
[b] Not elsewhere classified.

Table 2. Planned Job in 1941 and Last Main Job: Male Respondents

Planned Job	Last Main Job
1. *Executive, administrative, and managerial occupations*	
(33.82/17[a]) Managers, food serving and lodging estabs. ($n = 1$)	(47.60/22) Managers and administrators
(53.79/23) Accountant and auditors ($n = 1$)	(45.83/21) Managers, service organizations
(43.33/33) Purchasing agents and buyers, *n.e.c.*[b] ($n = 1$)	(49.99/413) Supervisor, firefighting and prevention
2. *Engineers, Architects, and Other Professionals*	
(69.92/48) Chemical engineer ($n = 1$)	(69.92/48) Chemical engineer
(66.55/55) Electrical and electronic engineer ($n = 2$)	(46.84/213) Electric technician
	(34.39/353) Communications equipment operator
(62.42/57) Mechanical engineer ($n = 1$)	(47.60/22) Managers and administrators
(64.56/59) Engineer, *n.e.c.* ($n = 5$)	(50.77/5) Administrators, public administration
	(62.25/43) Architect
	(71.48/44) Aerospace engineer
	(64.09/157) Teacher, secondary school
	(46.84/213) Electrical and electronic technician
(80.53/84) Physician ($n = 1$)	(71.48/44) Aerospace engineer
3. *Health-related professionals*	
(65.06/96) Pharmacist ($n = 1$)	(65.06/96) Pharmacist
4. *Teachers, post-secondary*	
(61.80/125) Sociology teacher ($n = 1$)	(61.80/125) Sociology teacher
(47.04/159) Teachers, *n.e.c.* ($n = 1$)	(65.06/96) Pharmacist
5. *Librarians and archivists*	
6. *Social scientists, lawyers, judges*	
(80.26/178) Lawyer ($n = 1$)	(80.26/178) Lawyer
7. *Writers, artists, entertainers*	
(43.35/194) Artist ($n = 1$)	(19.29/725) Metal/plastic machine operator
(54.79/195) Editor, reporter ($n = 2$)	(56.49/184) Technical writer
	(33.99/476) Manager, horticultural specialty farms
8. *Health technologists and technicians*	
(48.40/214) Industrial engineering technician ($n = 1$)	(54.06/148) Trade/industrial teacher
9. *Sales occupations*	
(38.51/243) Supervisor, sales ($n = 4$)	(55.18/13) Manager, marketing

(45.47/257) Sales occup., other business services (*n* =1)

10. *Admin. support, clerical*
    (31.06/337) Bookkeeper, accounting clerk (*n* = 2)

(33.82/17) Manager, food and lodging
(38.51/243) Supervisor, sales (*n* = 2)
(33.01/456) Supervisor, personal service
(38.51/243) Supervisor, sales

(50.77/5) Administrator, public admin.

(64.09/157) Teacher, secondary school

11. *Private household service*

12. *Protective and other service*

13. *Farming related*
    (27.60/473) Farmer, except horticultural (*n* = 9)

(33.82/17) Manager, food and lodging
(71.48/44) Aerospace engineer
(27.60/473) Farmer, except horticultural (*n* = 3)
(21.30/486) Groundskeeper, gardener (*n* = 2)
(19.41/688) Food batchmaker
(25.27/804) Truck driver

    (21.30/486) Grounds keeper, gardener

(38.51/243) Supervisor, sales

14. *Forestry and logging*

15. *Fishers, hunters, and trappers*

16. *Manual labor*
    (26.16/505) Auto mechanic (*n* = 2)

(47.90/15) Manager, medicine and health
(36.66/803) Supervisor, motor vehicle operator

    (39.72/515) Aircraft mechanic (*n* = 1)
    (30.10/516) Heavy equipment mechanic (*n* = 1)
    (20.00/877) Stock handler, bagger (*n* = 1)

(71.48/44) Aerospace engineer
(54.06/148) Trade/industrial teacher

(20.00/877) Stock handler, bagger

17. *Military*
    (905) Military, rank not specified

(NA/909) Not employed since 1984

---

[a] 1990 TSEI score/U.S. Census code.
[b] Not elsewhere classified.

Table 3. Planned Job in 1941 and Last Main Job: Female Respondents

Planned Job	Last Main Job
1. *Executive, administrative, and managerial occupations*	
2. *Engineers, architects, and other professionals*	
3. *Health-related professionals*	
(61.07/95[a]) Registered nurse (*n* = 5)	(61.07/95) Registered nurse
	(60.08/156) Teacher, elementary school
	(31.16/268) Sales worker, hardware and building supplies
	(36.11/628) Supervisor, precision production occupations
	(NA/909) Not employed since 1984
(65.06/96) Pharmacist (*n* = 2)	(65.06/96) Pharmacist
	(30.30/313) Secretary
(39.65/97) Dietician (*n* = 1)	(NA/909) Not employed since 1984
4. *Teachers, post-secondary*	
(64.09/157) Teacher, secondary school (*n* = 2)	(47.60/22) Manager and administrators, *n.e.c.*[b]
	(38.51/243) Supervisor, sales occupations
5. *Librarians and archivists*	
6. *Social scientists, lawyers, judges*	
(48.34/174) Social worker (*n* = 1)	(43.51/4) Chief executive and general admin., public admin.
7. *Writers, artists, entertainers*	
(44.39/188) Painter (*n* = 1)	(27.60/473) Farmer, except horticultural
8. *Health technologists and technicians*	
(38.51/207) Licensed practical nurse (*n* = 1)	(26.73/264) Sales, apparel
9. *Sales occupations*	
(38.51/243) Supervisor, sales (*n* = 3)	(50.01/158) Teacher, special education
	(38.51/243) Supervisor, sales
	(31.47/329) Library clerk
(24.87/275) Sales counter clerks (*n* = 1)	(31.06/337) Bookkeeper, accounting clerk
(34.90/277) Street and door-to-door sales workers (*n* =1)	(26.02/458) Hairdresser, cosmetologist
10. *Admin. support, clerical*	
(30.30/313) Secretary (*n* = 9)	(61.07/95) Registered nurse
	(30.30/313) Secretary (*n* = 6)
	(26.10/469) Personal service occup., *n.e.c.*
	(20.30/666) Dressmaker
(42.61/314) Stenographer (*n* = 1)	(44.40/185) Designer

(31.06/337) Bookkeeper, accounting clerk (*n* = 1)

(31.06/337) Bookkeeper, accounting clerk

11. *Private household service*

12. *Protective and other services*
(24.29/447) Nursing aide (*n* = 2)

(36.03/155) Teacher, kindergarten
(26.02/458) Hairdresser and cosmetologist

(13.85/449) Maids and housemen (*n* = 1)
(26.02/458) Hairdresser (*n* = 2)

(36.03/155) Teacher, kindergarten
(27.07/365) Stock clerk
(45.47/257) Sales, other business

13. *Farming related*
(27.60/473) Farmer, except horticultural (*n* = 1)

(29.96/274) Sales worker

(33.99/476) Manager, horticultural farm (*n* = 1)

(33.99/476) Manager, horticultural farm

14. *Forestry and logging*

15. *Fishers, hunters, and trappers*

16. *Manual labor*
(20.30/666) Dressmaker (*n* = 1)

(41.80/529) Telephone installer, repair

17. *Military*

[a] 1990 TSEI score/U.S. Census code.
[b] Not elsewhere classified.

Notes

1. INTRODUCTION

1. The identifier beginning with "denshovh" is a unique Denshō visual-history segment identification number. Readers who wish to view this segment or the narrator's entire interview can visit the Denshō Web site at <www.densho.org> and go to "Archives."

2. Currently there is considerable variation in the terminology used to describe events associated with the incarceration. For the purposes of this book, in an attempt to reflect more accurately what took place, we have generally chosen to use the terms "mass removal" and "exclusion" instead of "evacuation" except where the meaning would be unclear. In addition, we favor "incarceration" as compared with "relocation." As noted by other scholars, "evacuation" and "relocation" are euphemisms that the federal government utilized (Maki, Kitano, and Berthold 1999, 4–5; Commission on Wartime Relocation and Internment of Civilians 1997, xxviii). Also, "internment" is a long-sanctioned legal process usually referring to enemy aliens (Daniels 1995, 66). For this reason we prefer "incarceration" as applied to Japanese Americans, even though "internment" has been widely utilized to describe their situation.

3. At the time of this writing, the Denshō Web site contains over 110 interviews and 1,500 photographs and documents. It features an extensive multimedia presentation of events leading up to the expulsion and detention, the incarceration itself, and resettlement. For teachers, there are curricular materials on the site that were co-developed with the Stanford Program on International and Cross-Cultural Education (SPICE).

2. THE PRE—WORLD WAR II COMMUNITY

1. In our analyses, we refer to the entire sample as Nisei even though a small percentage actually have a different geogenerational status. We felt that since the small

number of non-Nisei were experiencing the same socio-historical events at a similar point in their lifespans, that their characterological structure would be similar to the Nisei.

3. THE INCARCERATION

1. As the term "assembly center" is a government euphemism, we put it in quotes or use the more accurate "temporary incarceration camp."

2. This phrase was used as a label for "loyals" and "disloyals" by Elmer Davis in a letter to President Franklin D. Roosevelt, October 2, 1942, President's Personal File 4849, Franklin D. Roosevelt Library, Hyde Park, New York.

3. Given that Tule Lake became a segregation center and had a very different history from Minidoka, we ran a mean comparison on the question regarding their overall feeling about their incarceration for those incarcerated in the two camps. There was no difference between those sent to the two camps in response to this question. Those sent to Minidoka had a mean score of 3.4, those sent to Tule Lake 3.3 ($p > .10$).

5. RESETTLEMENT

1. For a more detailed reconstruction of the movement of resettlers, see appendix B.

2. We directly tested for an interaction between the two wartime period variables, place first resettled (on or outside Pacific Coast) and planned occupation by computing an interaction term and including it in the regression equation. The place first resettled/planned occupation interaction was significant ($p < .05$). We did not similarly compute an interaction term for the other human capital variable, education, and place resettled because years of college education were principally gained during resettlement.

6. MARRIAGE AND FAMILY FORMATION

1. A potential methodological ambiguity in comparing our data with national census figures is that the age distribution of the two populations may be somewhat different. If one compares the 1940 census population age-sex pyramid to the Japanese American one for the same period, they are quite similar in the childbearing age groups (Thomas 1952, 10). This is probably due to the similarity of immigration patterns of Europeans and the Japanese, both groups peaking in the first decade of the twentieth century. Thus, any differences between incarcerees and national figures are not likely to be due to divergences in the age-sex composition of Japanese Americans as compared to European Americans and its subsequent effect on, for example, fertility patterns.

2. The TFR for any given year represents the number of births a group of one thousand women would have by the end of their childbearing years if they all sur-

vived and experienced the age-specific birth rates for that year. For a detailed technical note on fertility rate computations, see appendix C.

3. The rate and number of births in the United States actually fell between 1948 and 1950 after an initial spurt during the period from 1946 to 1947. This initial increase has been attributed to attempts to compensate for years of wartime separation (Bouvier and De Vita 1991, 4). It was not until 1951 that U.S. birth rates rose again and remained high until the early 1960s.

4. The national data for age of mother at birth of her children includes ever-married and never-married women. The Denshō sample for this analysis includes only mothers because none of the never-married Denshō women had children.

5. Anecdotally, it seems that the Nisei had many nicknames which were sometimes a response to the difficulty whites had pronouncing Japanese names. At other times, it appears that a different process was at work. Many humorous nicknames given by fellow Nisei "stuck," probably for complex reasons. Examples of these would be "Winky" and "Mochi" (Japanese rice cake). These types of nicknames were unique to the Nisei geogeneration.

8. RELIGION AND MAKING SENSE OF THE INCARCERATION

1. An earlier version of this chapter was published in the *Journal of Asian American Studies* 5 (2003): 113–38.

2. The small number of Catholics ($n = 8$ or 4.4% of the sample) was eliminated from the analyses to decrease variance on the religion variable. There were no Japanese American Catholic churches, unlike the Protestant case. In addition to Buddhists, Protestants, and Catholics, another 18.6% ($n = 34$) of the respondents listed "other religious preferences." We did not have more extensive measures of religiosity because of the omnibus nature of the Denshō survey.

3. For all three dependent variables, camp evaluation score, preferred leadership style, and involvement in the redress movement, controlling for the number of years incarcerated did not change the significance of any of the findings.

Glossary

baishakunin. A person who helps families find marital partners.

bosankai. Cemetery visiting group.

dekasegi. Internal migration for temporary work.

furo. Japanese style bath.

giri-ninjō. Attitude emphasizing obligation and human feelings.

go. Japanese board game.

hakujin. White person.

Issei. First or immigrant generation.

kenjinkai. Prefectural group.

Kibei. Nisei educated in Japan.

Nihon gakkō. Japanese school.

Nihonmachi. Japantown.

Nikkei. People of Japanese ancestry.

Nisei. Second or first American born generation.

obaachan. Grandma.

obachan. Auntie.

obaasan. Grandmother; elderly woman.

obasan. Aunt.

ojiisan. Grandfather; old man.

ojisan. Uncle.

Sansei. Third generation.

shigin. Type of singing.

shōgi. Japanese chess.

Yonsei. Fourth generation.

References

Ahlburg, Dennis A., and Carol J. De Vita
    1992   New realities of the American family. *Population Bulletin* 47:2–44.

Asai, Sadaichi
    1998   Creation, crucifixion, resurrection. Pp. 5–7 in *Triumphs of faith: Stories of Japanese-American Christians during World War II*, ed. Victor N. Okada. Los Angeles: Japanese-American Internment Project.

Baba, Harry
    1998   The long journey. Pp. 9–11 in *Triumphs of faith: Stories of Japanese-American Christians during World War II,* ed. Victor N. Okada. Los Angeles: Japanese-American Internment Project.

Baer, Hans, and Merrill Singer
    1992   *African American religion in the twentieth century: Varieties of protest and accommodation.* Knoxville, Tenn.: University of Tennessee Press.

Becker, Carl
    1990   Japanese Pure Land Buddhism in Christian America. *Buddhist-Christian Studies* 10:43–156.

Bianchi, Suzanne M., and Daphne Spain
    1986   *American women in transition.* New York: Russell Sage Foundation.

Bland, Richard, Brian Elliot, and Frank Bechofer
    1978   Social mobility in the petite bourgeoisie. *Acta Sociologica* 21:229–48.

Blau, Peter, and Otis Duncan
    1967   *The American occupational structure.* New York: John Wiley.

Bloom, Alfred
    1990   The unfolding of the lotus: A survey of recent developments in Shin Buddhism in the West. *Buddhist-Christian Studies* 10:157–64.
    1998   Shin Buddhism in America: A social perspective. Pp. 31–38 in *The faces of Buddhism in America,* ed. Charles S. Prebish and Kenneth K. Tanaka. Berkeley: University of California Press.

Bonacich, Edna
    1975   Small business and Japanese American ethnic solidarity. *Amerasia Journal*
            3:96–113.
    1980   Middleman minorities and advanced capitalism. *Ethnic Groups* 2:211–
            19.
Bonacich, Edna, and John Modell
    1980   *The economic basis of ethnic solidarity: Small business in the Japanese American
            community*. Berkeley: University of California Press.
Bosworth, Allen
    1967   *America's concentration camps*. New York: Norton.
Bouvier, Leon F., and Carol J. De Vita
    1991   The baby boom–entering midlife. *Population Bulletin* 46:2–35. Washing-
            ton, D.C.: Population Reference Bureau.
Breton, Raymond
    1964   Institutional completeness of ethnic communities and the personal rela-
            tions of immigrants. *American Journal of Sociology*. 70:93–205.
Brock, Rita Nakashima
    1996   Response: Clearing the tangled vines. *Amerasia Journal* 22:181–86.
Brodkin, Karen
    2001   How Jews became White. Pp. 30–45 in *Race, class, and gender in the United
            States: An integrated study,* ed. Paula S. Rothenberg. New York: Worth
            Publishers.
Bronfenbrenner, Urie
    1989   Ecological systems theory. Pp. 187–249 in *Annals of child development:
            Vol. 6. Six theories of child development: Revised formulations and current issues,*
            ed. R. Vasta. Greenwich, Conn.: JAI Press.
Broom, Leonard [Leonard Bloom], and John I. Kitsuse
    1956   *The managed casualty: The Japanese-American family in World War II*. Berke-
            ley: University of California Press.
Browning, Harley L., Sally C. Lopreato, and Dudley L. Poston Jr.
    1973   Income and veteran status: Variations among Mexican Americans, Blacks
            and Anglos. *American Sociological Review* 38:74–85.
Burton, Jeffrey F., Mary M. Farrell, Florence B. Lord, and Richard W. Lord
    1999   *Confinement and ethnicity: An overview of World War II Japanese American
            relocation sites*. Tucson, Ariz.: Western Archeological and Conservation
            Center, National Park Service.
Caudill, William
    1952   Japanese-American personality and acculturation. *Genetic Psychology
            Monographs*. 45:3–102.
Caudill, William, and George DeVos
    1956   Achievement, culture and personality: The case of the Japanese Amer-
            icans. *American Anthropologist* 58:1102–26.
Chang, Thelma
    1991   *"I can never forget": Men of the 100th/442nd*. Honolulu: SIGI Productions.

Chin, Doug

2001   *Seattle's International District: The making of a pan-Asian American commu-*
        nity. Seattle: International Examiner Press.

Coale, Ansley J., and Melvin Zelnik

1963   *New estimates of fertility and population of the United States: A study of annual*
        White births from 1855 to 1960 and of completeness of enumeration in the cen-
        suses from 1880 to 1960. Princeton, N.J.: Princeton University Press.

Coleman, James S.

1988   Social capital in the creation of human capital. *American Journal of Soci-*
        ology 94 (supplement):S95–S210.

Commission on Wartime Relocation and Internment of Civilians.

1997   *Personal justice denied: Report of the Commission on Wartime Relocation and*
        Internment of Civilians. Seattle: Civil Liberties Public Education Fund and
        University of Washington Press.

Cross, Susan, and Hazel Markus

1991   Possible selves across the life span. *Human Development* 34:230–55.

Crost, Lyn

1994   *Honor by fire.* Novato, Calif.: Presidio Press.

Culley, John H.

1984   Relocation of Japanese Americans: The Hawaiian experience. *Air Force*
        Law Review 24:176–83.

Daniels, Roger

1986   *The decision to relocate the Japanese Americans.* Malabar, Fla.: Krieger
        Publishing.

1993   *Concentration camps: North America Japanese in the United States and Canada*
        during World War II. Malabar, Fla.: Krieger Publishing.

1995   The internment of Japanese nationals in the United States during World
        War II. *Halcyon 1995: A Journal of Humanities* 17:65–75.

Daniels, Roger, Sandra C. Taylor, and Harry H. L. Kitano

1991   *Japanese Americans: From relocation to redress.* Rev. ed. Seattle and London:
        University of Washington Press.

Denshō: The Japanese American Legacy Project

1997   Seattle.

Dubrow, Gail

2002   *Sento at Sixth and Main.* Seattle: Seattle Arts Commission. Distributed by
        the University of Washington Press.

Duncan, William R.

1999   Camp Dharma: Buddhism and the Japanese American internment expe-
        rience. *Nikkei Heritage* 11:8–9, 15.

Duus, Masayo Umezawa

1983   *Unlikely liberators: The men of the 100th and 442nd.* Honolulu: University
        of Hawaii Press.

Duus, Peter

1976   *The rise of modern Japan.* Boston: Houghton Mifflin.

Duveneck, Josephine Whitney
    1978   *Life on two levels: An autobiography.* Los Altos Hills, Calif.: Trust for Hidden Villa.
Easterlin, Richard A.
    1987   *Birth and fortune: The impact of numbers on personal welfare.* 2nd ed. Chicago: University of Chicago Press.
Eitelberg, M., J. Laurence, B. Waters, and L. Perlman
    1984   *Screening for military service: Aptitude and educational criteria for military entry.* Washington, D.C.: Office of the Assistant Secretary for Defense.
Elder, Glen H. Jr.
    1974   *Children of the Great Depression.* Chicago: University of Chicago Press.
    1986   Military times and turning points in men's lives. *Developmental Psychology* 22:3–17.
    1987   War mobilization and the life course: A cohort of World War II veterans. *Sociological Forum* 2:449–72.
Elder, Glen H. Jr., and Susan L. Bailey
    1988   The timing of military service in men's lives. Pp. 157–74 in *Social stress and family development,* ed. David M. Klein and Joan Aldous. New York: Guilford Press.
Elder, Glen H. Jr., and Elizabeth C. Clipp
    1988   Combat experience, comradeship, and psychological health. Pp. 131–56 in *Human adaptation to extreme stress: From the Holocaust to Vietnam,* ed. John P. Wilson, Zev Harel, and Boaz Kahana. New York: Plenum Press.
Elder, Glen H. Jr., and Jeffrey K. Liker
    1982   Hard times in women's lives: Historical influences across forty years. *American Journal of Sociology* 88:241–69.
Elder, Glen H. Jr., Jeffrey K. Liker, and Catherine E. Cross
    1984   Parent-child behavior in the Great Depression: Life course and intergenerational influences. Pp. 109–58 in *Life-span development and behavior,* ed. Paul B. Baltes and Orville G. Brim Jr.. New York: Academic Press.
Ellison, Christopher G.
    1993   Religious involvement and self-perception among Black Americans. *Social Forces* 71:1027–55.
Embree, John F.
    1943   Resistance to freedom—an administrative problem. *Applied Anthropology* 2:10–14.
Emi, Frank
    1989   Draft resistance at the Heart Mountain concentration camp and the Fair Play Committee. Pp. 41–69 in *Frontiers of Asian American studies: Writing, research, and commentary,* ed. Gail M. Nomura, Russell Endo, Stephen H. Sumida, and Russell C. Leong. Pullman: Washington State University Press.
Endo, Russell
    1974   Japanese Americans: The "model minority" in perspective. Pp. 189–213

in *The social reality of ethnic America,* ed. Rudolph Gomez, Clement Cottingham, Russell Endo, and Kathleen Jackson. Lexington, Mass.: D. C. Heath and Company.

Espiritu, Yen Le

1992   *Asian American panethnicity: Bridging institutions and identities.* Philadelphia: Temple University Press.

Finnerty, Margaret

1991   *Del Webb: A man. A company.* Flagstaff, Ariz.: Heritage Publishers.

Fire for Effect: A Unit History of the 522 Field Artillery Battalion

1998   Honolulu: Fisher Printing.

Fong, Timothy P.

1998   *The contemporary Asian American experience: Beyond the model minority.* Upper Saddle River, N.J.: Prentice Hall.

Fugita, Stephen S., and Marilyn Fernandez

2003   Religion and Japanese Americans' Views of Their World War II Incarceration. *Journal of Asian American Studies* 5: 113–38.

Fugita, Stephen S., and David J. O'Brien

1991   *Japanese American ethnicity: The persistence of community.* Seattle and London: University of Washington Press.

Fugita, Stephen S., Tetsuden Kashima, and S. Frank Miyamoto

2002   Methodology of comparative studies of national character: West Coast survey. *Behaviormetrika* 29: 143–48

Fugita, Stephen S., S. Frank Miyamoto, and Tetsuden Kashima

2002   Interpersonal style and Japanese American organizational involvement. *Behaviormetrika* 29: 185–202.

Fujitani, T.

2001   The Reischauer memo: Mr. Moto, Hirohito, and Japanese American soldiers. *Critical Asian Studies* 33: 379–402.

Fukutake, Tadahashi

1989   *The Japanese social structure: Its evolution in the modern century.* 2nd ed. Tokyo: University of Tokyo Press.

Girdner, Audrie, and Anne Loftis

1969   *The great betrayal.* New York: McMillan.

Goldscheider, Calvin, and Francis E. Kobrin

1980   Ethnic continuity and the process of self-employment. *Ethnicity* 7:256–78.

Gordon, Milton M.

1964   *Assimilation in American life.* New York: Oxford University Press.

Gorfinkel, Claire, ed.

1995   *The evacuation of Hatsuye Egami.* Pasadena, Calif.: International Productions.

Grabill, Wilson H., Clyde V. Kiser, and Pascal K. Whelpton

1958   *The fertility of American women.* New York: John Wiley & Sons.

Grodzins, Morton

1949   *Americans betrayed: Politics and the Japanese evacuation.* Chicago: University of Chicago Press.

Groth-Marnat, Gary
    1992   Buddhism and mental health: A comparative analysis. Pp. 270–80 in *Religion and mental health,* ed. John F. Schumaker. New York: Oxford University Press.
Hansen, Arthur, ed.
    1991   *Japanese American World War II evacuation oral history project, parts 1–5.* Westport, Conn.: Meekler.
Harris, Catherine Embree
    1999   *Dusty exile: Looking back at Japanese relocation during World War II.* Honolulu: Mutual Publishing.
Hauser, Robert M., and John Robert Warren
    1997   Socioeconomic indexes for occupations: A review, update, and critique. Pp. 177–298 in *Sociological methodology,* ed. Adrian E. Raftery. Washington, D.C.: American Sociological Association.
Hayashi, Brian M.
    1995   *For the sake of our Japanese brethren: Assimilation, nationalism, and Protestantism among the Japanese of Los Angeles, 1895–1942.* Stanford, Calif.: Stanford University Press.
Hayashi, Chikio, and Yasumasa Kuroda
    1997   *Japanese culture in comparative perspective.* Westport, Conn.: Praeger.
Hodge, Robert M.
    1981   The measurement of occupational status. *Social Science Research* 10: 396–415.
Hogan, Dennis P.
    1981   *Transitions and social change: The early lives of American men.* New York: Academic Press.
Hohri, William
    1988   *Repairing America: An account of the movement for Japanese American redress.* Pullman, Wash.: Washington State University Press.
Ichihashi, Yamato
    1932   *Japanese in the United States.* Stanford, Calif.: Stanford University Press.
Ichinokuchi, Tad
    1988   *John Aiso and the M.I.S: Japanese-American soldiers in the Military Intelligence Service, World War II.* Los Angeles: Military Intelligence Club of Southern California.
Ichioka, Yuji
    1977   Japanese associations and the Japanese government: A special relationship, 1909–1926. *Pacific Historical Review* 46:409–37.
    1980   *Amerika nadeshiko:* Japanese immigrant women in the United States, 1900–1924. *Pacific Historical Review* 48:339–57.
    1986–87 A study in dualism: James Yoshinori Sakamoto and the *Japanese American Courier,* 1928–1942. *Amerasia* 13:49–82.
    1988   *The Issei: The world of the first generation Japanese immigrants.* New York: The Free Press.

Imamura, Ryo
   1998   Buddhist and Western psychotherapies: An Asian American perspective. Pp. 228–37 in *Faces of Buddhism in America,* ed. Charles S. Prebish. Berkeley: University of California Press.
Ito, Kazuo
   1973   *Issei: A history of Japanese immigrants in North America.* Trans. Shinichiro Nakamura and Jean S. Gerard. Seattle: Executive Committee for the Publication of Issei.
James, Thomas
   1985   "Life begins with freedom": The college Nisei, 1942–1945. *History of Education Quarterly* 25:155–74.
   1987(a) Exile within: The schooling of Japanese Americans, 1942–1945. Cambridge: Harvard University Press.
   1987(b) The education of Japanese Americans at Tule Lake, 1942–1946. *Pacific Historical Review* 56:25–58.
Kashima, Tetsuden
   1977   *Buddhism in America: The social organization of an ethnic religious institution.* Westport, Conn.: Greenwood Press.
   1980   Japanese American internees return—1945–1955: Readjustment and social amnesia. *Phylon* 41:107–15
Kashima, Tetsuden, S. Frank Miyamoto, and Stephen S. Fugita
   2002   Religious attitudes and beliefs among Japanese Americans: King County, Washington and Santa Clara County, California. *Behaviormetrika* 29: 203–29.
Kaul-Seidman, Lisa R.
   1999   The names which modern-day Zionist idealists give to their children. *Jewish Journal of Sociology* 41:81–101.
Kessler, Lauren
   1993   *Stubborn twig: Three generations in the life of a Japanese American family.* New York: Random House.
King, Rebecca Chiyoko
   2002   "Eligible to be Japanese American": Multiraciality in basketball leagues and beauty pageants. Pg. 120–33 in *Contemporary Asian American communities: Intersections and divergences,* ed. Linda Trinh Võ and Rick Bonus. Philadelphia: Temple University Press.
Kitano, Harry H. L.
   1976   *Japanese Americans: The evolution of a subculture.* 2nd ed. Englewood Cliffs, N.J.: Prentice-Hall.
   1993   *Generations and identity: The Japanese American.* Needham Heights, Mass.: Ginn Press.
Kramer, Kenneth P., and Kenneth K. Tanaka
   1990   A dialogue with Jodo-Shinshu. *Buddhist-Christian Studies* 10:177–86.
Lee, Sharon M., and Marilyn Fernandez
   1998   Trends in Asian American racial/ethnic intermarriage: A comparison of 1980 and 1990 census data. *Sociological Perspectives* 41:323–42.

Leighton, Alexander Hamilton
    1945   *The governing of men: General principles and recommendations based on experience at a Japanese relocation camp.* New York: Princeton University Press.
Levine, Gene N., and Colbert Rhodes
    1981   *The Japanese American community: A three generation study.* New York: Praeger.
Levine, Marci B., and Frank N. Willis
    1994   Public reactions to unusual names. *The Journal of Social Psychology* 134: 561–89.
Lieberson, Stanley, and Kelly S. Mikelson
    1995   Distinctive African American names: An experimental, historical, and linguistic analysis of innovation. *American Sociological Review* 60:928–46.
Light, Ivan
    1972   *Ethnic enterprise in America: Business and welfare among Chinese, Japanese, and Blacks.* Berkeley: University of California Press.
Linehan, Thomas M.
    1993   Japanese American resettlement in Cleveland during and after World War II. *Journal of Urban History* 20:54–80.
Loo, Chalsa
    1993   An integrative-sequential treatment model for post-traumatic stress disorder: A case study of the Japanese American internment and redress. *Clinical Psychology Review* 13:89–117.
Maeda, Wayne
    2000   *Changing dreams and treasured memories: A story of Japanese Americans in the Sacramento region.* Sacramento: Sacramento Japanese American Citizens League.
Maki, Mitchell T., Harry H. L. Kitano, and S. Megan Berthold
    1999   *Achieving the impossible dream: How Japanese Americans obtained redress.* Urbana, Ill.: University of Illinois Press.
Martindale, Melanie, and Dudley L. Poston Jr.
    1979   Variations in veteran/nonveteran earnings patterns among World War II, Korea, and Vietnam War cohorts. *Armed Forces and Society* 5:219–43.
Mass, Amy Iwasaki
    1991   Psychological effects of the camps on Japanese Americans. Pp. 159–62 in *Japanese Americans: From relocation to redress,* rev. ed., ed. Roger Daniels, Sandra L. Taylor, and Harry H. L. Kitano. Seattle and London: University of Washington Press.
Matsumoto, Valerie
    1984   Japanese American women during World War II. *Frontiers* 8:6–14.
Mayer, Karl U.
    1988   German survivors of World War II: The impact on the life course of the collective experience of birth cohorts. Pp. 229–46 in *Social structures in human lives,* ed. Matilda White Riley, Bettina J. Huber, and Beth B. Hess. Newbury Park, Calif.: Sage.

Miyamoto, S. Frank

1984 *Social solidarity among the Japanese in Seattle.* Seattle: University of Washington Press.

1986–87 Problems of interpersonal style among the Nisei. *Amerasia* 13:29–45.

1989 Resentment, distrust, and insecurity at Tule Lake. Pp. 127–41 in *Views from within: The Japanese American evacuation and resettlement study,* ed. Yuji Ichioka. Los Angeles: UCLA Asian American Studies Center.

Miyamoto, S. Frank, Stephen S. Fugita, and Tetsuden Kashima

2002 A theory of interpersonal relations for cross cultural studies. *Behaviormetrika* 29:149–83.

Modell, John.

1977 *The economics and politics of racial accommodation: The Japanese of Los Angeles, 1900–1942.* Urbana, Ill.: University of Illinois Press.

Moen, Phyllis, and Francille M. Firebaugh

1994 Family policies and effective families: A life course perspective. *International Journal of Sociology and Social Policy* 14:29–52.

Montero, Darrel

1980 *Japanese Americans: Changing patterns of ethnic affiliation over three generations.* Boulder, Colo.: Westview Press.

Moriyama, Alan Takeo

1985 *Imingaisha: Japanese emigration companies and Hawaii 1894–1908.* Honolulu: University of Hawaii Press.

Muller, Eric L.

2001 *Free to die for their country: The story of the Japanese American draft resisters in World War II.* Chicago: University of Chicago Press.

Musick, Mark A.

1996 Religion and subjective health among Black and White elders. *Journal of Health and Social Behavior* 37:221–37.

Nagata, Donna K.

1989 The long-term effects of victimization: Present day effects of the Japanese American internment. *The Community Psychologist* 22:10–11.

1990 The Japanese American internment: Exploring the transgenerational consequences of traumatic stress. *Journal of Traumatic Stress* 3:47–69.

1993 *Legacy of injustice: Exploring the cross-generational impact of the Japanese American internment.* New York: Plenum Press.

Nakagawa, Kerry Yo

2001 *Through a diamond: 100 years of Japanese American baseball.* San Francisco: Rudi Publishing.

Nakamura, Hajime

1968 Basic features of the legal, political, and economic thought of Japan. Pg. 631–647 in *Philosophy and culture: East and west,* ed. Charles A. Moore. Honolulu: University of Hawaii Press.

Ng, Wendy L.

1989 Knowing the past: Collective memory and the Japanese American experience. Paper presented at the annual meeting of the Association for Asian American Studies, New York, June 1–3.

Nikkei 2000 Conference

2001   *Nikkei 2000 conference: Summary and analysis.* San Francisco: The California Japanese American Community Leadership Council, The Nikkei 2000 Conference Committee, and The Japanese Cultural and Community Center of Northern California.

Niiya, Brian

2001   *Encyclopedia of Japanese American history: An A-to-Z reference from 1868 to the present, updated version.* New York: Facts on File.

Nishi, Setsuko Matsunaga

1998–99 Restoration of community in Chicago resettlement. *Japanese American National Museum Quarterly* 13:2–11.

1999   Generational legacies: Issei to Nisei and beyond. Paper presented at the Ninth North Park Korean Symposium, Chicago, October 16.

Nobe, Lisa N.

1999   The children's village at Manzanar: The World War II eviction and detention of Japanese American orphans. *Journal of the West* 38:65–71.

Norbeck, Edward

1972   Japanese common-interest associations in cross-cultural perspective. *Journal of Voluntary Action Research* 1:38–41.

O'Brien, David J., and Stephen S. Fugita

1982   Middleman minority concept: Its explanatory value in the case of the Japanese in California agriculture. *Pacific Sociological Review* 25:185–204.

Okamura, Jonathan Y.

2002   Baseball and beauty queens: The political context of ethnic boundary making in the Japanese American community in Hawai'i. *Social Process in Hawai'i* 41:122–46.

Okihiro, Gary

1999   *Storied lives: Japanese American students and World War II.* Seattle: University of Washington Press.

Osajima, Keith

1988   Asian Americans as the model minority: An analysis of the popular press image in the 1960's and 1980's. In *Reflections in shattered windows: Promises and prospects for Asian American studies,* ed. Gary Y. Okihiro, Shirley Hune, Arthur A. Hansen, and John M. Liu. Pullman, Wash.: Washington State University Press.

Pavalko, Eliza K., and Glen Elder

1990   World War II and divorce: A life-course perspective. *American Journal of Sociology* 95:1213–34.

Peterson, William

1966   Success story, Japanese American style. *New York Times Magazine,* 9 January, 20–21, 33, 36, 40–41, 43.

Prebish, Charles S.
  1979   *American Buddhism.* North Scituate, Mass.: Duxbury Press.
Prebish, Charles, and Kenneth K. Tanaka, eds.
  1998   *The faces of Buddhism in America.* Berkeley: University of California Press.
Putnam, Robert D.
  1995   Bowling alone: America's declining social capital. *Journal of Democracy* 6:65–78.
  2000   *Bowling alone: The collapse and revival of American community.* New York: Simon and Schuster.
Rindfuss, Ronald R., and James A. Sweet
  1977   *Postwar fertility trends and differentials in the United States.* New York: Academic Press.
Rindfuss, Ronald R., S. Philip Morgan, and Kate Offutt
  1996   Education and the changing age patterns of American fertility: 1963–1989. *Demography* 33:277–90.
Rindfuss, Ronald R., S. Philip Morgan, and C. Gary Swicegood
  1984   The transition to motherhood. *American Sociological Review* 49:359–72.
Robinson, Greg
  2001   *By order of the president: FDR and the internment of Japanese Americans.* Cambridge: Harvard University Press.
Rodgers, Willard L., and Arland Thornton
  1985   Changing patterns of first marriage in the United States. *Demography* 22:265–79.
Roos, Patricia A.
  1985   *Gender & work: A comparative analysis of industrial societies.* Albany: State University of New York Press.
Rosenfeld, Rachel A.
  1978   Women's intergenerational occupational mobility. *American Sociological Review* 43:36–46.
Rosow, Irving
  1978   What is a cohort and why? *Human Development* 21:65–75.
Ryder, Norman B.
  1973   *Towards the end of growth: Population in America.* Englewood Cliffs, N.J.: Prentice-Hall.
Ryder, Norman B., and Charles Westoff
  1971   *Reproduction in the United States 1965.* Princeton, N.J.: Princeton University Press.
Saiki, Barry, and Arthur Takemoto
  1999   Chicago resettlement. *Nikkei Heritage* 11:12–13.
Sale, Roger
  1976   *Seattle, past to present.* Seattle: University of Washington Press.
Schonberger, Howard
  1990   Dilemmas of loyalty: Japanese Americans and the psychological warfare

campaigns of the Office of Strategic Services, 1943–45. *Amerasia* 16:20–38.

Schuman, Howard, and Jacqueline Scott
  1989   Generations and collective memories. *American Sociological Review* 54: 359–81.

Seigel, Shizue
  1999   Incarceration and the church: An overview. *Nikkei Heritage* 11:4–5, 15–21.

Sewell, William H., and Robert Hauser
  1976   Recent developments in the Wisconsin study of social and psychological factors in socioeconomic achievement. Center for Demography Working Paper No. 76–11. Madison, Wis.: University of Wisconsin.

Shimabukuro, Robert Sadamu
  2001   *Born in Seattle: The campaign for Japanese American redress.* Seattle and London: University of Washington Press.

Shinagawa, Larry Hajime
  1994   Intermarriage and inequality: A theoretical and empirical analysis of the marriage patterns of Asian Americans. Ph.D. diss., Department of Sociology, University of California, Berkeley.

Sone, Monica
  1979   *Nisei daughter.* Boston: Brown and Little Company, 1953. Reprint, Seattle: University of Washington Press.

Spicer, Edward H., Asael T. Hansen, Katherine Luomala, and Marvin K. Opler.
  1969   *Impounded: Japanese-Americans in the relocation centers.* Tucson, Ariz.: University of Arizona Press.

Spickard, Paul
  1983   The Nisei assume power: The Japanese American Citizens League, 1941–42. *Pacific Historical Review* 52:147–74.
  1989   *Mixed blood: Intermarriage and ethnic identity in twentieth-century America.* Madison, Wis.: University of Wisconsin Press.

Stevens, Gillian, and Monica Boyd
  1980   The importance of mother labor force participation and intergenerational mobility of women. *Social Forces* 59:86–92.

Suzuki, Lester
  1979   *Ministry in the assembly and relocation centers of World War II.* Berkeley: Yardbird Publishing.

Takahashi, Jere
  1997   *Nisei/Sansei: Shifting Japanese American identities and politics.* Philadelphia: Temple University Press.

Takami, David A.
  1998   *Divided destiny: A history of Japanese Americans in Seattle.* Seattle and London: University of Washington Press; Seattle: Wing Luke Asian Museum.

Tateishi, John
  1984   *And justice for all: An oral history of the Japanese American detention camps.* New York: Random House.

1991   The Japanese American Citizens League and the struggle for redress. Pp. 191–95 in *Japanese Americans: From relocation to redress* (rev. ed.), ed. Roger Daniels, Sandra C. Taylor, and Harry H. L. Kitano. Seattle and London: University of Washington Press.

Teachman, Jay D., and Vaughn R. A. Call

1996   The effect of military service on educational, occupational, and income attainment. *Social Science Research* 25:1–31.

Teixeira, Ruy A.

1992   *The disappearing American voter.* Washington, D.C.: The Brookings Institute.

tenBroek, Jacobus, Edward N. Barnhart, and Floyd Matson

1954   *Prejudice, War, and the Constitution.* Berkeley: University of California Press.

Thomas, Dorothy S.

1952   *The salvage.* Berkeley: University of California Press.

Thomas, Dorothy S., and Richard Nishimoto

1946   *The spoilage.* Berkeley: University of California Press.

Tuck, Donald R.

1987   *Buddhist churches of America: Jodo Shinshu.* Lewiston, N.Y.: Edwin Mellen Press.

Tule Lake Committee

2000   *Second Kinenhi: Reflections on Tule Lake.* San Francisco: Tule Lake Committee.

Uchida, Yoshiko

1982   *Desert exile: The uprooting of a Japanese American family.* Seattle and London: University of Washington Press.

Umemoto, Karen

1989   "On strike!" San Francisco State College strike, 1968–69: The role of Asian American students. *Amerasia Journal* 15:3–42.

U.S. Bureau of the Census

1973   *We, the Asian Americans.* Washington, D.C.: Government Printing Office.

1990   *Current population reports.* P-20, no. 450 (March). Washington, D.C.: Government Printing Office.

1991   *Current population reports.* P-20, no. 461 (March). Washington, D.C.: Government Printing Office.

1993   *1990 census of the population, Asians and Pacific Islanders in the United States.* CP-3-5, Table 5. Washington, D.C.: Government Printing Office.

U.S. Department of Health and Human Services, National Center for Health Statistics.

1985   *Vital statistics of the United States, 1981, Volume I: Natality.* Hyattsville, Md.

2000   *Vital statistics of the United States, 1997, Volume I: Natality.* Hyattsville, Md.

Wada, Yori

1986–87 Growing up in Central California. *Amerasia Journal* 13:3–20.

War Relocation Authority

1946(a) *Community government in war relocation centers.* Washington, D.C.: U.S. Department of the Interior.

1946(b)   *The evacuated people: A quantitative description.* Washington, D.C.: U.S. Department of the Interior.

1946(c)   *The relocation program.* Washington, D.C.: U.S. Department of the Interior.

Weglyn, Michi

1976   *Years of infamy: The untold story of America's concentration camps.* New York: William Morrow.

Weinstein, Neil D.

1980   Unrealistic optimism about future life events. *Journal of Personality and Social Psychology,* 39:806–20.

Wierzbica, Anna

1991   Japanese key words and core cultural values. *Language in Society* 20: 333–85.

Wilson, Robert A., and Bill Hosokawa

1980   *East to America: A history of the Japanese in the United States.* New York: William Morrow.

Winter, Jay M.

1985   The demographic consequences of the Second World War for Britain. Occasional Paper 34, British Society for Population Studies.

Wollenberg, Charles

1976   Schools behind barbed wire. *California Historical Quarterly,* 55:210–17.

Yamamoto, Virginia Swanson

1998   Terminal Island days. Pp. 163–65 in *Triumphs of faith: Stories of Japanese-American Christians during World War II,* ed. Victor N. Okada. Los Angeles: Japanese American Internment Project.

Yoo, David K.

2000   *Growing up Nisei: Race, generation, and culture among Japanese Americans in California, 1924–49.* Urbana and Chicago: University of Illinois Press.

Index